Leave It To Me...
My Life In Music

"LEAVE IT TO ME"

LYRIC
DICK GAUTIER

MUSIC
DONN TRENNER I.A.S.C.A

DON'T_ LET THE BLUES UP-SET YOU   JUST_ COME TO

ME.   HERE'S_ THE GOOD NEWS, I BET YOU   I'LL_ SET YOU

FREE.   SO_ IF THEY START TO GET YOU

LEAVE_ IT TO ME.   JUST_ TAKE THE

SUN AND SHAKE IT   OUT_ OF THE SKY.

THEN_ GRAB THE RING   AND TAKE IT   WHEN_ IT GOES

Leave It To Me...

My Life In Music

By Donn Trenner
with Tim Atherton

BearManor Media

2015

Leave It To Me... My Life In Music

© 2014 Donn Trenner with Tim Atherton

Registration #: TXU001918084

For information, address:

BearManor Media
P. O. Box 71426
Albany, GA 31708

bearmanormedia.com

Typesetting and layout by John Teehan

Published in the USA by BearManor Media

ISBN—1-59393-173-5
978-1-59393-173-5

*To Sara Elizabeth, who brings me great joy,
and for the inspiration of all the friends
and musicians who have
enriched my life.*

Table of Contents

Prelude

THANK HEAVENS THERE ARE KIND PEOPLE in the world. Donn Trenner is at the top of my list. There are fewer really talented people who are also kind. Donn is at the top of my list. Now add "funny, warm, witty, silly, and gifted jazz musician" and the number of candidates narrows dramatically. Donn is at the top of my list. Toss in composer, arranger, orchestra leader, supporter and mentor, and you begin to get a sense of the remarkable set of qualities that set Donn Trenner apart from most of the planet's population. You might also get a sense that I really like this guy.

Donn is my longest and dearest friend. I first met him at the age of fourteen when he was the pianist with Les Brown and His Band of Renown. Les was the studio band leader for my father's television program, *The Steve Allen Show,* with NBC in Burbank, California. I grew up in the wings of Dad's stages and would always be nearby when celebrities were on the shows. I never lost the excitement a regular fan feels when meeting a famous personality. My father always felt that as well, and was thrilled to share the stage with great talents.

Dad played piano and was an accomplished composer and lyricist. His relaxing hours were spent noodling alone at the piano with a tape recorder running. Each hour often generated a new song to add to the hundreds he wrote during his career. But, if he found a bassist, drummer, guitar, clarinet or horn player, he could literally jam all night with no audience. Playing was truly a passion.

As gifted in many areas as Dad was, he was an even better judge of consummate performers and exceptional musicians. Though I think he had a blind spot when it came to rock and roll. His favorite music was jazz and Donn Trenner was the natural choice to be his Musical Director, and would be integral to the production. Steve Allen hosted the first of the 1950's TV shows to feature jazz and often black artists on television. He was committed to making sure that great musicians had a venue for a mass audience. I'm sure Dad also had them on the show just so he could stand close to the giants and a new star on the upswing. He also hoped for an opportunity to sit in with the likes of Miles Davis or Stan Getz, and share his love of music on live television.

Donn also worked with Dad when he sparked my interest in building electronic Heathkits.

– Steve Allen Jr., MD

I MET DONN WHEN I WAS A NEW RECRUIT in the US Air Force in 1946. His genuine caring nature was immediately displayed at our first meeting, when he helped and guided me - a perfect stranger – far beyond what I could describe here. From that moment, and during our sixty-nine year most revered friendship, I have been privileged to have met many of his friends and associates both here and abroad, including many who are the subjects of this book.

The list of people who love Donn is too long to name here, but it is an unquestionable truth that his concern and desire to help almost everyone he encounters is beyond description. It perhaps explains why those whose lives he has touched think so highly of him.

I believe this book, written with humor and compassion as well as fact, shows beyond a doubt what a great man he is. Additionally, his place as a pianist, conductor, and arranger is already recognized by most top tier musicians as exemplary. It is inevitable that he will reach the highest place possible in modern musical history.

– Leo Adelman

DONN TRENNER. Those two words hold a lifetime of memories.

New York City, March 10, 1964 and I was nineteen years old. My mouth was dry, my heart was pounding, and my breathing was shallow and fast. Was I surrounded by sharks gnashing at my rubber raft? Practically. I was in a big TV studio at ABC at Columbus and 66th street. I was booked to sing in front of millions of people on a show called *ABC's Nightlife*. I was about to make a big fool out of myself.

The orchestra was taking their places and warming up. Whoa, the sharks were circling me now. Suddenly, there he was… shirt casually open, California tan, smiling face.

"Hi there, I'm Donn Trenner the musical director of the show. And you must be our singer."

"Oh, I guess. Hi, I'm B. J. Ward."

"That's quite a name you have there, BeeJay. What does the B. J. stand for?"

"Basically Jewish." I said. He laughed. "I love it. Do you have charts?"

"My charts? Uh… what do you mean?"

"Your charts, arrangements?"

My shaky hand held out a homemade lead sheet with chords and lyrics. "Here's what I have."

He took my music. It looked so flimsy in his hand.

"This is your chart? Well, not to worry, BeeJay." said the cool Donn Trenner, "We can work with this."

He turned toward the band, now awaiting his instruction. To the bass player he said,

"Gimme a four bar intro in Bb. I'll play the verse rubato." To the drummer, "Mel, how about a ching a ching a ching ching ching. Strings? Listen to the melody and give me whole notes starting at bar sixteen. Okay everybody, let's do it. A one. A two. A one two three."

We were off and just like that there was music. Wow! I admired his musical acumen, his mastery of the piano, his sense of humor, plus he was very sexy. That's when I came up with the idea of marrying him. I didn't tell him, of course. What are you kidding? We just met.

We married a year later, and I moved to California. We had so many adventures over the years, too numerous to recount here. (All of that will be in *my* book.) We traveled together. He played and conducted. I put together vocal groups to back up the Stars in their Main room acts from Las Vegas to Reno to Lake Tahoe. In Europe, he played and conducted in Sweden, in London at the Palladium, The Concertgebouw Orchestra in Amsterdam, and Nor Deutsche Rundfunk in Germany. What a travelogue of experiences we shared. We also learned to fly airplanes together, built a recording studio together and raised hunting dogs together. (Well… that was a big mistake!) We love each other today as we always have.

I'm so proud of Donn for writing this book, for chronicling this moment in musical history. The Big Band Era is where Donn honed his craft with the giants of the musical scene. Found his style, polished it, and learned his way of communicating the Gift.

We all hope to leave something behind... a tiny footprint in the ocean of time... a pebble, a ripple we send out that reverberates somewhere to someone that says, "I was here." Just as this great Era will never come again, there will never be another Donn Trenner.

–B. J. Ward

1

Persistent Jim

I WAS WORKING AT CAESAR'S PALACE with Ann-Margret when I got a call from BJ . We were no longer together, but we were always in touch. She asked, "How's the fire?" I had slept late that day and had no idea what she was talking about. Her voice was shaky, "The fire, the MGM Grand is ablaze." I had worked there many times. It was diagonally across the street on the corner of Flamingo Road and Las Vegas Boulevard. I walked out onto my balcony and saw helicopters lifting people off the roof of the twenty-six-story MGM Grand. It was a horrific fire and a lot of people perished.

My early involvement in the Las Vegas scene began with Steve Allen. He, his wife, Jayne Meadows, and I went there to perform. On occasion, we attended the shows of other artists and afterwards there would be much discussion on what worked, what didn't work, and why. Jayne had strong opinions and was not shy about sharing them.

I saw Nat Cole at the Sands Hotel. Aside from his remarkable musical talent, there was his gentility and lack of any evident ego. With many performers, what you see from the audience perspective is just veneer, not the true person. Nat was the real deal. Years later, I sat on a piano bench with him as we were preparing for his guest appearance on a TV show. He was just as classy and genuine as he appeared in his nightclub act. In Las Vegas, he had a notice put up that no "blue material," meaning nothing profane, was permitted from any act that opened for him. I still feel a great reverence for him.

Nat Cole's demeanor and stage presence stands in stark contrast with that of Don Rickles, who we also saw in Las Vegas. The first time I watched him, he was just a local lounge act known as the "Sultan of Insulters." Don literally made his living by insulting people. He was outrageous, severe, and abrasive, but the audience found humor in his act and he became quite popular. I much preferred the engaging style of Mr. Cole.

Las Vegas had become an amazing, thriving center for entertainment. So many celebrities and musicians worked there. I would be in Las Vegas for as many as eighteen weeks a year when I was with Shirley MacLaine. I usually had a week to get prepared followed by a four week engagement, with no nights off. I had a similar schedule with Ann-Margret. It was intense, but I loved performing. In the beginning, I played primarily at the Flamingo Hotel, but my favorite was Caesar's Palace. Las Vegas was still in its infancy compared to what it is today. There were only six major hotels then, and the Dunes, Desert Inn, and Sands are gone now.

The Las Vegas lifestyle never appealed to me. I performed there, but I didn't frequent the casinos or simply pass time in the hotels. I would rather be on-stage, than just hanging out there. Regulars who go to Las Vegas usually have two goals: what can I win and what can I get for free? It showed in their faces. I've seen emergency vehicles come for people who won big and lost big. I've never been interested in giving my salary to support real estate development in Vegas.

Both Las Vegas and Los Angeles have always lacked a certain sophistication you'll find in New York, but working in Vegas was great. Unlike now, from the 1950s through the 1970s, there were quite a number of orchestras employed. Many top-notch musicians came to Las Vegas because there was a volume and density of available work that didn't exist in other places. The union scale was higher there than perhaps anywhere else in the world. As time went on, all of this continued to grow because there were more hotels with big showrooms being built. Many years later, the Tropicana Hotel would change everything. They brought in a show from France, *Folies Bergere*, and decided to tape the orchestra. If they could get away with hiring a few live musicians to supplement the pre-recorded sound accompaniment, it would be much less expensive. A musicians' strike ensued, but the establishment prevailed. The union dropped its demand to restrict taped music and now canned music is prevalent.

Living in Las Vegas required me to be nourished by something other than slot machines and the night life. I started building electronic kits, such as television sets, in my hotel room. Early on in my life, I developed a love for what made things work, maybe because I came from a family that showed quite a bit of disrepair, and I felt a sense of having to get things done.

As a young teen, I figured out how to rewire our lamps because I knew the frayed cords were a fire hazard. I had an erector set and a chemistry set that went their normal course. I didn't come close to blowing anything up. I just had some fun with these things, as many children do. I was fascinated with trolley cars, buses, trains, airplanes, and automobiles. I heard the laboring of car engines because somebody was staying in first gear too long, or being in third gear far too soon. Later, when I got into putting my own band together, I built my own bandstand fronts.

During the summer, when I was boy, a family outing meant that we packed a picnic, hopped on a trolley, and rode out to a public park. There were places that were a real treat because they were two trolley fares away, like the local beaches for swimming. The family outings were primarily geared for me. I don't think they were nearly as enjoyable for my parents, but they did it because they thought that's what they should do.

The places of my childhood became so important to me that whenever I came back to New York, if I had a day off, I rented a car and drove up to New Haven. I would spend a few minutes meditatively sitting in the car in front of our old house. Sometimes it cost me a couple of hundred dollars for a rent-a-car, motel, and food, but I felt compelled to return home.

In the beginning, we lived on Carlton Street in Hamden, just outlying New Haven, in an area called Whitneyville. I loved living there. The house my parents built was lovely. We were there from the time I was three until I graduated from grammar school. Then along came the problems of the Depression and they were not able to hold on to it. They sold the house and we moved several blocks away so I could stay in the same school. After a while that didn't work financially and we moved into New Haven.

As a kid, my health was generally very good, but I had a real susceptibility to poison ivy. I remember several summers when my mother wrapped my whole body in gauze and then poured a purple solution called potassium permanganate onto that gauze because I was covered with blisters. My fingers would actually attach themselves. I looked like a web-footed duck. My face had also swollen up so much that my eyes closed and I had to drink through a glass tube. It was awful. Later on, I used to take poison ivy injections in the winter. That would cause my arm to break out with poison ivy for a few minutes and then it went away. I wasn't tremendously athletic and never broke a bone. I did play some outdoor sports, but I would rather have been practicing piano.

My father was a volunteer fireman when we lived in Hamden. Every Monday night, he went over to the fire station to play penny-ante poker. It was the most important day of his week. On that day, he exhibited a definite personality change. I actually saw him kiss my mother on the cheek. My mother used to say that if she died and the funeral was on a Monday, he probably wouldn't show up.

My mother, Florence Muriel Goldbaum, was born in 1898, and my father, Henry H. Trenner, was born four years before that. Dad was out of New York and my mother was from New Haven. I was not told the story of their romance, but she must have been twenty-nine years old when she became pregnant because I was born in March of 1927. Perhaps this made them a bit older as parents for this time.

I remember my paternal grandparents; I didn't spend nearly as much time with them as I did with my maternal grandparents, but we all lived close geographically. My mother's mother, Hattie, drove a car. I was apparently well aware of where we were going because when my grandmother wasn't sure, I could tell her which way to go. She told everyone that I had a great sense of direction. I had lots of aunts and uncles in the New Haven area. My mother's parents were quite comfortable and my grandfather, Jacob Conrad, or J.C., was known for thoughtful charitable acts. He did little things like going into a cafeteria, and when leaving, he would take a couple of muffins, put them in his pocket, and find somebody on the street that needed something to eat.

I used to play piano for my grandfather. He would stand in this big doorway and tap dance while I played "Top Hat." He was a handsome man. I thought he looked like a movie star. One day, when he saw me looking at myself in the mirror while combing my hair, he proclaimed, "Men aren't supposed to do that, that's mollycoddle stuff." Ever since then, when I look in the mirror, I never see my whole face. If I'm shaving, I see where I'm shaving. If I'm brushing my teeth, I see my teeth. He told me only sissies look at themselves in the mirror.

Television hadn't come out yet, so we used to go over to my grandparents' to listen to the radio. My grandmother used to love Mr. Keen Tracer of *Lost Persons* and *The Shadow*. I used to stay up with her every Sunday to listen to her programs. One evening when I was ten, I heard the Hindenburg pass over the house. It was reported on the news that it would be traveling over our vicinity, so we went outside to listen for it. A couple of hours later, it exploded while attempting to dock with its mooring mast at Lakehurst, New Jersey.

My father was a free spirit, who became a salesman and worked hard, but never made much money. Still, he loved to go to work. He would get up and leave earlier than he needed to because he'd rather be there than any other place. He was a totally different person while at work. He became a character with a big personality, and everyone loved him. Coming home was actually difficult for him.

In the beginning, he was employed by my mother's parents' store, The People's Clothing Company, in New Haven. It was one of the first clothing stores that offered credit. As a boy, I used to go down there to play. I found a typewriter and taught myself to type. Across the hall was another big space that my grandfather called J. C. Goldbaum Woolens and Trimmings. He was a supplier to tailors throughout Connecticut for whatever goes into a tailor-made suit: under-collars, collars, threads, buttons, and cloth. Dad stayed there for quite awhile, and then he worked for a few jewelry stores.

After that, he tried to start his own business called the New York-New Haven Messenger Service. He provided a courier service for jewelers in town who needed to have jewelry taken to New York, or picked up and brought back. He would take the Bankers express every morning. The train left New Haven at 8:00 and got to Grand Central at 9:18. Strangely enough, there isn't a train that fast now because there are so many more stops. He used to go down daily and return home between 4:30 and 5:00. It was a thankless job.

We just got by. We were never hungry, but I don't remember any surpluses. You couldn't say we were poor, but I realized that if I wanted anything that wasn't an absolute necessity, I needed to pay for it myself. I remember my dad always calling me "Persistent Jim," because if I wanted something, and expressed a need to have it, and he wasn't able to provide it, saying that became sort of a stern reprimand, "Persistent Jim, get off my back."

Looking back, I think I may have been a bit precocious with my many interests. I had a magazine subscription business. I found things at my grandfather's business, like the typewriter, that allowed me to become organized. I maintained a file card on each of my costumers. I sold the *Saturday Evening Post, Ladies Home Journal,* and others, until my interest in music began to take over.

I felt many of my friends and their families seemed to do more with their lives than we did. My parents never owned a car or even drove, so there wasn't a car in my family until the minute I was sixteen years old. I went out immediately and bought a car with the money I had been saving. It was a deep blue 1936 Ford Phaeton.

Much of our economic difficulties came from the Depression, but my father did not have enough training to do anything else except be a retail merchandiser, and I think there were disconcerted feelings about his inability to make more money. As my career got started, he was always interested in how much money I made. In the beginning, I used to resent that a little, but I would share that information with him anyway. I think it was a vicarious pleasure for him, knowing that his son was able to do better financially.

My mother was busy most of her life trying to be nice to everyone. She was gracious and charming, with a terribly low estimation of self-worth. She was insecure, a bit downtrodden and full of complexes, more than any human being I have ever known. I think a great deal of my mother's problems came from the way she was treated by her own parents. They had three children, two girls and a boy, and her captivatingly attractive sister was the fair-haired favorite child of the family.

My mother took the bus into town by herself to go to the grocery store and carried all the bags back, sometimes in inclement weather. She was not a well woman and suffered a lot from arthritis. I always thought she was a chronic complainer. I don't ever remember my mother when asked, "How are you today, Florence?" ever saying, "I'm fine." She always managed to somehow portray the ills and pain that she felt. And now, I feel badly, and perhaps a bit guilty, that as a child I seemed to think that wasn't so real.

She was always late, chronically tardy. It used to drive my father crazy. But again, back to no car, it was the trolley. If my mother missed the trolley car or the bus, my dad might be waiting downtown for half an hour or more, getting angrier by the minute. They used to bicker all the time and it would always become argumentative. I hated that because I could see my mother getting upset. I became angrier at my father than I was with my mother for how harshly he spoke to her. It was a normal kind of marital flare-up in their peculiar relationship, but there was never a physical exchange.

I began to see my mother doing strange things that indicated that she was getting mentally confused. One day, I found a letter that my mother had written to a famous syndicated columnist in one of the New York newspapers named Westbrook Pegler. In this letter, she accused him of referring to her every time he mentioned General MacArthur. I didn't understand what the cause was, but eventually figured out what the reference was. My mother was a fairly attractive woman and carried herself in a stately and polished manor. She was a bright lady, but not necessarily formally educated, though she did go through high school. The key to this mystery was her rather large nose, which came to a big point; the same nose as General MacArthur. My mother, being so paranoid, used to think she was being followed. She had all kinds of persecution complexes. When I saw that letter she had written to the columnist, I knew how far out she had become. Then I realized that this contributed to the general state and condition of my parents' interpersonal relationship.

To me, this seemed like an irregular problem that needed to be taken care of. I didn't know how to negotiate it, but became fascinated by it. I needed to analyze why they did not get along, and why there was so much turmoil. There was a high school English teacher, Dr. Walsh, who I respected and trusted. I felt he was someone who had the answers and could offer advice. We met after school a couple of times and I expressed my concerns. He told me that, at fourteen, I was too young to be a psychiatrist.

I felt my father was unfair to my mother. She was a vulnerable and fragile person, and he disregarded her as though she didn't matter. Maybe this later had the effect of making me deferentially considerate to the women in my life, perhaps causing a degree of dysfunction in my personal relationships. To an extent, I often became an enabler, or I tried to take care of people instead of respecting their independence. I wanted to overcome deficiencies in my relationships by trying to fix things on my own, instead of recognizing the appropriate time to get help from someone with an education and experience specializing in such matters.

I believe that maybe being an only child within this kind of family dynamic caused me to grow up too quickly, feeling as if I alone carried the burden of their dysfunction. I also believe being an only child had its advantages. Both of my parents were caring and affectionate to me. I was the center of their collective focus. Had there not been me in that picture, I think they would have dissolved the relationship. As it was, they stayed together right to the very end. My father was so proud of me that it was embarrassing at times. Early on, they would have preferred me to pursue a classical career, but it was never put upon me as though I was going in the wrong direction. They supported me in everything I did, even when I eloped.

2 Potato Pancakes

No one person stands out as my musical mentor. I pursued what I determined necessary for my musical growth. I remember liking my first piano teacher, Lillian Langrock, but my teachers didn't get the best out of me. I was learning a piano sonata from lesson to lesson. They were happy with that and would just go on to something else, instead of helping me refine the piece or instruct musical subtlety.

Having perfect pitch and a photographic memory was a great help to me musically. My mother discovered this when I was five years old and had me tested. My perfect pitch was accurate enough that somebody could sit at the piano and I would tell them what the bottom and the top notes were in a resounding chord. My mother had some musical background. She wanted to be a singer and played piano a little bit. I would be in the other room correcting her note mistakes. Sometimes she sat in the room while I practiced. I had memorized the piece I was playing and she would be looking at the music, but got lost while trying to follow along. As I was playing, I said things to her like, "It's on the right hand page, second staff down, third measure. That's where I am now." For me, there is an auditory and visual connection between perfect pitch and a photographic memory; one can signal the other.

My mother somehow was able to find enough money for me to continue with my lessons. My father might have felt that he didn't have the money, but she eked it out somehow. She also managed to take me to symphony concerts at Woolsey Hall on the Yale campus. The concert-

9

master was Hugo Kortzshok, and Harry Berman played in the violin section. Harry Berman's cousin, Sonny Berman, played trumpet and became important in the jazz world through his association with the Woody Herman orchestra. Sonny played in my first band.

When I was growing up, we didn't listen to a lot of music in the house. I bought the family's first record player when I was about fifteen and got recordings of the bands that came through the Shubert Theater in New Haven. However, we did listen to the radio broadcast of the Metropolitan Opera. My mother told me that as a young boy I used to stand in the sun parlor on Saturday afternoon conducting along with the music.

Music seemed to come rather easily to me, and I acquired a relatively solid classical background. At my eighth grade graduation, I played Mendelssohn's Rondo Capriccioso. It was also around this time that I started to become interested in popular music. I wanted to have a rehearsal and see if I could put a band together. I got a couple of stock arrangements from Goldie's, a local music store. One of them was "Alexander's Ragtime Band." I assembled this small group of musicians, probably not well balanced, like piano, bass, drums, a couple of horns, and who knows what. They came over to my house and we started to read this music. Shortly, I excused myself from the room, went into the kitchen where my mother was, and said, "These guys are awful!" That was my first rehearsal.

New Haven was a fertile area for music and all the name bands were coming through. The Shubert Theater was an important venue and booked name bands from New York, and those passing through on tour. Tony Pastor, Bob Chester, Shep Fields, Charlie Barnet, who I would later play with, and Glenn Miller, whose band became particularly significant to me. Going to see these bands became a passion. I strongly felt a need to learn about the tonal colors and rhythms of jazz music. I developed an ardent fascination with the big bands.

My mother took me to New York City by train to see Duke Ellington at the Zanzibar. I, of course, was underage, and my mother had maybe consumed two ounces of alcohol in her life, and both were related to a toothache. All I can remember is being in this exotic nightclub and being excited by the Ellington Orchestra. To my surprise, out of the ceiling came this large circular platform and on it was Mr. Ellington playing a piano.

My parents were American born, as were several prior generations of our family and our minor religious involvement was with Reform Judaism. I attended Sunday school, but learning Hebrew was optional and it served no purpose in my life. It was common in that Sunday school to be confirmed, but rare to have a Bar Mitzvah. It just wasn't in the cards for me. The rabbi refused to confirm me because I had missed too many Sunday mornings. I was starting to play dances on Saturday nights, which made it difficult for me to get up early the next morning.

The rabbi was a devoted jazz fan and, years later, was on the board of directors for the Newport Jazz Festival. He was personal friends with Benny Goodman and Count Basie. I would skip classes at Sunday school to hang out with him and talk about jazz because I found his knowledge intriguing. I also accompanied the kid's choir in some of the assembly programs. My parents often attended the adult services on Friday night. On one such evening the rabbi delivered a sermon where he talked about youth culture and the kids in Sunday school. At this point, he spoke with much concern about the young pianist, who was now accompanying the choir because he seemed to be jazzing up the sacred hymns. Given his appreciation of jazz and our long talks, I was surprised and angry that he would handle it that way, rather than just talking to me about it.

Coming from a family that supported the Jewish faith, I realized the horrors of World War II, the whole period of Adolph Hitler, and the millions of people who had been killed in concentration camps. My parents knew of those who were murdered and there were people in our community who lost family and friends. I was aware of what was going on from reading the newspapers and was terribly upset by it.

Growing up, I didn't feel deeply connected to the Jewish community, but there was something profoundly disturbing and distressing about my own cultural identity being used as a reason to kill innocent people. It was not just my connection to the faith, but a feeling of connection to humanity. Most people didn't know I was Jewish and I heard a lot of anti-Semitism in conversations around me. When I first went out on the road, I was at a military base in Walla Walla Washington, and the band stayed overnight in the barracks. I remember being in tears lying in bed. The older guys were playing cards down the hall and making horrible anti-Semitic comments and jokes. Two other men in the orchestra, Hy Rubenstein and Mel Epstein, overheard this, as well, put their notices in the next day, and returned to New York.

Since then, I've talked about it with friends who lived through World War II in Germany. When visiting close friends in Munich, Peter and Felicitas Dietsch, I had just been to the Anne Frank museum in Amsterdam the week before. Peter said to me, "Donn, there is something you must do.

You must do it for yourself, but you have to do it for me, as well. You need to drive down a couple of kilometers, to a street called Dachauer Strasse, turn right, and follow the signs to the concentration camp. I want you to go through that." Peter, like many Germans, felt incredible guilt for what had happened. It is one thing to imagine the horrors from a distance, but it's a horrendous realization to go to these places.

By the time I was a teenager, both my mother and father had recognized my devoted interest in jazz, especially after going to hear the bands every Sunday at the Shubert Theater. I couldn't get enough of it. It was a joyful period of learning and figuring out what the musical "ingredients" were that created a specific, easily identifiable sound. In those days, every name band had a signature sound, something that made them unique. Many people could identify the Glenn Miller sound, even if they didn't know why. It came from the way the woodwind section was voiced. The melody was played by a lead clarinet, instead of the lead alto sax, as was the norm for most orchestras. The fourth sax or second tenor doubled the lead, playing one octave lower. That was the key to the Miller sound.

The Glenn Miller Orchestra was stationed at Yale University. Mr. Miller was at the peak of his career when he went into the service. "String of Pearls," "In The Mood," and all those tunes that we're so tired of playing now, but are still consistently popular, were significant then. "At Last," made famous by Etta James in 1960s, was also a big hit for the Glenn Miller Orchestra in the 1940s.

I attended James Hillhouse Comprehensive High School, which was located essentially in the center of the Yale campus. I used to see Glenn Miller walking to work in the morning. We would also see actor Broderick Crawford coming out of his barracks since he was stationed there as well. There were all of these incredible musicians that we got to know. Players, such as pianist/arranger Mel Powell, bassist Trigger Alpert, Hank Freeman who was one of the great lead alto players, Zeke Zarchy, a wonderful trumpet player, and Willie Schwartz, who was the lead clarinetist in that trademark Glenn Miller sound, were all associated with the orchestra that was stationed in New Haven during 1943 and 1944.

I was impressed with the whole feeling of how that orchestra existed. I think part of it was the decorum and the management. They didn't look like some of the bands that I played with later, where their tuxedos were old and shabby, or were wasted from alcohol, or perhaps drugs. I didn't get that feeling with Glenn Miller. They had refinement. I got a feeling of real importance and substantial musical endeavor.

My mother asked me if I would like to have any of these gentlemen from the band over to our house for dinner. I said, "I'd love to have Mel Powell and Trigger Alpert." I wondered if I could get them to come. Mel Powell at that point had just left the Benny Goodman Orchestra. He was a stellar player. He wrote some really fancy piano pieces. One was called "The Earl." It was a marvelous piano piece that he did with Benny Goodman.

Mel Powell and Trigger Alpert were both Jewish, so I asked them what they would like for dinner and if they had any special foods that they would like. They said potato latkes.

I said, "Potato what?"

They said, "Potato latkes. You know like potato pancakes."

Well, my mother wouldn't have known anything about that. I called my grandmother, who lived a mile away, and she made the potato pancakes. I brought them back in my car, and my mother kept them warm in the oven. They were sitting at opposite ends of a rectangular table. Mel said something to Trigger about passing him some more pancakes, and Trigger picked up a couple of latkes and flung them across the table at him. I think my mother was probably shocked, but she took it all in stride.

I was tall at fifteen and looked older than I was. I got a call to work with a well-known group called the Yale Collegians. They had all of these arrangements from a small Black orchestra called the Savoy Sultans. It was to be a summer job in a little resort near my house, not far away, and my mother agreed to let me go, so I took the job. It paid $15 a week. This was the first time I'd ever seen chord symbols. I learned what chord symbols meant by just playing what I was hearing. Then I looked on the page and discovered it was the same thing that I was hearing and playing. My ears did it for me. However, having perfect pitch makes it almost impossible for me to transpose the music I am reading because I'm pre-hearing what is already on the page.

I was an honors student in high school until I started to write arrangements. Then I went to just passing. My focus went totally into music. I just wanted to be around a band and play. One of the most meaningful and exciting events in my life at that point resulted from meeting Perry Burgett, who was an arranger for Glenn Miller and later became a staff writer for Skitch Henderson and *The Tonight Show* band. At that time, Perry was stationed at Yale, and he took an interest in me as a young musician.

He said, "If you write an arrangement in the Glenn Miller style, bring it over and I'll get the Miller band to rehearse it."

I said, "Are you kidding me?"

So I wrote an arrangement of "I'm in the Mood for Love." I brought it in and they rehearsed it. A while later, the band came over to play an assembly program at my high school and they performed my arrangement. I couldn't believe they actually played it. It was one of the thrills of my life. As a result, I formed my own band.

Some of our first gigs were at my high school. The athletic boosters gave me $15 to bring a small combo of five musicians to play after the basketball games. I brought fifteen musicians and paid them each $1. I wasn't a great businessman, but I was organized, and determined to have my own orchestra. I bought my band fronts with my own money. I made a stencil out of cardboard with my initials DT and painted them on. I had business cards printed that said, "Donn Trenner and his orchestra, featuring trumpeter Sonny Berman." On our opening night at my high school, I was in the hospital after an emergency appendectomy. I was lying in bed talking to Sonny on the phone to learn if the job went well. I fell asleep with my ear resting on the phone.

The Sonny Berman story is rather sad. We went to the same high school, but he was two years older. Sonny was a natural jazz musician and destined to be one of the better known jazz trumpet players. He had this great harmonic and melodic ability to instantaneously compose what he perceived. Sonny went with the Woody Herman Orchestra and there's a particular recording he did with them, "Sidewalks of Cuba," where Sonny played spectacularly. He's still known today as one of the stellar jazz players. On occasion, Sonny and I would ride the train to New York. We went down on some premise that was satisfactory to our parents, and after we got there we went to the burlesque shows. It was three days after the last time I saw him when he died. Sonny had gone to visit baritone saxophonist, Serge Chaloff, also of the Woody Herman band. Apparently they experimented with drugs. I don't know how much he had been using before, but apparently he had injected some heroin and a bubble went to his heart. Sonny was twenty-one.

After a year, my band was pretty good and we were getting some work. We performed anything from Liszt's Hungarian Dance to Glenn Miller tunes, using charts that I had written in high school instead of paying attention in class. I started writing a lot of arrangements. I felt different from my peers. I remember walking the hallways of Hillhouse

With my first band in 1943.

High and seeing posters for upcoming dances. At the bottom was, "music by the Donn Trenner Orchestra." I never went to the dances other than to perform. I didn't develop a typical high school social life. Music and my orchestra was the soul motivation. The typical profit from a show was $3-$4 per person. The money was unimportant to me. I just wanted to have an orchestra and play for people.

In addition to playing high school and local college dances, we also did shows. I put a USO show together and chartered a bus with my own money. I had a big sign made to hang on the side of the bus, the Donn Trenner Orchestra. The Ink Spots, a four-man vocal group, was well-known at the time, so we had The Four Southern Echoes and they were comparable, if not better than The Ink Spots. We also had a girl singer and a seventeen piece orchestra. I knew a kid from high school who was really funny, so I used him as a comedian. We did a show at Wesleyan University on a Sunday in April of 1943, to raise money for the Wesleyan Naval Flight Preparatory School. It was easier to get around and organize things because I had gotten my driver's license just three weeks before.

Milt Zudekof, from New Haven, was the lead trumpet player in my band. His brother, Moe Zudekof, was a legendary trombonist and band leader, better known by his stage name, Buddy Morrow. Buddy had a long career as a studio musician in New York. He had a reputation of being able to execute anything written for any instrument on the trombone. A little later on, I would be lucky enough to go out on the road with Buddy's orchestra.

At this point, I was a junior in high school. I went with another musician down to New York and heard Dizzy Gillespie on 52nd Street. At that time, bebop was becoming more well-known and accepted. It is a highly intellectual genre of jazz music. It is particularly challenging melodically and harmonically. It requires musicians to hear more advanced chordal substitutions for the melody of the song they are playing, so the improvisation is more complicated and more technical than playing in an earlier style.

I was probably the youngest person there, but at 6'2", I looked old enough to get in. I didn't drink, so my parents were not worried about me. We went to The Onyx, The Three Deuces, and then Minton's Playhouse up in Harlem. At the Deuces, some girl singer came out after being introduced, and Dizzy, with his devilish sense of humor, turned his horn around and sort of goosed her with the mouthpiece. It was Billie Holiday.

There was a small bandstand at the front of a narrow room with just enough room for the musicians to come out of a side door and go over to the bandstand and play. The bar stood at the other end and the rest of the room was jammed with tables and people who were coming and going. Dizzy made me laugh, and that impressed me. I love the ability to mix humor with almost anything. I've seen it work well, even in moments of tragedy. Humor is so important. Musically, he was marvelous. He was playing this new and exciting kind of music that was filled with rapidly changing harmonies. Sometimes, if the tempo wasn't too fast, each beat would change harmonically, which I loved because I could hear what was going on.

I didn't know much about Billie or the significance of her fame. She had this little gardenia in her hair. Stylistically, she was quite wonderful, but really loose. At sixteen years old, it was hard to understand the difference between a style and the effects of intoxication. I wondered if it was her style, or the result of alcohol and drugs. Billie's pitch was a little bit careless, but her feeling was so different. She would take an up-tempo tune and sing it so loosely it felt like, if you transferred the time machine behind it, it could have been a ballad. As I listened to her later in my life, and heard some of her recordings, I thought she did well with delivering a lyric. I don't think I was ever that impressed with her, as perhaps some others, for being a master of storytelling. I think she was so influenced by the music behind her that she just went along with the moment. Some of her utterances seemed almost unmusical, but they worked and became part of her style. I only heard one set that night because I didn't have enough money. Most of the clubs had cover charges and a drinking minimum. I just slipped in there to listen for as long as they'd let me.

I sat in for a couple numbers at Minton's Playhouse in Harlem. Like most nightclubs, it was dimly light, but unlike many other clubs, it wasn't just some little rental area that had been adapted into a nightclub. Minton's seemed bigger because it had a stage and more tables for people to sit and listen. It was an intense place and I'm not an aggressive person, so for me to go up and ask to sit in, meant somebody must have been egging me on. It was scary. The piano player moved out of the way and there I was, with Fats Navarro playing trumpet. I didn't stay long. I just remember that listening to, and playing with, the legendary Fats Navarro was an amazing experience.

I wasn't able to attend my graduation from high school in 1944. I had completed school, but there was a week between the ceremonies and when classes ended. I sent my parents to pick up my diploma because I had taken a job in Myrtle Beach, South Carolina with the Johnny Bond Orchestra. There was an Italian trumpet player named Agio Davido Bonafede, who was known as Johnny Bond. He was a funny guy and appealing to a variety of women, including one of The Andrews Sisters, Patty, who adored him. We were booked at the Ocean Forest Hotel in Myrtle Beach and this was my first trip away from home. I drove my blue Ford down south, where I saw my first signs of serious racial prejudice and discrimination. I couldn't believe it. Two separate water fountains and three rest rooms. I was confused, appalled, and hurt. I was brought up differently than that.

I went into town one day, taking the bus that ran from the resort into town. The driver was a young lady and kind of cute. I was minding my own business, when an older Black lady got on the bus. There was no place for her to sit, so I got up and gave her my seat. The girl bus driver saw this through her rearview mirror and stopped the bus. She made a big announcement in front of the whole bus, "You see the bar that goes across those seats back there? Coloreds sit behind that bar, not in front of it! I'm not going any further until you get out of that seat. You don't belong there." I felt terrible for this lady. I couldn't believe anyone could be so insensitive, crude, and cruel. With a devious plan, I decided to disingenuously ask this girl bus driver for a date. I took her out one evening and we drove to some establishment. When she stepped out of my car, I drove away leaving her there.

After I returned from South Carolina, I went down to New York to audition for Juilliard. This was to appease my parents more than anything else because I had already more or less decided to follow another opportunity. I had been accepted at Julliard and was offered a generous scholarship because of my auditory abilities, but as I was walking up to the room to play my classical piece, I heard another student playing so incredibly well that I turned around and walked out the door. The pianist was much further advanced in his classical pianist abilities. I knew I didn't belong there. I had stopped classical training when I was thirteen and needed to follow my own musical passion.

I knew turning eighteen years old meant I would be drafted into military service. I went home and discussed two possibilities with my parents. One was to go to Julliard, and the other was an opening with Ted Fio Rito and His Orchestra. Ted Fio Rito wrote hit songs, such as "Toot Toot Tootsie Goodbye." He was a fine pianist and a nice fellow. Manny Albam, Frankie Socolow, Doc Severinsen, and many other really good jazz musicians went with that band. My parents were not thrilled when I decided not to attend Juilliard. At the time, they would have preferred I go on to become a classical pianist, but as I became involved in the musical experiences of my young life, they were completely supportive.

3 With Love, Lt. Moore

THE 1940S WERE A FERTILE PERIOD for the big bands. There were numerous orchestras traveling throughout the country, and they were prosperous. There were a large number of ballrooms and theaters throughout the country. People who liked to dance would come out and dance, and those who just liked to hear the big bands would come out to listen. The music was structurally well-conceived, written by highly skilled writers and played by distinctly talented musicians. The public followed the bands like major and minor league sports teams. It was a vibrant period that was supported by people who attached importance to listening. People just wanted to be there to feel the whole presence of a group of musicians who would get into a bus and go from one night to another, showing pride and dignity in their profession.

The Ted Fio Rito Orchestra paid about $85 a week, which was relatively good money then. We traveled on a bus and stayed in hotels, three, maybe four nights a week, not more than that because they worked it out so we traveled at night after the gig to eliminate a night's rent. We used to share a double room, which was about $5 for a double or $2.50 for each person. I lived frugally on the road and managed to send home $35 or $40 a week. I thought it would help for two reasons: psychologically, it would help my parents understand that I was accomplishing something more than just having a jam session every night, and it proved I was a young man starting to make a little bit of a living. It was also nice to give something to them. I was never a big spender on the road, and as a kid I had learned to save for things I wanted.

19

With the Ted Fio Rito band in 1945.

Besides establishing myself as the pianist, I was writing some arrangements for the band. I started to notice that Ted liked to get off the stage during a four-hour engagement. Being seventeen, I didn't know anything about this kind of activity, but Ted was a gambler. I don't know how it happened, but before I realized it, I had become the assistant leader of the orchestra. He would disappear, and I would run the band for a whole set or for whatever needed to be covered. Being a leader was not unfamiliar territory to me. I had already had a band, just didn't know how to make money with it. Well, as openings in the band came up, I started bringing in musicians that had played with me back home. Over the course of about a year, I created a nucleus of players from my original band.

One of my close boyhood friends was Hal Geary. He was older than me and was into literature. My mother adored him and felt he was a good influence on me. Hal became the drummer with my band. At that point, he had already gone to California, but I sent him a wire asking if he would be interested in playing the summer with me. I got a wire back from him, "I'll be on the next train." I got him on the Ted Fio Rito band initially as, what we called, "property manager," which for lack of another term is "band boy." When the drummer left, Hal quickly became the best drummer they had had. Later on, he became Les Elgart's drummer, so our paths continued to cross for a while and later he became more involved in business endeavors.

Gene Cipriano was a year younger than me and had never traveled before. He said, "You'll need to convince my parents that things will be okay."

I had to go over to his parent's house to get him on the band. I told them, "Don't worry. He's out with a group of us from home here and we'll take care of him. I'll make sure everything is fine."

Gene had never been with a lady, so one night I went to Gene and said, "I've got a girl for you, it's time." I set this whole thing up. I told him after work to go up to my room and she would be there waiting for him. I said, "There's only one thing, she's a little funny about the lights. So just go in, turn them off, and make yourself comfortable." I had half of the band hiding in the bathroom and under the bed. He came up, took his clothes off, and got into bed, and it was the other tenor saxophone player, Jimmy Hanson, who was in bed. Thankfully, Gene had a good sense of humor.

Gene Cipriano became well known in California. He plays good jazz and is a wonderful saxophone player, who uniquely doubles on oboe, a difficult instrument that is a rare double for a saxophonist. He did a lot with Henry Mancini; Hank loved him. Gene may have one of the largest retirement pensions from the Musician's Union that anyone will ever receive. He was in most of the good studio orchestras, doing motion picture after motion picture. I was fortunate that he was one of the original members of my first band, and over the years we've have worked together a great deal. He is fun to be around and acts so carefree that you feel like you're still talking to a sixteen year old kid.

My first time in an airplane was with Ted Fio Rito. I'll never forget it. Because I was interested in the mechanics of everything, I got to sit up front with the pilot and co-pilot. It was a twin engine military airplane that came out to take us from Topeka to Salina, Kansas to play a function at an officer's club. The co-pilot was a girl from the Women's Auxiliary Ferrying Squadron. On route, we lost the left engine. I remember them going through all kinds of checks to figure out what had happened. All the time they were checking this out, we were losing altitude fast and, although the crew was calm, it was clear we were in trouble. They were flipping toggle switches, working quickly through a series of maneuvers. They told me to pass the word back to start throwing stuff overboard. There were para-chutes on board and a band boy had mistakenly picked two parachutes up by the ripcord, so those were no longer any good. We were getting close to the ground and I said, "Where are you going to land?"

He said, "We'll land on the road down there."

I said, "How about the telephone wires and the telephone poles?"

He said, "We'll cut those with our wings."

We were very close, maybe at three hundred feet, and the engine caught again. We got to the gig and I remember Ted Fio Rito introduced the pilot and co-pilot as heroes.

On April 12, 1945, the band was scheduled to play in Walla Walla, Washington at the air base there. From time to time, we did these shows sponsored by Coca Cola called *The Victory Parade of Spotlight Bands*. They would bring bands in to do shows at military bases, but they canceled the show because President Franklin Delano Roosevelt had died that day.

On my eighteenth birthday, we were traveling on the West Coast, playing the normal circuit of ballrooms and civic auditoriums, sometimes concerts and sometimes dances. We were playing at a place called Janson Beach Ballroom, outside of Portland, Oregon. Ted said, "Come here, I want you to meet somebody." I knew we were losing a trumpet player and he had to replace him. I went over to meet Doctor Severinsen, a dentist, his wife, and their son Carl, who played trumpet. Carl Severinsen, who later became known as Doc, after his father, joined the band. He was a couple of months younger than me and we headed down to San Francisco to play the Golden Gate Theater along with the fabulous vocal group as-sociated with Tommy Dorsey called The Pied Pipers.

We were housed in several hotels. The whole band couldn't stay in one hotel because there were not enough rooms available. Carl had a young lady friend from Oregon that he brought down to California to be with him. I called over to the front desk of his hotel and asked for his room.

He answered, and I said, "Is this Carl Severinsen?"

He said, "Yes."

I said, "This is Lt. Moore. I'm from the 14th precinct and I under-stand that you have transported a young lady across the state border. I just want you to know that we're aware of this. This is a felony and you're in a lot of trouble. I would like very much for you to get yourself a representa-tive. We will meet you tomorrow morning in the lobby at 10:00 to discuss this matter."

I don't know what made me do something this cruel, but there was someone else in the room when I made this phone call egging me on, once I came up with this idea.

The band manager was an attorney, and I knew that's who he would get. The next morning, a bunch of us went over to his hotel. We sat in the lobby and saw Carl and the band attorney, Bill Cantalupo, coming down the stairs. Doc Severinsen remembered me as Lt. Moore for many years. I used to send him opening congratulatory wires saying, "Hope everything is well with you. Love, Lt. Moore"

We did the two week engagement at the Golden Gate Theater in San Francisco. The Pied Pipers stood behind me on a little platform. I remember the hair on the back of my neck just bristling, they sang so well. I loved what a great vocal group sounded like with those close harmonies. Across the bay in Oakland, there was a place called the Mondre Café that featured late afternoon band presentations and some dancing. Jimmy Hanson and I had met a couple of girls, so one afternoon we went over there on a date. I was driving and looking in the rearview mirror. Jimmy was in the back seat with the girl I was really attracted to. Her name was Helen Carr, and somehow I hooked up with her and we started to date. I didn't know she sang until after we started going out. She just didn't talk about it. Then I discovered she had a unique job. There was a telephone service in bars and late-night clubs where one could dial up a song. You told the operator what song you wanted to hear and they would play it from their central station. Helen was one of the operators.

After finishing the Golden Gate Theater engagement, I walked into a government building in San Francisco to register with the Selective Service and bam, I was drafted.

4 Special Services

I WAS FIRST STATIONED AT SHEPPARD FIELD in Texas for about eleven months, and then I was shipped out to Scott Field, which was in Bellville, Illinois, not far from St. Louis. As it turned out, the war was pretty close to being over, so I didn't go in at a time when my life would be endangered by being shipped overseas. Even so, I didn't want to be an infantry soldier. I wanted to do what I knew how to do.

I went to Fort Devens in Massachusetts for my induction, and after that they put us on a troop train. No one knew where we were going or which branch of the service we would end up in, maybe the infantry, but nobody knew. The train ride lasted for two and a half days. We wound up in Wichita Falls, where we discovered we were in the Army Air Corps, which is what that branch was called before it became the Air Force. Here, I went through basic training and classification, where they try to figure out what it is that you're qualified to do.

I was out on the field with a few thousand GI's and we were doing what was required, like jumping-jacks and push-ups. I was wearing my dark glasses as many others were. The drill sergeant was up on this great big podium so he could see over the heads of everybody. He was yelling commands and going through all the authoritarian intimidations that soldiers with stripes on their shoulders do to corporals who have nothing on their shoulders. He sharply shouted, "Hey you, you with the dark glasses"! At first, I didn't know who he meant.

Someone next to me whispered, "I think he means you."

I pointed to myself.

He said, "Yeah you."

I said, "What?"

He said, "Do some push-ups for me."

I was really embarrassed. I knew I was going to be made a spectacle of myself, so I did some push-ups.

He said, "You know what you look like? You look like a monkey fuckin' a football."

I knew at that point that I had to get out of there.

Then we went through bivouac training, which, of course, is long days out in the field with barbed wire and live ammunition. I felt I was headed for trouble with this and it certainly was not going to help my career, so I marched over to special services and exclaimed, "I'm an entertainer, I'm a musician, I'm in entertainment, I'm an orchestrator and an arranger, I play piano, and I don't want to do this stuff anymore." I was exceedingly fortunate with their reaction. My classification was changed to 442, which was "Entertainment Specialist."

I had purchased a trombone while in high school and played in the high school band, having taught myself. So I played a little trombone when I first got into the field band, but shortly got switched to mallet percussion. They had us play at a presentation for some important general who came out to Sheppard Field. We were out there marching along in response to a series of whistle commands. I was trying to play the glockenspiel on this particular drill and was confused by the commands. The band is marching around in different directions and I was just kind of following them wherever they went while reading my part. The next thing I knew, I looked up, turned around, and saw the band going away from me in the opposite direction. I was marching straight ahead on the field all by myself. I ran back to the band with this big glockenspiel bouncing in front of me.

Soon I was assigned to Special Services, where I wrote for three band libraries. Each library was fifteen to thirty arrangements of songs. I chose a variety of popular songs because jazz was not well accepted by the military at the time. However, I did manage to sneak some swing feel in along the way. Every arrangement was handwritten on score paper, which was twice the height of a regular piece of paper. One arrangement could be thirty pages for a three minute song, so it was a time-consuming process. After writing the orchestral score, I would take one line, which might say "Trumpet 1" and copy it onto staff paper, and so on, until each musician had parts for all the music that would be played. It was helpful that I was able to write a complete arrangement from hearing a song just one time.

I also produced a weekly show called Shep Parade. During the week, I auditioned people on the base who seemed to have any kind of talent at all. A small budget allowed me to bring in some acts from Fort Worth and Dallas. We put the show together and did it on Monday and Tuesday nights at the theater on the post. I invited Helen Carr to come down and sing in the show.

One day, I was sitting at the desk, and a small fellow walked in and said, "How can I get in the band?"

I said, "Well, what do you do?"

"I'm a trumpet player."

"How well do you play?"

"Pretty good."

I said, "Okay, fine, we'll do it."

Leo Adelman had just arrived and he weighed about 140 pounds soaking wet. His gear hadn't come in yet, like his duffel bag and all the accoutrements that they assign to you when you first get in the service. He was probably not even big enough to carry it. A day later, it was delivered to the loading dock over where the train came in. He stopped by my desk and said, "My stuff is here. I don't know what to do about getting it."

I said, "Don't worry; leave it to me."

Because I was now in Special Services, I had a hat with a band insignia, which was not significant of any special status, but it looked like a warrant officers cap. When I would leave the post, instead of having to show my pass, they would actually salute me. I could get on and off the base easily with this cap. I borrowed the Lieutenant's car and we drove over to the loading dock. We loaded his gear into the car and brought it over to the band barracks. I walked in with Leo and, as soon as I walked in, some soldier yelled, "Ten-hut" because they thought I was an officer.

I was carrying Leo's duffel, and said, "Where would you like it Leo?"

He said, "That's my bunk down there."

I said, "Fine."

I brought it down, dropped it at his bunk, said "At ease," and walked out.

I lived in the band barracks along with Bill Byers, who was a fine jazz trombonist and played in the band I directed. He became a legendary arranger and was a ghost writer for Quincy Jones. Bill was a unique and strange man. I've never known anyone that wrote music quite the way he did. He could sit in a room, watch a ball game while listening to some music, and write horizontally across a score page in ink a lead alto part, then the second alto part, then the first tenor part, then the second tenor part, and then the baritone part. All this, while doing several other things at the same time.

Billy was the first person to turn me on to grass. He had marijuana planted all around the band barracks. There was an old staff sergeant there, and Billy got this lifer to water his plants. He told him it was some exotic plant from somewhere and he would go around with a watering can and water Bill's plants. We were standing outside a USO Hall in Wichita Falls. He said, "Come on let's smoke some of this."

I said, "I don't think so."

He continued, "Oh come on man, you are always so negative about things. You got to do this. It's important to your life. Try it."

So I decided to try it, but I would fool him somehow and expel it out the corner of my mouth so he wouldn't see it. I can't remember if it was in cigarette form or a pipe, but I took a little puff on it and, not knowing how to smoke anyway, I just sort of got rid of it.

With Special Services in 1946.

I was in the service for fifteen months all together. After eleven months at Sheppard Field, I was transferred to Scott Field for the remaining four months. In the band, there was Don Helfman, a.k.a. Don Elliott. Don was an incredible talent and great to have in the band because he was so versatile. He was primarily a trumpet player, but he also sang and played vibraphone and mellophone, a brass instrument similar to a French horn. Don had a hit with his comedic vocal creation, "The Nutty Squirrels," which was actually a respectful tribute to Charlie Parker. He became the second pioneer of multi-track recording, with Les Paul being the first. He was also an important producer of commercial jingles and contributed vocal work for Quincy Jones' film scores.

Helen and I were going together by now and she moved to be near me. We got a little place by the famous Chase Hotel in St. Louis. They had a venue called the Steeplechase Room with a trio lead by a great guitarist Joe Schirmer. That's where Helen learned one of Cole Porter's lesser-known songs, "Down in the Depths (on the 90th Floor)." The song has three different segments; it's not written as a standard thirty-two bar song form. It tells a story, which requires a distribution of different emotions within the lyric content. There's a line I often think of because of the way she sang it, "With a million neon rainbows, burning below me." It takes a certain kind of vocalist to pull it off. Helen Carr was that kind of vocalist.

With that sultry quality in Helen's voice, you could hear Billie Holiday's influence. Helen was more of a soprano, but not a high-pitched soprano. She didn't have an enormous range, but she maximized her talents in the way she approached a song. Helen could interpret music with great feeling. She had wonderful rhythmic timing and excellent pitch. Helen taught me a lot of songs.

I went into town to be with her as often as I could and would catch a bus back to the post when I needed to. It was pouring rain one morning while I was waiting at the bus stop, and I wrote a song called, "Memory of the Rain." Helen and I would record that song. In the 1990s it was re-released in a Bethlehem Complete Works CD collection. We continued to date, and after I got out of the service I brought her to New York.

5 Ritual Fire Dance

HELEN CARR'S STRIKING BEAUTY rivaled that of Lana Turner. However, Helen was limited as an entertainer because she frequently sang songs like "Trouble is a Man" and "Lover Man," and although they were beautiful, highly sophisticated selections, they were not well-known at the time. People wanted to hear popular tunes.

I was still nineteen when I got out of the service in the fall of 1946. We rented a little flat, a room on West 86th Street, and started looking for work. A few months later, Helen and I decided to elope. We went down to Elkton, Maryland and got married. It was a romantic time and we had, as many couples do, our favorite song: "More Than You Know." Later on, when I was traveling and playing radio shows with Les Brown, I could send her a signal by playing the first four notes from that song. I would throw that in when I was playing a solo knowing that she would hear it.

While we were dating I noticed Helen reacted in negative ways whenever she was in the presence of other women, but I thought she was just a little insecure. At the time, I believed it was a relatively minor problem that could be overcome, but early on in our marriage the problems set in, and I began to realize that it was something more than just jealousy. I had to rush home after engagements if she was not with me. If the gig was over at 1:00, and it was a thirty minute drive, and if I wasn't home by 1:35, allowing me five minutes to get to my car, I had to explain where I was. It was neurotic, really. I was not able at the time to fully analyze how destructive this was going to be to our relationship.

I began playing with a series of bands, and Helen and I, out of necessity, often traveled together. It was always fun when we worked together, but it got to a point where I couldn't take any engagements unless there was a performing role for her. I worked with The Tommy Dorsey Orchestra for just one week. Without a place for Helen in that band, I knew it would not work out. I was invited to audition for the newly reorganized Glenn Miller Band under the direction of Tex Beneke. They were playing in Auburndale, Massachusetts at a place called the Totem Pole. Someone called me to go up and audition because their pianist, Henry Mancini, was leaving the band. Ginny O'Connor, the girl singer for the band, had returned home to California. Hank and she wanted to get married, so he was moving out there, as well. I was offered the job, but I couldn't take the position because it was too much traveling and they already had another singer lined up to replace Ginny. We had this kind of situation in our marriage; if she wasn't there, I didn't go. I became conditioned to turning things down even though we needed the money.

For our need of money, I went out with one of the worst hotel orchestras I ever heard, Blue Barron. We used to call these kinds of sweet-sounding novelty groups "Mickey Mouse Bands." It required me to play a real "boom chuck" style. I told the leader, Harry Friedland, "I can't do that, that's not music," but we agreed to disagree. Again, I needed the money. But this time the circumstances would lead to Helen and me working together. She had gotten a job with another one of these bands under Chuck Foster. Through a series of phone calls ,we worked it out so that the pianist with Chuck Foster would go with Blue Barron, and I'd join Chuck Foster.

We played the Blue Room of the Roosevelt Hotel in New Orleans, and Helen was with us. Chuck's dance band was fairly well-known in the hotel circles. In those days, the hotel's dance orchestra was also likely to be called upon for a show. For several days, we rehearsed for a variety show. There was an opening act that used the "Ritual Fire Dance," which had a written-out piano solo that was technically difficult. The choreographer, Donn Arden, was spending a lot of time working out the dance steps. The orchestra was on hold. Fifteen or sixteen musicians were sitting there waiting for him. It was hard for me to sit in front of a piano without playing a little bit, so I started lightly practicing. All of a sudden I heard Arden yell at me, "Stop that noodling!" They went on working and we went on waiting. Awhile later, I absent-mindedly started to play again. Arden this time screamed in his abrasive, obnoxious voice, "I told you to stop that noodling!" He kept us waiting and we were getting restless. Of course, at

On the road with Chuck Foster and Tony DeNicola in 1947.

some point I started playing again. He whipped around and said in a patronizing tone, "Why don't you just practice the "Ritual Fire Dance" and get that under your fingers instead of noodling all the time?" I was really embarrassed.

Afterwards, I was out in the lobby waiting for an elevator and noticed Arden was standing with his back to me. I reached around to the front of him, grabbed him by his shirt, and whipped him around. "Don't you ever talk to me like that again or you'll be playing the 'Ritual Fire Dance." I let him go and walked away.

In 1947, after a few months of playing hotel gigs with Chuck Foster, I got a call from the Buddy Morrow band. Helen was able to get on the band with me and we went with the band for about six months. I wrote a few charts for Buddy's band that Helen could sing. This was before his famous "Night Train" recording and the band didn't yet exist on a regular basis. Periodically, an agency would organize tours and put dates together. We did a lot of those summer resort ballrooms. I remember doing parties at country clubs around Detroit, playing straight-ahead promotional dances, where the band had been booked on a specific date, at such and such a location, from 9:00 pm to 1:00 am. They developed a whole itinerary of those, maybe five or six a week. Those bands had to work a lot in order to maintain the salaries. They were the same kind of gigs as with Ted Fio Rito.

One night in Buddy's band, at a hotel in Indianapolis, some of the boys got together in my room after the gig. I had a finger-painting set. Someone had given it to me and I just took it along on the tour. The gentlemen were smoking grass. I guess by this time, I had learned a little bit about how to administer it properly. I remember standing up and making a speech, "You guys really cause so many problems for yourself. I don't know what you're talking about. This stuff does not do anything for you. It's all a figment of your imagination. I can't possibly believe that you even spend time doing this." To prove my point, I took a couple of hits. I don't remember much after that, but I do remember we went out to a little restaurant and I ate four large ham sandwiches.

Some of the boys stayed behind in my room. When we got back, I found them locked in the bathroom and I could hear them giggling and making a lot of noise. They had taken the finger-painting set out and totally destroyed the bathroom. Paint was all over the walls and somehow on the ceiling. Helen and I didn't know what to do. We just started scrubbing, trying to clean it up, with little success. The next morning, we checked out of the hotel mincingly and quickly got out of town. Lucky for us, we didn't hear any more about it.

Life on the road can be difficult. Money is often narrow. We lived in tight quarters with lots of people and dealt with different personalities. We would arrive at our hotel in the early morning after riding on a bus overnight. Usually the rooms wouldn't be ready and it was noisy. Musicians generally don't dwell on the difficulties. Part of being in the club of musicians is about seeing the humor in almost everything. It was never boring and practical jokes are part of the experience.

I enjoyed being with Buddy. On the bus at night, I enjoyed going up to the front, where he always sat, to talk with him, sometimes for a couple of hours. I had some serious conversations with Buddy, the personal nature of which I never had with anyone else before; just never felt comfortable or had the opportunity. There were problems in my relationship with Helen that I didn't understand, and Buddy would patiently listen. Even with the complications of my marriage, this was actually a wonderful period in my life. I was young and in love, and most of the time I enjoyed my work.

After Buddy's band, Helen and I headed to San Francisco. She was from that area and that's where we had met. I knew she had a child from a previous marriage, but I didn't know much about her past. Her son, Gordon, was still out there, and that was one of the reasons that we centered back there in 1948.

I had become close to a couple of musicians, who had been on the Chuck Foster band. Drummer Tony DeNicola and saxophonist John Setar followed us out to California, and *The Donn Trio and Helen* was born. We had some photos taken to help promote the group. Tony would later go with jazz saxophonist, Charlie Ventura, and The Harry James Orchestra. John Setar is a versatile musician with a strong sense of harmonic constructs, which makes him a great jazz player. Like John, students often learned clarinet in school and then pick up the saxophone; alto, tenor, or baritone, and sometimes bass clarinet. Few musicians can play all of these instruments as well as John. He later became my orchestra contractor, and good friend. John's easy-going personality made him especially effective in dealing with television executives in our later adventures. That was my trio, without bass, just piano, drums, and John, who played all the reeds, with Helen.

We put in for our union cards in San Francisco, which was a restrictive process. At that time, there was a six-month period of waiting for all the amenities afforded to a full member of the local. During the first three months, musicians could only do casual club dates; no steady engagements were allowed. After the third month, we could take a steady engagement. During that time, the four of us rented two rooms at the Hotel Continental.

With John Setar, Tony DeNicola and Helen.

We had one bathroom in between the two rooms. We used to stash milk outside the window with bread and bologna, or whatever else we could make sandwiches with. We lived a carefully planned financial existence, playing club dates while waiting for our union cards.

I was called to do a single, a date playing as a solo performer. There was a new pianist coming into town, who was just starting to get some notoriety. He was booked into a club that only opened for this engagement, strangely enough. He was George Shearing, and I had to open for him. I sat up on stage at the same piano he played on and no matter where I looked my eyes seemed to always land on him, and I really got nervous. He introduced me with his wonderful British accent, "And now ladies and gentlemen, the twelve magic fingers of Donn Trenner." I used that as a quote in newspaper advertisements for other engagements.

In San Francisco, I also put together a band of three White and three Black gentlemen, which was unusual at that time. Alto saxophonist Paul Desmond and trumpeter Alan Smith were in that group. We did a little skit on a tune that we used to do as a showcase. Paul and Alan Smith would go out front and dance the eight bar bridge. We had fun doing it, and the audience enjoyed it.

Paul was one of the most lyrical musicians I've ever heard, and truly an intellectual.

Many years later, I visited with him just a week before he died. Someone called, who knew that I knew Paul, and said that if I was to be in New York anytime soon, I'd better see Paul because he was gravely ill. I went up to see him. He was sitting in his living room, looking worn out and emaciated. There was a coffee table with about five packages of Merit cigarettes, one opened and the others not yet. I knew my usual need to say something and hoped it would be a little bit amusing, but what came out was not the least bit funny. I said, "Is there really any merit in all of that?" A week later, while traveling with Shirley MacLaine, and driving somewhere after the show, I was listening to Paul playing on the radio. The announcer came on and said, "And that was the late great Paul Desmond." I was deeply saddened by the loss of a friend and a genius musician.

I received a call to go down to Los Angeles to do a session with Charles "Baron" Mingus. I don't recall all the details of this date, only that we recorded a few tunes with saxophonist Buddy Collette, who was well-known there. We did put down "Boppin' in Boston" where we had to scat sing the syllables: sha-bah-bah-a-da-la-clee-blo ta-bloo. With Helen, we recorded "Say It Isn't So." It was not documented, but after listening to the

Paul Desmond and Alan Smith

recordings years later, I believe I am also the pianist on "Mingus Fingers" and "These Foolish Things."

The Donn Trio and Helen lasted about a year, until I wound up going out on the road with Charlie Barnet. Charlie had been traveling with a ten-piece or eleven-piece orchestra for a while. That phase of touring was ending, and he reorganized the big band in Sacramento. They came into San Francisco and I guess he heard me, or maybe somebody had recommended me. He asked if I would be interested in going with the band. Of course, and because the offer also included Helen, I said yes. We went out on the road with that band from 1950 to 1951. He was a fascinating individual with a good fiery orchestra. Trumpet player, Al Porcino, and several other fine players were in the band. We did some things that were really fun to play, like a recording session with strings.

We were still living in San Francisco at the time. One night when Charlie's band was in town, I was invited to a hotel room. I was told there was someone I needed to meet and was ushered inside. One of the musicians, Red Kelly, who had been on the Ted Fio Rito band with me, was lying down on the bed face up with a towel covering most of his face. They drew two eyes and a nose on his chin. It became an improvised comedy routine. You asked this creature questions and it answered you back in a strange voice as it smoked a cigarette. It was hysterical. These kinds of skits were a common part of our lives. Years later, Red started a nightclub in Olympia, Washington, and he ran for governor.

There is a famous recording of "Early Autumn" that was done by Woody Herman, with a wonderful tenor saxophone solo by Stan Getz coming out of one of the choruses. One particular night, we were lying there and Red was stoned out of his brains lying on the floor. Everybody thought he was asleep, when all of a sudden he got up off the floor and said, "I got it! I got it! I know what Stan Getz was saying in that solo." Red had composed a lyric for Stan's tenor solo on "Early Autumn."

> Oh, good mornin', How the fuck are you this very lovely day.
> You gotta get up. You gotta get up today, gotta get up.
> You know lately you've become a sort of a sleepy head,
> It's true, can't blame you. But let me tell you bros,
> Time to get started, time for the gig to start,
> And you know how the old man flips if anyone's late.

It works perfectly to that solo. One night, some years later, I sang this to Sammy Davis Jr. at a party in his Las Vegas hotel suite.

The Band traveled doing many, many one-nighters. With Charlie Barnet, there was a tendency to go into more jazz clubs because Charlie's band was much more representative of being a jazz orchestra. Charlie had an arranger from California, Paul Villepigue. Paul also wrote original music, including a song called "Lonely Street" that Charlie recorded. He was an unusually good writer who was strongly influenced by the Ellingtonian style, and Charlie Barnet adored Duke Ellington. Paul understood Ellington dissonances and could create that effect. I remember a scene that took place in Charlie Barnet's apartment one night while we were there. He was playing his Ellington recordings and Rita, his third and fifth wife said, "Oh Charles why do you always play that? It's so blasé."

He really got angry, went over to her, stuck his finger in her face, and said, "Rita, don't you ever say Duke Ellington is blasé."

When he wasn't on the road, Charlie lived in Sherman Oaks. He had three cages of monkeys. He had trained one of them to use the toilet. It would actually go upstairs and use the toilet and push the lever to flush it, but wouldn't take his hand off of the handle, so Charlie had to go up and release it from its hand. He also had one monkey that didn't like Rita at all. That monkey was often up on Charlie's shoulders with its front paws laced into Charlie's hair. When Rita walked into the room, he felt like the monkey was going to pull all his hair out. He claimed that often the monkey would put his hand behind itself, defecate and throw it at Rita. That's true love!

The Barnet band toured from coast to coast. There was a club on 49th street in New York that was upstairs over a well-known restaurant. It was called Bop City. One night, we were there with Charlie Barnet and the whole orchestra. Many people came in to hear the band and we went through our normal concert sets. Whatever set we were playing, we knew that on the next number Charlie would be playing his tenor sax.

This particular night, he grabbed his soprano saxophone and everybody in the band was looking at one another wondering what he was up to because this tune required the tenor. He made an announcement to the audience. "Ladies and gentlemen, I know I've said this before, but I want to make it clear. I will never set foot in front of a band again. And for those of you who are disbelievers… ." He lifted up his knee, took his soprano saxophone, and whack, the horn was ruined. Then he walked off stage. We were shocked. The club had to return money to the people who had paid cover charges. Earlier that night, Charlie found out that his wife was seeing Billy May, a good friend of Charlie's. Billy is still referred to as one of the great arrangers. He worked for Frank Sinatra, Nancy Wilson, Charlie, Sammy Davis, Jr. and many others. It seemed this incident would end the tour, but Charlie got over that in a day or two and we went on to finish the dates.

I recall sitting somewhere with the band in a hotel room and Charlie was sitting on the bed with me, and my back was up against Charlie's. Two or three of us were sitting on the bed listening to some music or something and Charlie turned around over his shoulder and said, "You know what? You're the greatest fucking musician I've met in ten years." Well, I didn't know quite to how take that. I was somewhat embarrassed, but felt flattered anyway.

While Helen and I were still based in San Francisco, we played a few dates down in Los Angeles. I used a saxophone player on those dates named Bud Shank. This was before Bud became so well-known for the work he did with Shorty Rogers and all the West Coast Jazz recordings. We had talked about moving down to Los Angeles, and after Charlie Barnet I wanted to get out of San Francisco to further my career. First, we had to go to court to get permission that would allow us to take Helen's young son out of the selected jurisdiction of Contra Costa, Alameda and Oakland Counties. We got permission and moved down to Los Angeles.

From 1952 to 1954, I worked with various people in the Los Angeles area. Jerry Gray was an arranger who wrote for a lot of bands. His billing read, *Jerry Gray and his Band of Today*, and we used to call it, "Jerry Gray and his Band of Yesterday." He wrote a lot of famous arrangements for Glenn Miller, such as "String of Pearls." I didn't travel with Jerry's band. I worked locally with him, mostly on club dates, but we did play the Hollywood Palladium several times, which was a thirty-minute drive from where I lived. I also came to play regularly at the Hollywood Palladium with Les Brown. Les Brown's orchestra had a consistently tight rhythm section. In an orchestra, the rhythm section is usually made up of piano, bass, drums, and sometimes rhythm guitar. It has to be almost perfect. If it doesn't come together really well, then the orchestra can't swing. The rhythm section is the "motor" that supplies the energy. One person can ruin an entire rhythm section, so the players depend on each other. There's an incredible trust that builds over time. When it isn't working, it doesn't feel right. You can't fake it. If the rhythm section isn't cohesive then the arrangements won't work. When it's right, we've always called it playing in the "pocket."

Around this time, I played an engagement with saxophonist Georgie Auld, Red Callender on bass and Larry Bunker on drums. Georgie was well-known in Chicago, New York, and all the jazz circles. Georgie was a big personality and a prominent tenor player. Later in his career, he appeared in the film, *New York, New York* (1977). We played for about two weeks at The Haig, a Hollywood jazz club that was well-known at the time. Georgie put together this combo with piano, bass, and drums, and he was the soloist. We mostly played blues tunes and well-known jazz standards, such as "How High the Moon."

I also recorded with Georgie. Our record producer, George Kates, had a concept for tenor sax with singers. He used a vocal group as an orchestral arrangement. They became the background for Georgie's solos. Vocal groups, when they're good, are harmonically inviting and a real pleasure to work with. It's like putting a string section behind a singer. It was an unusual setting for a jazz soloist, but it worked out well.

George Kates was a talented producer but an obnoxious man. He didn't know how to talk to people or direct musicians. I was playing piano once and he came over my shoulder and started playing the piano to show me how a piece should be played. It was bizarre. Kates eventually became involved with the Lawrence Welk Orchestra and their television show. They had a huge listening audience. It was a wonderful gig for the local musicians. The pianist, Bob Smale, was on the band for years. His answering machine message was an imitation of Lawrence Welk's unusually funny accent and phrasing. There are many Welk-isms out there: "Now ladies and a gentlemen, we'd like to play a famous… uh… Duke Ellington song, 'Take A Da Train.' And here's a selection from World War i."

An association with the Tiffany Club developed within that first year in Los Angeles. The owner, Chuck Landis, was interested in bringing in some great names in jazz, and that's what he did for a while. I was lucky enough to play there with a couple of the best.

Cliff Aronson called me about putting a group together for an engagement with Charlie Parker and later for Stan Getz. Cliff was the West Coast representative of Associated Booking Corporation. ABC was owned by Joe Glaser, a tough manager. A fifteen-word conversation with Glaser often had twelve profane words in it, but he was hugely successful. For years, he booked two musicians who were not signed but represented on a handshake only basis. One was Louis Armstrong and the other was Les Brown. I got a call from Cliff, and we talked about putting the group together for Charlie Parker. There was some discussion about using Chet Baker because Charlie knew of him. Chet was attracting a lot of attention in the jazz world and I thought he would be a good choice for the engagement. Circumstances were also that I had known Chetty. I first met him in San Francisco at a jam session when he was in uniform. He was stationed at the Presidio. I didn't go to those jam sessions often, but I met him there one night and then I knew him in passing in Los Angeles. I went ahead and hired the musicians and one of them was Chet Baker. With Bird and Chet, I had Lawrence Marable on drums and the bass player was Harry Babasin. With Stan Getz, it was just him and a trio, with Jimmy Pratt on drums and Gene Englund on bass. Each engagement was for fifteen days with Mondays off.

Late in May 1952, we set up and rehearsed on a Tuesday afternoon and opened that night for the run. Parker had been working everywhere but New York, due to the loss of his cabaret license. I was pretty naive as to the extent of Charlie Parker's habits. It was fascinating really. At the rehearsal, we spent over two hours sitting there watching him drink tumblers of bourbon and everyone was calling him "Bird." He didn't even take his horn out of the case. Eventually he said, "I guess we better run over a couple of tunes." Finally he took his alto out and said, "Let's do 'The Song Is You,'" which is a wonderful tune with a difficult bridge, and he counted off a very bright tempo. We played that, and rehearsed a few

With Bird and Chet in 1952.

other tunes. Bird had some more bourbon, and was taken to his hotel where he dressed and came back for the gig.

My impression of Bird was that he was a true genius. I learned some bebop tunes with him because I didn't have the opportunity to learn them any other way. I already knew "Groovin' High" and other standard bebop heads that all the musicians were now playing, but I had not gotten into some of the deeper compositions of Parker. I got through the engagement playing whatever was necessary. We played tune after tune after tune, and it was a thrill to work with him.

On the Monday nights off from the Tiffany Club, we played at another club in Inglewood, just outside of Los Angeles, near the airport. In addition, Sonny Criss would appear as a guest. One of those Monday dates was recorded and later released as an album titled, *On the Coast,* the Charlie Parker All-Stars with Chet Baker and Sonny Criss. After all these years, I was shocked to learn it had been recorded.

During intermissions, Bird used to love to eat spicy Mexican food and drink. Many musicians came in just to hang out with him. I'm not a good representative of what it felt like to be social with Bird; same with Stan Getz. I was naive as a young adult because I didn't hang out. "Hanging out" was a term that was unimportant to me. "Let's hang out."

And do what, was always my first thought. *What are we going to do if we hang out?* The idea of going to a bar and drinking never appealed to me. I was involved in other things, whether it was my life at home or building something, or just wanting to be at home. To "hang out" just had no context for me. Let's go drink and waste some time? Maybe it was unfortunate that the whole social essence of that period might have escaped me.

I heard Stan Getz on jazz radio programs while driving. I listened to a lot of music in my car because there were good radio stations in California. I was certainly enamored with his playing. I thought there was some kind of extended genius in what he was doing. I never heard anything come out of his horn that didn't feel like it had gone through a mistake filter; it was flawless. Of course it was extemporaneous, immediate, and wonderful, but it sounded perfect. I found his personality diametrically opposed to what I felt from his playing. I had heard from other people that he could be onerous, but I didn't really see this come through until many years later when I did a jazz festival in Sweden and got to be around him again. Stan was socially ostracized because of this. It didn't make sense to me that this wonderful warm soulful player wouldn't be a wonderful warm soulful person, as well.

Helen and I finally did an album on Bethlehem Records. Prior to that album, though, Helen and I signed with a record company called Trend, which recorded and developed jazz artists. Albert Marx, also owner of Discovery Records, was the first to record The George Shearing Quintet in this country. Albert phoned us, we went over to his house, and he signed us to a record contract. He frightened me. For whatever reason, he was so intimidating I couldn't exist around him. We let a whole year go by without doing an album and just let the contract expire. We finally got a chance to record our first album for Red Clyde, who was the Artists and Repertoire (A&R) man for Bethlehem Records' West Coast operations. Helen and I recorded "Memory of the Rain." The title tune of the album was the Cole Porter song, "Down in the Depths (on the 90th Floor)." On this album we had Charlie Mariano on alto sax, Don Fagerquist on trumpet, Stan Levy on drums, and Max Bennett on bass. There are some wonderful solos by Charlie and Don on this first album.

I bought my first house with a $25 deposit, and a friend loaned me the rest for a $185 down payment. It was in Reseda, just outside of Los Angeles, in the San Fernando Valley. It had three bedrooms, one bath, and a one-car garage. It included a Westinghouse washing machine in the garage. The lot was 50' wide and 150' front to back. It cost $9,200 and the payments were $52 a month PITI on the GI Bill, which meant principal, interest, taxes, and insurance. That monthly payment would fluctuate; some years it would go up as high as $53. The house was actually very nice and I stayed there for several years.

There was a pianist in Los Angeles by the name of Geoff Clarkson, who had been on Les Brown's band for many years. Les' band played great dance music and was booked to play a couple of nights at the Zenda Ballroom, right across the street from the Biltmore Hotel. Geoff was unable to play that engagement, and they asked me to fill in. Many of the pieces written for Les' band had rhythm section solis, with piano and electric guitar written together. Solis are written solos, not improvisations, performed by more than one player, usually a section within the ensemble. I went in having to sight-read the book. Somebody called me later and told me that I sounded like I had been with the band for twenty years. I guess they were complimenting my reading ability, which I appreciated. Then I got a call shortly after that saying Geoff was not going to work with the orchestra any longer, and would I like to go with them. I jumped at the opportunity.

6

Give Me an 'A'

I WAS WITH LES BROWN and His Band of Renown during much of 1954 to 1961. When we were not playing the Hollywood Palladium or performing for The Bob Hope Show, we'd go on tour. With the Palladium being just a half hour drive from home, our three-week or four-week engagements there were especially easy for me. For the sake of Helen's career, and for our relationship, I needed to leave the band for a short period to go to New York. Then I returned home to California and rejoined the band. It was difficult for Helen when I was playing for Les because she wasn't working, and felt the need to be with me all the time. Her constant distrust continued to put a serious strain on our marriage.

Work was fairly steady with the Les Brown band. We did a lot of touring, but for the most part, the tours weren't too bad for the guys with families. We didn't go out for long stretches and had nice breaks in between. We often did ten-day tours using a chartered DC-3, playing college dances and concerts. The one extended stretch each year was the summer tour, with over seventy one-nighters and often no days off. Those were exhausting tours, but they were an important part of our earnings.

The salary was good, not great, but good, around $250-$300 a week at the time. In addition, the band was also employed by Bob Hope, which made it financially rewarding. The whole time with Les' orchestra was a really wonderful experience. The music was always good. Sometimes it was great and sometimes it was sensational. There were so many outstanding players and the repertory represented exemplary writing from many great composers and arrangers.

Ray Sims, brother of legendary tenor saxophonist Zoot Sims, was on the band. Besides playing in the trombone section, he sang "Flamingo." Ray was a nice trombone player even though he may not have had a great command of the instrument, which comes from the intellectual approach of studying an instrument formally. He cracked notes on occasion, but that was just a lack of proper training, nevertheless he played with a warm soulful feeling. Dave Pell, another great player, was on tenor sax. We had players like Don Fagerquist, who was one of the great trumpet players of all times. He had a natural talent for being a jazz player. His compositional efforts, in the realm of improvisation, were lyrically expressive. He was easy to accompany and fun to trade eight-bar and four-bar phrases with.

After Don Fagerquist left Les' band, he became involved in the studios. When he was doing The Red Skelton Show, I'd to go over to the studio to see him every once in a while and he would be buried in this maze of playing cues and utilitarian musical commitments. Of course, Don was fully capable, but the work wasn't particularly fulfilling, and it certainly didn't utilize his vast talent as a creative musician. Eventually he drank himself to death.

I played at Don's funeral and was worried because it was in a Catholic Church. I didn't want to do anything that upset the protocol, but I really wanted to play "Young Man with a Horn" in remembrance of Don, which may not have been appropriate in the eyes of the church. I remember sitting up at the organ and my hands were shaking. I was afraid I would miss the keys, but I played the song anyway. He was a close friend and indeed a sweet man with an incredible talent, one of the best.

There was a sax player with Les' band from Connecticut who played lead alto. Sal Libro was famous for creating nicknames for the guys. It took him a while to come up with one for me, and what he came up with was classic. When I first joined Les' band, I was young and couldn't help myself when it came to correcting notes. I'd yell out, "Second trumpet, it's C-natural not a C-sharp!" It would just come out of my mouth without thinking. Anytime a new chart was brought in, and something was wrong, Les would look over at me expecting me to correct it. Also, I've always had a chocolate addiction, so I was often seen eating chocolate of some kind. My mother fed me a lot of it because she frequently made chocolate cakes. Sal finally came up with a nickname for me, Herschel Hawkshaw the Tune Detective. Herschel was for Hershey and Hawkshaw after the comic strip character; hence, the tune detective.

Several people in the Les Brown band became quite important to me. One in particular was Butch Stone, who was well-known in the band business. He played baritone sax and sang a couple of novelty tunes, such as "A Good Man Nowadays is Hard to Find" and "Robin Hood." As road manager, Butch was a master of psychology. He could deal with the orchestra and the pitfalls of each day, anything from a difficult schedule to hotel logistics to problems in restaurants, when the food wasn't good or we couldn't get waited on, or any of the various challenges of being on the road. Butch had a natural talent for coming up with one clever sentence that would make everything right. He also used to stand in front of the bus and make speeches to the orchestra. After a strenuous day, he would wait until we had packed up, boarded, and Les was seated. Then Butch would walk up the steps, turn left and put his hand on the back of Les' chair, so that Les couldn't see his facial expressions. He then did a routine like: "Gentlemen, I just want to thank you, and Les particularly wants to thank you, for being so cooperative today under such arduous conditions." He would lean back to look at Les' face. The guys in the band would be breaking up because Les would already be deep into his book. "Les also wanted me to tell you that he really appreciated the problem with the rooms not being ready today… ." He could do comedic bits like this that

With Les Brown's band, Butch Stone on baritone sax.

just broke us up. He was so clever in being able to take a hard day, and with his sense of humor, defuse the tension and make it all right. I learned a lot from Butch Stone about handling orchestras and handling people in a leader capacity. This became enormously valuable to me later on.

The front seat on the right side of the bus was Les Brown's. He had an array of bridge and golf books and a donut cushion. Les never knew where the band was going or where it had been. He was totally involved in bridge and golf. I sat opposite Les, right behind the bus driver, and became the assistant bus driver. Les woke up one night and saw me driving. I thought he was going to lose it. I drove the bus on several occasions because we had a bus driver who apparently had some kind of allergic reaction to certain foods. I watched him one night as his face just got so absolutely swollen his eyes closed. I said, "You can't even see. Do you want me to drive?"

He said, "Can you handle this bus?"

I said, "Of course."

I had never driven a bus before in my life, but I knew how to do it because I had been watching him and my ears told me where all the RPM ratios were for the gear shifting. I really enjoyed it.

We were on the road one summer and Helen was with me, so I drove my own car and was not traveling on the bus. This was one way of mitigating her jealousies. Whenever I could, I just took her with me. At least she appreciated my sense of humor and was a willing participant in some of my pranks. One night after we played a show, Helen and I walked a couple of blocks away to a restaurant to get something to eat. I used to get out of the hall quicker than everyone else. I never used the piano book because I knew the charts from memory, so I did have anything to pack up like the horn players or the drummer. We were already finishing supper when the bus showed up with the rest of the band. On a lark, Helen and I took the bus and hid it. I drove it back over to the auditorium, backed it down the loading ramp, got in the car, and quickly left town.

It was frustrating for me out on the road because I was the only musician who would go to work on any given night and not know how good or bad my instrument was going to be. I got really angry about the fact that pianos were so poorly maintained. There was a piano that I played in Balla, Ontario that I wanted desperately to throw into Balla Bay. This venue was located in a beautifully romantic area that was a regular tour stop for name bands during the summer. I wanted to see that piano sail down the river; it was just awful.

On more than one occasion, I set pianos on fire. I can remember one place in Ventura, California. Les wasn't there yet, but everybody else was standing around listening to how bad this instrument was. Where the piano lid lifts up and folds over there's a hinge. I realized that if I took a cigarette lighter and lit the varnish, the varnish would burn. I only got about two feet of it burning, but we all had a good laugh. I had to put the fire out because it smelled terrible. Sometimes we would take the piano lid off totally, so that it didn't acoustically destroy the sound for the rest of the rhythm section. If it was really bad, I would go out and buy some popcorn and throw some on the strings. I'd play along and all of a sudden I'd hit a big chord and the popcorn would come flying out of the piano.

We were working at a place in St. Petersburg, Florida and the piano was essentially unplayable. I was not going to be able play that thing for four hours. A trumpet player named Wes Hensel was on the band at the time and, wanting to check the pitch of his horn, said, "Give me an A." I reached in and tore a damper off and threw it at him. Before the evening was over he had several dampers. Wes carried them around in his trumpet case for years. By the time Les got there, we had already played the first set without him. I walked up to him and said, "This piano is unplayable. I'm sorry I can't play it." I thought I was doing some sort of benevolent favor for the rest of the piano players who might be coming in because the piano was now so far beyond repair that nobody in their right mind would allow it to stay; the piano would have to be replaced. Was I wrong. The next year, we were booked in the same place, and sure enough the same piano was there, now missing the dampers that I had pulled out, and I had to play it again.

Les' band was not a big recording orchestra, but we did do several albums, including the *Les Brown Song Book* and a couple of All-Star albums with Buddy DeFranco and Zoot Sims. The Dave Pell Octet, which became viewed as a noteworthy Los Angeles jazz ensemble, came about as a result of Dave's entrepreneurialism. He was a member of the Les Brown orchestra so these things were done as an extension or auxiliary to the Les Brown schedule. We recorded several albums in Hollywood. The music was terrific and the sessions were fun to do. Shorty Rogers, Marty Paich, and Johnny Mandel wrote most of the charts, and Wes Hensel also wrote a couple. Interestingly, in my travels through Europe I found the Dave Pell records to be well-known among jazz musicians there.

We worked a few dates with Dave's group, playing concerts and clubs. Dave didn't have to conduct on anything, but he did have to cut the band off. He would stand up there and, without any preparatory anticipation; attempt to cut the band off. Nobody knew where the cut-off was. Dave was very nice guy and aggressively involved in business ventures. Before he did the octet he was into photography. He would have several cameras stashed under his music stand and between tunes he'd pull them out and take pictures.

After a while, Helen did a second album titled *Why Do I Love You*. I helped put it together, but I didn't play on it. We used bassist Red Mitchell and trumpet player Cappy Lewis, who did a lot of dates with Nelson Riddle, and guitarist Howard Roberts, who was well-known on the West Coast. After this release, we decided to go back to New York again to see if we could get something going with her career. I took leave from Les Brown's band and we headed back East, and that's when our marriage really got rocky.

7 Out of the Bushes

HELEN'S ALBUM WAS OUT NOW, and we thought that maybe we could get some mileage by getting her more known in New York. We packed up and drove the car back across the country with her son, Gordon, and our German Shepard, Prez. Gordon was about fifteen years old, and we placed him in a school on Long Island. I started looking for work.

I got a call to play with Art Mooney at the Glenn Island Casino on Long Island Sound in Westchester County. Art had a good commercial orchestra and it was a nightly job for a couple of weeks. On some evenings, the Glenn Island Casino was rented out to a large private party and closed to the general public. On other nights, they had people come in to direct audience participation games. In the middle of the second week, two people came in and created a silly balloon game. People danced with a balloon pressed against each other's forehead and their arms behind them. The object was to see how long they could dance without losing the balloon. For some reason there was an uninflated balloon up on the piano, right on the music rack. Well, how long can a person look at an un-inflated balloon without doing something about it? Being the clown that I was, and perhaps because the music was just so un-stimulating, I picked up the balloon, looked over to see that the big and tall Art Mooney wasn't watching me, and blew it up. Whitey Mitchell, our bass player, was blowing up balloons, too. I let the balloon go and it took off, as a balloon will do, and it came right back and landed on the piano rack.

I played a little more and I kept looking at the balloon. I decided I had to do it one more time. This time I started to inflate the balloon and, as I did, realized there was a piano solo coming up. I didn't have time to take the balloon out of my mouth so I was sitting there with a half inflated balloon sticking out of my mouth as I played the piano solo. I looked up at Art and it didn't seem like he had noticed me doing this. After I finished my stupid little eight-bar piano solo, I blew the balloon up again. I let it go again and it took off straight for Art and hit him square in the face. He came right over to the piano. It felt like he was twenty feet tall as he stood over me and said, "I can't believe anybody with your reputation, who has worked with all the people you have worked with, would do anything like that!" He kept going on and on.

Finally, I said, "Please stop. Let's talk afterwards. I'm wrong and you're right. Let's discuss this later." I felt like I had a hot ring around my neck, I was so embarrassed.

I was going through some serious emotional pain because of my marriage. Things were not good with us and it was just a terribly difficult time. At any rate, I went up and talked to Art afterwards. I apologized and I explained what I was going through, not that it was any excuse for my behavior, but I guess it certainly was a contributing factor in my looking for a moment of levity. He was fine and accepted my apology.

On one of our days off, I got a call to work with a wonderful bassist, Oscar Pettiford, so I didn't go back with Art Mooney. The engagement was at a jazz club with Oscar and Ron Jefferson, a wonderful drummer, who was one of the thinnest people I've ever seen. Anita O'Day was on the bill with us and would come up to do part of each set. I went to Philadelphia with Oscar, and that's where my marriage really came flying apart.

I don't know how many people are aware of this, but I guess anybody who worked with Anita knew that she had a metric problem. She could get so laid back and free with improvisation that she would kind of fall too far behind and lose a measure or a beat here and there. One night when it happened, she turned around and glared at me as though I had done something wrong. Afterwards, I had a little moment with her. I told her, "Don't you ever do that again or you'll be working up here alone. We were all fine. The trio was where it was supposed to be." Somehow we got things straightened out.

While I was in Philly, it was three days before Mother's Day, so I went into a greeting card store. I was looking around for a card for Helen and this girl came up to me and said, "My, you look troubled. Is something wrong?"

And I said, "No, just troubled."

She was personable and we talked for a few minutes in the store. She told me her name was Joan Martin, and she knew a few musicians like Stan Getz and other people. She said, "If you feel like you need to contact someone here, I'll give you my phone number."

She wasn't soliciting a date and it didn't come across that way. With things being so awful with Helen and me, I felt the need to talk to someone. I called her one night and met with her the next day. We talked for a couple of hours and I went back to my hotel room.

We had come to the end of our two weeks in Philly and I was preparing to go back to New York. My transportation was all set; I would be going back with Oscar. Then Helen called me and said, "I'm coming there to pick you up."

I said, "There's no need for that. I've already got a ride back."

She insisted on coming to get me. I decided to write a note to Joan and thank her for her kindness. I didn't know when Helen was going to arrive. The note was incomplete and, being taken by surprise when she suddenly arrived, I stuffed it under a pillow. Well, Helen found it and with her propensity for being mistrustful, the fireworks started. It was late in the evening when we got into our blue Buick to drive home. Within a few minutes it became a screaming match.

We were approaching the expressway outside of Philly and by now it was just terrible in the car. She was hitting me over the head with her shoe while I was trying to drive. Just as we were about to get on the expressway, I pulled the car to the side of the road, jumped out, and ran like a wild animal into the bushes to hide. She got to the toll entrance of the expressway and they let her turn around to come back out. I saw her from the bushes, going back and forth looking for me. Finally she got back on the expressway and sped off.

I didn't know what I was going to do. It was two in the morning. I had a pocket full of money because I had just been paid. I didn't have any clothes with me because they were in the car. I crawled out of the bushes and started walking back toward the city. A police officer pulled up and asked me what I was doing. Trying to catch my breath, I replied, "I have money in my pocket. I have identification. I finished a performance with Oscar Pettiford and just had a screaming match in the car with my wife!" I told him I'd like to go back to the hotel where I had been staying because the night's rent was already paid. What I really needed was some sleep and some time to figure things out. He took me to a cab and I headed back to Philly.

The next day, I tried to reach Joan, but she wasn't there. I remembered she was a close friend of Chan Parker, Charlie Parker's wife, and that Chan lived in New Hope, Pennsylvania. Joan had mentioned that Chan owned an ice cream parlor called the Bird's Nest. I called Chan and found Joanie. She returned to Philly right away and took me to her place. Joanie had practically no money, but she went out to a delicatessen and bought a big turkey leg, some coleslaw, and brought it back. She made me eat and then said, "I'll be right back." She went out again and had a key made. "This key is yours." She knew that I had to go back to New York to honor some other engagements and to settle whatever was going on, but she said, "You can come here as much as you need."

Joanie had been a photographer's model in Philly and she also posed nude at the art schools. She had a slender figure and a lovely face. Then she moved to New York and became the caretaker of Lenny Bruce's children. Many years later, we had a short-lived romance, but it didn't ever materialize as a relationship. We stayed friends and wrote letters. I would always see her to say hello when I came back to New York. A little later on, I helped Joanie when she moved out to California. She had an understanding with Lenny that if she went to California with him, he would buy her photography equipment in payment for her taking care of his children. Joanie became a highly regarded photographer. I got her an account with Steve Allen. She spent a week with Steve and his family. Joanie didn't want anything posed. She would go to the market or the bank or whatever and be constantly shooting with her Hasselblad. She took a lot of pictures of musicians and a lot of pictures of my band. She remained a friend of mine right through to her death. Many years later, I received an alarming call from her neighbor. I went to her rental home to find she had died. Joanie was never into drug use, but lived a subsistence lifestyle with little regard for her health. The neighbor had actually stolen jewelry off her body.

My relationship with Helen had completely deteriorated. I had been faithful to her throughout our marriage, but her obsessive distrust had gotten worse over time. Helen was several years older than me and she had never been honest about her age. Maybe that contributed to her insecurities. When I was looking for some things in the house, I found papers proving Helen had never actually gotten divorced from her first husband. I was able to have the marriage annulled after all those years. After we broke up she stayed in New York. Eventually she went out with Barnet's band again. They did a seventeen-day tour, and during that time she found out that she had cancer. There was no evidence of any illness while I was with her. She passed away maybe two years after we separated. One of the last people she dated was Zoot Sims. My mother was one of the last people to see Helen alive, and I visited her in a New York hospital about two weeks before she died. Gordon was now eighteen years old and in the service. He called me after the funeral and he told me he arranged to have my picture put in the coffin with her, which he must have thought was important.

After all the painful emotional difficulties of my marriage, I needed to get away. Someone in New York offered me an engagement on a ship, the SS Independence. So I took a voyage. It was a twenty-one-day round-trip excursion from New York to Naples, Italy. It was nice trip, but the ship had a strict policy that we were not allowed to socialize with the passengers. I have always enjoyed getting to know people, hearing their stories, and sharing an appreciation for music. So that was a little difficult for me, but I got through it. After that, I returned to California and Les Brown.

8

Snack Bar

EARLY ON, LES BROWN'S BAND did the weekly Bob Hope radio show at NBC Studios in a building on the corner of Hollywood and Vine streets. It contained a number of rooms large enough to put a big orchestra in for studio work. Those radio days were a lot of fun. We had special guests and a regular singer named Margaret Whiting. She was a wonderful singer. We used to call her "One-Take Maggie." When we went in to do these radio shows, if a number didn't work well, we could redo it. We never had to with Margaret; she'd get it on the first take and made it easy. Just hand her the chart, play it down once, rehearse it a little and it was in the show. She's one of those singers who had built-in pitch that she didn't have to work for.

Many stars were guests, such as the "Richard Burtons," the "Elizabeth Taylors," and folks like that. We also did skits where they'd bring a sound effects unit in and create an auditory set. If a door was involved, they had a little door that they opened and shut, or sirens, or any other kind of extraneous noises, creaking if it was a mysterious skit, horns blowing, or whatever. If there was a fight, they had sounds that could match somebody getting punched in the jaw.

Bob lived near the NBC Studios and that was convenient because NBC was like Bob's second home. This was a transitional period, where we continued to do the radio shows and also started producing his television variety show specials, one every six or seven weeks. This was nice financially because it meant extra money in addition to our regular orchestra salary.

The Les Brown and Bob Hope association impacted all subsequent events in my career. I worked with so many wonderful people during those Bob Hope years: Dorothy Lamour, Ginger Rogers, Rosemary Clooney, Janice Page, Grace Kelly, David Niven, Jimmy Durante, the list goes on and on. I got to spend time with each guest during the rehearsal period.

I also spent a lot of time with Bob and we developed a positive working relationship and a warm friendship. Bob also brought me along for private engagements. We went into area hospitals to entertain. They would move a small upright piano around to the different wards. In Japan, on one of the Christmas trips abroad, we did a couple of hospitals in a town called Itazuke that had a US Air Force Base. The full show didn't go to Itazuke. Bob and I took a cab from Tokyo, which was a long journey. In about eleven seconds we discovered the rules of the open road there. If it's open, use it. It was a scary ride.

Back in the US, Bob and I did a series of one-nighters. We were in Boise, Idaho, one evening and Bob asked me to take a walk with him after the show. We were meandering through the empty streets of Boise sharing stories and a few laughs when we happened upon the local police station. Bob casually suggested, "Let's go inside and say hello to the fellas." The officers on duty could not believe their eyes and were just thrilled that he took the time to do something like that.

For the television specials, I would get the call for a ten-day or longer rehearsal schedule. In the first stage, I would meet in a rehearsal hall with the director and the assistant director. We would discuss the overall theme and then what some of the musical numbers should be. We looked at pacing and cohesion and the need to make sure the songs we chose reflected the talents and abilities of the artists. A lot of consideration and creative effort went into this process. Once in a while, Les Brown would be in attendance, but not often because he was playing golf much of the time. Les didn't care to go to meetings.

In the next stage, I would go into the studio and meet with the choreographer. Then we would start to lay it out, discussing songs and the music, and I would start playing some things on the piano. As we went along, the choreographer would start putting the steps together and I would sketch out the instrumental accompaniment. Then we'd bring dancers in and start to rehearse. We rehearsed them on a schedule of six to eight hours a day; three or four hours in the morning, take a break, and go on into the afternoon. It was strenuous with a lot of repetition, a lot of 5-6-

7-8, the way dancers count. I enjoyed the intensity of the work and the camaraderie that quickly evolved.

Ten days seems like a long time for a TV show rehearsal, but it was like creating a short Broadway musical in under two weeks. We needed to build numbers around the featured performers, particularly when we had a variety entertainer like Ginger Rogers. We would develop a special song and dance number where she could both sing and dance. We always had eight to twelve, sometimes more, dancers with a well-known choreographer, such as Nick Castle. Nick was pretty strict, as many choreographers were, but he had a sense of humor. With the girls, he did this funny bit where he'd throw his hotel key down on the rehearsal hall floor and say, "We can work on this later," and jokingly point to the key.

I was there every day writing these long sketches. It seemed like everyone working, including all the artists, got to know each other on a first name basis. I can't exactly explain why this was the case, but when it was Ginger Rogers, everyone addressed her as "Miss Rogers." There seemed to be this natural sign of respect to dignify her that way. She certainly didn't demand it because she was sweet and personable. I really liked her and enjoyed our conversations during those periods we worked together. She asked me to go out on the road with her a couple of times to do a traveling show, which I wasn't able to do, but my drummer, Bob Neel, who was also my drummer on The Steve Allen Show, went out on the road and worked with her as her musical director. Miss Rogers was a lovely lady.

The schedule is a factor and there are only so many hours available. Often it was impossible for the rehearsal pianist to do everything. There wasn't time for me to write the full arrangements for all these big production numbers because I needed to be in the rehearsal hall, so I wrote four-line or five-line sketches, indicating the voicing and instrumentation, and then hand it off to the orchestrator. An orchestrator was someone who could take the sketch and transcribe it into detailed instrumental parts with a complete score, and then send the score to whoever our staff person was for copying parts, and we had great copyists.

I worked closely with Frank Comstock, who was our orchestrator. Frank had been associated with Les Brown for many years before I joined the band. Frank arranged many of the semi-classical pieces that Les performed, like "Slaughter on 10th Avenue" and "The Nutcracker Suite." When I was touring with Les, we played a serious musical segment on every dance engagement. Les would call it his concert section. He would position a half-hour to forty-five-minute showcase in the program to present these large pieces, and Frank's orchestrations were often featured. Frank was an extraordinary arranger and wrote for most of The Bob Hope Shows.

Usually, in a television show or special, the quest celebrity would be placed in a musical setting with both singing and dancing. The vocal and dance segments were constructed with precisely planned choreography, which had to be conveyed in well-structured music. This was something I could have difficulty with because some choreographers would disregard metric necessity. We would put this together in the rehearsal hall and sometimes it became argumentative. A seven and a half-bar phrase didn't thrill me a lot, or even more difficult, seven and three-quarters. I got into emphatic debate with some choreographers. But, there were some who truly understood and respected the need for those additional two beats, or that we needed to take two beats out in order for the phrasing to be symmetrical, and accomplish proper metric musicality. It could be exasperating to write choreographed music unless the choreographer has an intuitive jazz sense. With an astute metric sensibility he can often translate this musicality to his necessity for dance steps. Then the two beats and the steps become an amalgamation.

Often, I fought for what I knew was best musically because the choreographer wanted important moves caught in the orchestration, and sometimes it can be interruptive. I composed numerous fifty-bar and sixty-bar segments, where in the middle of the tune it would become the dance segment, taking away, for the moment, from the singer. This could happen anywhere in the music, on the head, in the tail, or in a sung reprise.

I spent a lot of one-on-one rehearsal time with artists and sometimes I needed to coach them on how to get by their metric problems, so they could sing a tune and have it come out correctly. I remember going to Lucille Ball's house to rehearse with her, when she was married to Gary Morton, and I had problems with her. She was a talented performer, but had serious metric problems. I had to approach the issue gently with as much diplomacy as possible. It was necessary to create some busy fills in the music so she wouldn't dare sing. In other words, I could control her entrances so that metrically it would come out correctly. She had some pitch problems as well, so it was important to keep the melodic theme present in the writing to guide her.

On the first day of full rehearsal on the set, the orchestra would come in and the copyist would bring in the parts and the score. If Les was there, and if I was lucky enough to get his attention for a minute, because he was always socializing, I'd say, "Les, come here, look at this. When you get to this point in the score there's a trap. Be careful. It goes into 3/4 then back to 4/4." Sometimes I just felt he wasn't even listening to me. I did what I had to do and of course he'd get trapped.

At that time, prior to videotape, television was filmed in kinescope. We'd go through two days of full production rehearsal and then film the show twice, with two different audiences. The audiences attended free of charge. Often we filmed in Studio 4, the same studio that was later used for *The Tonight Show* with Johnny Carson. The audiences could be totally different in their reaction. Bob Hope and I used to talk about this and he blamed it on the configuration of celestial bodies. Sometimes they were wildly entertained and sometimes it felt like they just got out of a boring executive meeting. Bob thought it was definitely the result of the alignment of the moon and planets.

Frequently, I went up to Frank Comstock's house. I was so impressed with his sound system. There wasn't stereo sound at that point. It was strictly monaural, but not for long. He showed me this gear he called the Wappy 2. The model was a WAP 2, and it was a little golden-faced pre-amplifier. He made it from a kit the Heath Company sold for $19.95. I was immediately hooked; I had to build some sound equipment.

I started ordering Heath kits regularly and would take them on the road with me. While some of the musicians played cards or went out for the evening, I built receivers, two television sets, and various other pieces of electronic equipment. I spent many evenings in a hotel room with an array of parts spread on the floor around me while I soldered things together. It was such a joy when I finished playing to go work on these kits. They had good quality components and the people who put the manuals together were brilliant.

The directions were extremely accurate, but you had to follow them precisely or it wouldn't work. Cut a wire 6 inches long. Strip a 1/4 of an inch of insulation from each end and attach one end to C1. C1 was like a little horseshoe terminal and the directions showed how to wrap the wire around that terminal. Then it says NS which stands for 'not soldered.' At this point attach the other end to Q4, and it showed a great pictorial of where Q4 was, S1, solder one wire. Now you would go back to that first point where it said NS and maybe three more wires would be wrapped around it and it would say S4, meaning solder 4 wires. The beauty of it was in the end, it either worked or it didn't. Of course, if it didn't work, it was disappointing. However, usually if I went back over the steps, I would find one or two errors that I made, like some little thing that didn't get soldered. Then it would work and it became my friend.

I remember telling the musicians in the band, "You record your music and you can't even hear music properly. You ought to build some of this equipment." When some of the fellows in the band couldn't afford to buy the kits outright, I'd use my Heathkit credit card. Not many people had them, but I had become a regular Heath customer, so I used to get the kits for them. I'd have to do a little accounting. They would always pay me, but they'd pay a little each week. I'd send in the bills and keep everything together.

On occasion, while traveling with Les Brown, we went through Benton Harbor, Michigan, where I visited my friends at the Heath Company. One of the Heath executives, Matt Cutter, became a friend and visited me in California from time to time. Whenever we were in the Benton Harbor area, Matt would personally deliver kits for the musicians to build.

The gentlemen in the band did a terrible job of soldering. I spent a lot of time after the gigs back in the hotel room holding circuit boards up in the air with the soldering iron under it letting gravity pull out the excess solder, which had slopped all over the circuit board. I was doing service calls all night because I had so many people building Heath kits. If anybody came in my room they would say, "What's that funny smell?" Surprisingly, the answer would actually be solder.

The view from the stage.

The band with Bob Hope and Jayne Mansfield at the Bayonet Bowl.

When we went on the Bob Hope tours, I would have someone take a photograph of Miss America and me, with her holding this little portable FM radio that I had built. I would send the pictures to Matt and he would hang them in their employees lounge. As a result, I developed quite a rapport with the people at the Heath Co. and they did a story about me because I had purchased over $20,000.00 worth of gear.

The Bob Hope Christmas trips were incredible. They provided an opportunity to go to places that were so obscure. Besides locations in Europe, we went to Alaska, Africa, Korea and Japan. We traveled to Keflavik, Iceland as well. You couldn't be blasé about looking out and seeing thousands of soldiers sitting in the snow, if necessary, to see a Bob Hope Show.

We flew to South Korea just after the war and there was still a great deal of tension. There was a line of demarcation where we couldn't go any further. We played one concert in a place called Bayonet Bowl.

Actress Jayne Mansfield and Mr. Universe Mickey Hargitay were married and on this trip. We stopped in the Midway Islands to refuel on our way to Korea and she went swimming in an angora bikini. There was a large group of service men there with their cameras. I took a picture and sent a copy to the Heath Company and became a hero for having a picture of Jayne Mansfield bathing in the waters of Wake Island. At that time,

Jayne Mansfield and Mickey Hargitay

Jayne was considered the most photographed person ever. You would hear the sound of thousands of camera shutters clicking as she walked on to the stage.

Technically the shows filmed overseas were not actually USO shows. They were Bob Hope productions. He made a lot of money doing these shows, but he also invested a lot of money to make these productions work as well as they did. All of those trips were done with Military Air Transport Service, which was a great airline. The whole production traveled in two airplanes. One was for the celebrities and upper crust. The other was for the orchestra, the crew, and the press. We would leave from Burbank right around the sixteenth of December and come home around the twenty-eighth, having missed Christmas with our families. We did our holiday shopping in the Post Exchanges because we were within military facilities at all times.

A lot of wonderful actors and entertainers went on those trips. We almost always had Miss America, and Les Brown was always chasing after her. I remember giving a dollar to Dorothy Lamour because she didn't have any cash with her. Sometime later, without ever thinking about it,

I got a thank you note from her with a dollar in it. Jerry Colonna was a comical singer. He had a big thick mustache, and eyes that he could enlarge. He'd sing the first word of a song and his eyes would become huge and he held the note for about a day and a half, until he was ready to explode. He was kind of a sidekick for Bob Hope and he did all of those trips with us. Of course the press traveled with us. The journalists, as I saw them, were freeloaders. If there was any free food around, they had their faces in it immediately.

Bob Hope and Jerry Colonna

Each of the two Military Air Transport Service planes had two stewardesses. On a trip to Berlin, one was very attractive and the other didn't smile at all. I jokingly referred to her as Hatchet Face. I decided that I was going to make her smile before the trip was over. The seats are backwards in Military Air Transport Service. You sit with your back going in the direction of the plane. If there was an accident, they believed there was a better chance of survival if your back was supported from that position. We were ready for take-off and I had an empty seat next to me. As this stewardess was walking up the aisle, I pulled her down and said, "Fasten your seatbelt." She sat next to me and I said, "Now listen, we're going to have a good time on this trip and you're going to smile if it's the last thing I do." I kidded around with her and we had a nice flight.

In Berlin, the band was staying at a military hotel. Bob Hope, Les Brown, and some of the celebrities stayed at the Berlin Hilton. We had a night off and Les and I had bought some alcoholic beverages. I'm not exactly sure why because I really didn't drink very often, probably just to bring home for gifts. I brought home lots of things from the post exchanges. Les had some liquor up in his room that belonged to me. This particular night, I asked my charming Hatchet Face friend out for a date and she agreed. We went to a small club in Berlin where they had a little band. I really got the feeling that I wanted to play. I don't really speak German, but, when coming back from a break, I went up to one of the musicians and said, "*Spiel ein bisschen?*" Roughly translated means "play a little." He gave me a firm no. Even so, not to be deterred, I approached the piano and started to play a little. Suddenly everything changed and they were fine with letting me play with the band.

It came time to go back to the hotel and see what might develop with this girl. I had prearranged with Les that I could get my cocktails up in his room and perhaps use his room depending on how things might progress. We went up to his room and just had a couple of drinks. When we were leaving, I went to the elevator and mistakenly pushed both up and down buttons. This meant, of course, that any elevator passing would stop at this floor, as well. Here I was with this young lady on my arm and the doors opened and there's Mr. Hope with our other stewardess on his arm. The doors opened and the doors closed. You could hear the two of them laughing as they proceeded up the elevator shaft while we stood there.

During this time, I had dated a girl who was a student Emory University in Atlanta. By Christmas, she was back at home in Baltimore. We were on our way to Europe with Bob Hope, and I knew that our airplane was going to stop at Andrews Air Force Base. I called her and said, "We'll be passing through and we won't be there very long, but if you'd like to come over we'll probably be there for a couple of hours." Our plane landed and we went to the commissary and there she was, waiting for me. Bob noticed this, but he didn't say anything and I introduced her to him. After this stop, we took off for Spain.

There was another girl I had dated who had a girlfriend I also knew. She was apparently working for the military and was stationed in Madrid. She knew I was coming over. When we got to Madrid, someone entered the airplane and asked, "Is there a Donn Trenner here?"

I said, "Yes, I'm here."

He said, "There's a girl downstairs screaming. She's nuts she wants to see you so much."

This girl somehow got to the bottom of the metal staircase that they wheel out to the airplane so you can exit. Hope saw this, as well. From here, we went to Nouasseur Air Base near Casablanca. There, I met a young lady, who worked at the Post Exchange, while buying some Christmas gifts. She was nice and I asked her if she wanted to watch the taping. She came to the show and, of course, Hope saw her there. After this, I

Bob Hope in Morocco.

brought her out to breakfast one morning where we were all eating. Seeing this, Bob made the remark to one of his chief writers, Billy Larkin, "I think Donn Trenner is trying to turn the whole world into a snack bar."

In Morocco, at the Neuesseuer Army Air Force Base, we had Ann Miller on the show. Ann was a wonderfully stylish tap dancer and famous for her legs. That was her trademark. She wanted to do "Too Darn Hot," which was apparently her big song and dance number in the MGM movie, *Kiss Me Kate*. Andre Previn had scored it so they sent me up to Paris for a couple of days to work with him on a reconstruction of that scene for the television show. The studio orchestra for the motion picture was huge. With Les' big band we also had brought strings, winds, and a harp, so I could adapt from the movie score. I re-orchestrated what was necessary from that score, keeping the sequence and honoring what the soloist needed from the film scene, while at the same time creating more of an augmented big band sound. I flew back and got that together with Les' band and we performed it. Ann Miller had never done kinescope taping before. She and producer Jack Hope, Bob's brother, were almost fighting because she didn't understand why she couldn't redo, and redo, and redo her number until it was perfect.

I had met a girl named Peggy King. She was known as Pretty Perky Peggy. She used to do The George Gobel Show and was also called the "Hunt's Tomato Sauce Girl" because apparently that was his sponsor. She was cute and a good singer. I dated her briefly after we did a tour with several engagements, going all the way up to Seattle. I took my bass player, who was also to be the bass player for Steve Allen's television show, Bob Bertaux. Anyway, we started to date. At her home in Beverly Hills, she had a pantry filled with cases of tomato soup. There was a picture of Andre Previn over her fireplace because they were close for a while. They had broken up, but she left the picture up. Whenever I would go over to her house, she would say things like, "Andre did this. Andre did that. No, this is Andre's." I was living in the shadow of Andre Previn.

She was also really possessive. Once, when I was traveling with Les, she called me up and said, "I'm coming in with a white dress and a rabbi."

I said, "Wait just a minute!" She even called my mother and told her that we were getting married. She was quite aggressive about this relationship. Eventually, it came to an amicable ending.

In Paris, I related a little of this to Andre, casually mentioning, "I've been seeing Peggy. She's really a trip isn't she?" I knew immediately it was the wrong thing to say. He became defensive and supportive of her. I should not have said anything that subtly implied any negativity. He was quick to let me know that he didn't want to hear any of it. We didn't talk about that any further.

Musically, Andre is a great orchestrator and a fantastic symphonic conductor. As a pianist, I heard him play some jazz once. I could hear the classical influence. Technically it was flawless, but his time felt nowhere connected with the pocket and it didn't swing. However, sometime later I heard an album where he was right in the pocket. My friends Bob Bertaux and Bob Neel toured and recorded with him over the years.

On these Christmas tours, we had hardly more than a modicum of time for ourselves. I love to do things for other people and I love to spend money on them. When I was going to Japan, I asked, "Is there anything you want that I can bring back."

Somebody said, "Yeah, I need some new china."

This was ironic, china from Japan, but Japan actually had wonderful china.

Again, we always took two airplanes: plane-one carried the celebrities with the technical crew, orchestra and press in plane-two. Hedda Hopper was a well-known gossip columnist that traveled on several of these trips. Hedda was considered more of a celebrity than press, so she usually traveled in plane-one. I think it was also to keep her content. On our way home, we went through Honolulu. We were all exhausted. It had been a strenuous trip and we all had bought a lot of stuff, particularly me. I had several complete china service sets for twelve, and all kinds of other gifts. Hedda could not help herself and complained to one of the customs agents, "You know we're really very tired and I'm sure you're not going to make us unload this whole airplane, are you?" Well that's all it took. We had to unload the whole airplane. Mr. Hope teased me about how much belonged to me. They had to get a larger cart to hold all my presents.

9 Nothing Is That Important

THROUGHOUT MY CAREER, in addition to being fortunate enough to work on shows and in the studios, I have always played private parties and taken gigs in small jazz clubs and restaurants. These engagements can be enjoyable and provide an opportunity to make music a little less formally. They could be artistically rewarding depending on whether I was booked directly, when I used my own musicians, or was hired just as a sideman. Private functions could be financially meaningful, but casual club dates, while appreciated, never paid particularly well.

I played Sammy Davis Jr.'s wedding reception with my jazz quartet at the Beverly Hilton Hotel. Sammy's wedding was controversial because he was marrying a Swedish woman, May Britt. Interracial marriage was still illegal in most states. The wedding created a media feeding frenzy, and May Britt was so frightened by it she did not attend her own wedding reception. Robert Mitchum, Frank Sinatra, and many of Sammy's well-known friends were there. Sammy had a lot of friends.

During this period, while continuing to work for Les Brown, I started taking calls for studio sessions. I did several for Bethlehem Records, in New York and Los Angeles. One was an album with vocalist Betty Roché. There's a song on it that I wrote, but Helen Carr is listed as the author. I don't know how that happened, but she probably helped with the lyric. The tune is called "I Just Got the Message Baby." It's kind of a cute tune. Betty Roché's recording was titled *Take the A Train*." Conte Condoli played trumpet and there was a wonderful vibraphonist on it named Eddie Costa, who was becoming well-known in jazz circles.

I also did a recording with show tune singer Frances Faye, titled *Relaxin' With Frances Faye*. She's on a wonderful Bethlehem album with Mel Torme, which was a tribute to Gershwin's *Porgy and Bess*. She was outspoken, funny, and quite a character as a piano player and singer. Her voice was a bit raucous, but she was a good interpreter of music. An album with bebop trumpeter, Howard McGhee, titled *Life is Just a Bowl of Cherries*, was just another call that I got from Bethlehem.

I did a recording with legendary tenor saxophonist, Ben Webster, and strings on the newly founded Reprise Records, called *The Warm Moods*. I had developed an association with Johnny Richards, who was involved with Stan Kenton's band. Johnny was a great arranger and composed the music for Sinatra's big hit, "Young at Heart." Johnny wrote the string orchestrations for Ben Webster's album and requested me for the session. It was recorded at Radio Recorders Annex, which was in Hollywood.

Also, in the early 1960s, I worked with Mel Tormé recording several tunes, including "Don't Let the Moon Get Away" heard on the Verve album titled *Swingin' on the Moon*. I also worked with Mel a few times when he appeared on *The Steve Allen Show* and also a Bob Hope Special. Later on, I worked for Jack Jones and ran into Mel again when he was doing a show with Jack. Mel was a talented man and did many different things. I don't know if I necessarily approved of everything he did. To me, it all became a little over-showy. He would sing and then run up to play drums, which he did well. It's not really fair of me to be critical because Mel was an extraordinary musician.

He was a talented composer. We all agree, "The Christmas Song" is melodically and harmonically beautiful. Mel also liked to conduct and write arrangements, but he was not a skilled arranger. He had some workable ideas, but the ensemble writing was awkward. He brought charts in for sessions that needed editing, which took up rehearsal time. Nevertheless, Mel was musically brilliant and was truly one of the great singers. He had tremendous ears with an ability to improvise and maintain pitch. Stylistically, he projected a swing feel that was just wonderful.

I first met Rosemary Clooney at her home in Beverly Hills, when I was asked to work on some projects with her. On another occasion we were rehearsing for a Bob Hope Special. I'll always remember her entrance on one particular rehearsal day. We usually rehearsed at NBC, but sometimes a studio wasn't available. We were using a big rehearsal hall in the Masonic Temple on Hollywood Boulevard. At the opposite end of this rehearsal hall was a doorway that came in from the parking lot. The door opened and in walked Rosemary Clooney with a gentleman on her arm and her two Great Danes. To my surprise, the gentleman was Sy Berger, one of my friends from the days of my first orchestra in New Haven. Sy was a wonderful trombonist and played with *The Tonight Show* orchestra. Sy, I guess, had a long-running romance with Rosemary.

In 1963, I played on an album with Rosie and Nelson Riddle titled *Love,* on Reprise Records. It was a large production, including strings. Of course, Nelson's writing was just wonderful. Nelson also had a romance with Rosemary. She was a beautiful and charismatic woman. I was doing a few club dates with Nelson and one night I was struck when I got a glimpse of him from the side. Nelson's profile had an incredible resemblance to Sy Berger. I later mentioned this to Rosie and she agreed.

I was contacted by a songwriter, who wanted to produce an album of her tunes as sung by Rosemary Clooney. I spent quite a bit of time working with her on her songs. There were spots that needed to be repaired. Not lyrically, but if there was a trap somewhere, and it doesn't work out melodically or harmonically, two bars may have to be changed. I tried to do as much as I could for the tune without changing someone else's song. The album was produced privately, and, to my knowledge, never released. Rosie sounded wonderful on it.

I was concerned about Rosie's health. It was difficult for her to get from the studio into the control booth because she had gotten so heavy, but the gentility of her personality came through in her singing. When she sang, it seemed effortless; it never sounded forced. Even when she was struggling to get around, her true personality came through in her voice and that made it a joy to be around her. She was one of those people who never took advantage of others and no one in her presence ever felt pressured. Both the musicians and the technical crew looked forward to working with her because her kindness permeated her whole existence. She was a lovely human being. I can't say enough nice things about her. I'm sorry that I didn't work with her more.

I recorded for Nelson Riddle on his theme song for the weekly CBS television series *Route 66,* where I played the iconic piano fills written by Nelson. I also did an ABC television show, *Follow the Sun,* with Sonny Burke, who became the musical director of Reprise Records and was one of Les' closest friends. We used to record Les' band with him a lot. Sonny was a fabulous writer and bandleader, who co-composed "Midnight Sun" with Lionel Hampton and Johnny Mercer. An earlier CBS sitcom I played for was *Hennesy* starring Jackie Cooper, who played a naval doctor. Sonny

Burke also wrote the nautical musical theme that was employed through each episode. The melodic motif was also used as dissolving music, going from one scene of the show to another.

A dissolve is a cue that carries you from one mood into the next setting of shots. Cues are short segments of music that are used for many things. We did lots of little thematic skits with Bob Hope. The characters might go from one room to another room, and there would be the need for a little piece of music between the two scenes of the sketch. We would call that cue a dissolve. Where the scene is transitioning from one set to another, you play a short piece of music that doesn't have a full cadence. It usually ends on some suspended chord which gives you the feeling of continuity and sometimes foreshadows the mood of the next scene. This leads the preceding theme and feeling to the new feeling and location.

A tag is a cue you would play concluding the sketch or for an exit. There are all kinds of cues for color and musical enhancement of the moment. We would do mystery cues, stings, little inserts of music to embellish the act, the performance, the comedic element, or the dramatic aspect of what was taking place.

Dramatic play-ons were used for people like Elizabeth Taylor. She would come out to do a sketch with Bob, or some little comedy bit, and we played her on with a grandiose piece of music with lots of strings, while she walked out looking beautiful.

Sometimes taking these studio calls caused difficulty with my traveling schedule. One summer, Les Brown toured with cars because Plymouth was a sponsor of the Bob Hope shows. The band was traveling with a really silly wardrobe. We wore linen jackets, the rhythm section wore light blue, and the saxophone section wore pink. They arranged to get us six new Plymouths to do our summer tour. Lou Hagopian was a friend of Les'; I think they were country club buddies. They used to play bridge and golf together, and Lou was an executive of Chrysler, in the Plymouth division. That was the year that they developed a car called the Valiant. I decided I wanted to get a new car. I was in New York and I called Lou. He said, "Sure, on your way back you can pick up a new Valiant. I'll take you through the factory and you can drive it from Detroit back to Los Angeles." I didn't even have time to do the factory tour. I had to hurry back to do a recording with Jackie Cooper. Jackie liked to play drums and he didn't play that badly. I mean you could actually sit down and play a little with him. This was to be a jazz album of music from the Hennesy show and he was going to play on it.

The recording date wasn't flexible, and it was now close to the time that I picked up the car in Detroit. I was determined to drive the car non-stop across the country in time to make the recording date. I almost made it. Somebody had given me a couple of Dexedrine tablets, which I had never taken before because of my fear of pills. When I got near home in California, I started to hallucinate. I had taken one of these tablets after falling asleep at the wheel three times over the last couple of hours and it scared me, but after a while I fell asleep again. I must have been going at a leisurely pace because the car just slowed to a gentle roll and went up a small embankment on the opposite side of the road. I realized that I was spent. Somehow, I walked from there to some little restaurant. I went in and sounding like a zombie said, "Here's a dime. Please call this number and tell them where I am." I went back to the car and fell asleep. The next thing I remember two friends picked me up and drove me home, which was only twenty-five miles away at that point. I drank some coffee, washed my face, drove down to Hollywood and recorded with Jackie Cooper. Sonny Burke used to tell people that story concluding with, "Nothing is that important." He used to say that to me frequently. "Nothing is that important."

I began a romantic involvement with an attractive young woman in Chicago while on tour with Les Brown's band. Her name was Mary Ann Lewendowski, but she was known as Mary Ann Leslie. We were married for about four and a half years until her religious roots bit back at her. She was Catholic and she wanted to have a Catholic wedding. I talked with a priest in Chicago, who was a good friend of hers, Monsignor Halpen. He put me in touch with some people in California. I was going to try to accommodate her need for a Catholic ceremony. The archdiocese in Los Angeles put me through the ringer. They weren't about to "let me in" without doing some serious research. They wanted to go back to Helen. They wanted to go back to Helen's parents. They wanted me to do this and that. It just got ridiculous. Finally, I realized there was nothing more I could do. I told the priest, "I don't even want to be part of this. It doesn't sound like my religion at all." There was no openness or sense of welcoming. Mary Ann agreed to a non-religious wedding. We got married in a little chapel at an office building in Chicago and my parents came out to the wedding. We built a house in Woodland Hills, California.

A couple of years into our marriage, Mary Ann went back to Chicago to visit. I was really glad when she came home. I asked her how everything went, "Did you see your close friend Monsignor Halpen?"

She said that she had.

"Did you tell him how things were with you and how happy we were?"

She said, "Well, he told me I wasn't really married as far as the church was concerned."

That had a serious effect on her, and on me. Everything just sort of declined from there and the marriage dissolved.

I don't remember the exact circumstances that led me to finally leave Les Brown because I really liked being there, but I had been turning down some engagements with Les because of other projects that were coming my way. And sooner or later, I wanted to go back to New York and get my union card.

Shortly after I left Les, I got a call to go with Lena Horne as her pianist. I started with her in Palm Springs and then we went on to Las Vegas. Lena's husband and musical director was Lennie Hayton. After work, we would frequently go over to their house to have something to eat because they liked to have their people around. She used to call Lennie "Poppa." "Let's go back to the house Poppa," she would say. I saw Billy Strayhorn there a couple of times. There was a close friendship between Billy and Lena.

Lena was not a dynamic singer, but her beauty and her mannerisms gave her a remarkable stage presence. She exuded a kind of introspectively dramatic charisma. When I was in Las Vegas with her, Ella Fitzgerald was working down the street. Paul Smith was Ella's musical director and we got together one evening and compared their stage presence. We agreed that Lena was the essence of refined femininity on stage, and Ella's incredible talent was uninhibited and based on her jazz affinity. With her scat singing she sounded more like a musical instrument. Lena was more theatrical; Ella was more musical. Lena was a strikingly beautiful work of art. She was tall and slim and dressed elegantly. She knew how to gracefully float on stage. Lena could do the smallest burlesque bump and it was like a bomb went off, but knew right where the line was and never crossed it on stage. Lena also had a knack for lyric delivery and, with her expressive face, was a powerful storyteller. It was never overdone, but it was all-powerful. It was interesting to be on stage and watch how people, both men and women, responded to her.

Her husband, Lennie Hayton, was famous for his musical work in motion pictures. He was a highly skilled orchestrator and conductor. Lennie was interesting be around. It was difficult for me to watch how he worked with an orchestra. He created so much tension and turmoil. He was not at all a kind person in front of musicians. I don't know whether it was a Napoleonic complex, but he never treated his players nicely or showed them any respect. Most of the orchestra members feared him, and I hated that. It is the wrong way to deal with musicians. You're not going to get the best from them musically if they feel like there's a dark cloud hanging over them. Nevertheless, I stayed there and watched.

I got a chance to observe the relationship between Lena and Lennie when I spent time with them at the house they were renting in Palm Springs. He was milk toast around her. It was a matriarchal relationship. Lena was a strong lady and she was kind to him in their private life. He was sweet and was acquiescent toward her in every way, but when he was in front of an orchestra, he turned into an ogre. This is where the counter balance in his personality would come out.

In Las Vegas, we worked the Sands Hotel. Many live albums were done there, Frank Sinatra and Count Basie, among others. While I was there, I received a telegram from the Westinghouse Corporation and it said, "You have just been selected as Musical Director of the new Steve Allen show." This would be a nightly television production with five shows a week. I couldn't believe it.

I went to Lennie and told him. We had only done twelve performances together, but I wanted to work through the required two-week notice. He went up to Lena's dressing room before the show that night and told her. Lena was really angry, and from a woman who was so refined, I heard some profanity like I'd never heard before. I didn't understand why she couldn't reflect back and think about those rare moments in one's career when something big happens. I thought they might be happy that someone they were working with had been selected. Bass player, Bob Bertaux, had come to Lena's band through me. I asked him to join me on Steve Allen's television show and he administered his notice the next night. The profanity continued.

Las Vegas 1961

10 Leave It To Me

AT THE BEGINNING OF our professional association, Steve Allen called me into his office and said, "We've got an engagement in Vegas. Would you like to do it?" From there, the two of us planned the whole show. He sent me to Las Vegas to audition a girl for a part in a Count Dracula sketch that we would do on stage. They built three black coffins and mounted them on stands so that instead of being horizontal and on the floor they were almost standing up straight, so it was like a strange-looking telephone booth. In the skit, Steve played Dracula's nephew. He walked in with this girl on his arm to greet Dracula and said, "I'd like you to meet the Count."

Her line was, "Glad to meet you Mr. Basie."

At the end of the show, Steve acknowledged me. "Perhaps you wonder where all those luscious arrangements came from." After a slight pause he continued, "I would like you to meet the lush who wrote them," and I stepped out of the coffin. This was typical of the kinds of parody we would do on the television show, and Steve was generous in his acknowledgement of my work.

In addition to playing piano, directing the band, and appearing in skits, I also did work in the control booth, which included the directorial staff and the audio crew. I helped the sound engineer get a better balance on the band. It was helpful for them to know when certain sections of the orchestra were featured, or a solo instrument needed to be captured. There was a lot of running around, even when it's not being televised. I

A piano duo with Steve Allen.

would move to different parts of the hall during a rehearsal to hear where things need to be adjusted. I've always enjoyed the variety of my work and the fast pace. With advances in technology, resulting in different systems being used at different locations, and the unique challenges that came with each production, I was always learning something new.

After a year of doing the weekly ABC shows, we began the new nightly television show. I hired most of the orchestra by telephone while at the Sands Hotel with Lena Horne. I called the famous jazz trombone player, Bob Enevoldsen, who is still known internationally. Bob played valve trombone a lot like Bob Brookmeyer. He also played tenor saxophone and bass, and was a highly skilled arranger. He and I would write the music for the Steve Allen shows together. That's how things started at *The Steve Allen Show*.

When I chose my guitarist, Herb Ellis, he was working with The Dukes of Dixieland at the Metropole Cafe in New York. He had to complete that engagement, so I needed another guitar player to start the show until Herb was available. I took a chance and hired Joe Pass, who was in

Synanon at the time. Synanon was a Santa Monica rehabilitation organization for recovering drug addicts. In my first meeting with the band to discuss schedules and what was going to be happening, Joe came with his sponsor because that was the only way that they would let him leave the center. He was deeply involved with that organization and it helped him improve his life. Joe started with us and did the first couple of weeks. I remember when I hired Herb Ellis, he said to me, "I would really love to do the show, but my eyes aren't that great." Meaning, I don't read musical notation that well.

I said, "Don't worry we'll work it out."

I had the same problem with Joe Pass, too, but we worked it out. In the beginning, Bob and I managed to write as few things as possible that would require strict notation, but I did like to write for guitar because it gave me a fifth voice. I could write guitar with the four horns and get some five-part harmony creating different colors. It was fun to have Joe there for the first couple of weeks. Joe and Herb were both remarkable players.

I hired Jimmy Zito on trumpet, who was a well-known studio player. He was married at one time to movie actress, June Haver, who had sung with Ted Fio Rito. That marriage was an important part of Jimmy's resumé. He had a warm ballad sound and was a strong lead player for this setting. Playing lead here required a little more lyrical approach than playing lead with a big brass section. He played well, but was a bit volatile. Jimmy would get irritated if somebody walked out of the stage door during rehearsals, leaving the door open. It might get drafty and his horn would get cold. He made a big fuss out of that. One day, in the middle of the show, he threw his horn into his music stand and angrily declared, "I can't take it anymore," and quit. He was replaced with Conte Condoli. We only had that one personnel change in the band.

The rest of the orchestra included Bob Neel on drums, Frank Rosolino on trombone, and John Setar on reeds, who would continue to be my California contractor. Whenever I did anything that needed an orchestra, John and I put it together. He was like my "right arm." John was also my contractor, when I later went to New York to do another television show, *ABC's Nightlife*. Bob Neel and bassist, Bob Bertaux, were both on the Les Brown band, and we also had worked frequently as a trio. That was the orchestra. It was just an octet, but we sounded bigger than that when we needed to. We handled the forthcoming musical diversity well.

The schedule was quite nice and worked out wonderfully for us. We did five shows a week in the beginning, working Monday through Friday. Each day, Bob Enevoldsen and I would write as much of the show as needed. Our copyist, Dick Guyette, was always on time with beautifully prepared parts. The show was an hour and forty-five minutes each night which meant that often we could have four or five major guests: a musical artist, a comedian, an actor, a political figure, and some kind of kooky personality.

A lot of my work was coordinating ahead of time, before the guest came in to do the show. I was working in preparation a week prior to the taping of certain artists. Most of the time, I was able to contact the guest in advance so we could get their music ready. It would be in any one of four forms: terrible, in need of repair, okay, or good. We did whatever was needed to make it playable. Sometimes we took lines from sections in their music, like the brass section and the fills, so they could make enough sense out of the charts they already knew, but we would use a different voicing and a different feeling because of the size of the orchestra. When it actually came time to rehearse their material with the band, we had created some semblance of familiarity for them. It all seemed to work well, and everybody seemed to be happy. The orchestra developed a national reputation as an excellent TV band.

I had my own office at the Steve Allen Playhouse in Hollywood on Vine Street. I worked a full day, every day because I had all of this advance work to do. I had a secretary, which was helpful. There was a lot of

With the band in rehearsal.

Our TV band.

telephoning and a lot of sending messengers out to pick up music. Earlier on, there were daily meetings with Steve, and later on, he wasn't around as often. Meetings were primarily with the comedy writers. I spent a lot of time with them working out what the shows were going to be. By this time, I'd had a great deal of experience in this kind of planning and development, having been with Bob Hope.

The taping usually started around 1:00 in the afternoon with a studio audience and the show would be over by 4:00. Later, when we started taping two shows on the same day, we would break for dinner and then tape an evening show with a second audience. Either Johnny Jacobs, our announcer, or I would go out and greet the audience and do the warm-ups. Sometimes we shared it. It was fun for me and I enjoyed it.

I selected almost everything the band did and we played a lot of my tunes. "Leave It To Me" happened on that show, which we used as the commercial break tune. We did another song called "Top of the Morning." It meant a lot to me because I was a member of ASCAP. I remember the first ASCAP check I got after being on the air. At first, I thought it was a filing number. I couldn't believe it. It was a lot of money, over $3,000 in mechanical royalties, just for playing my music on the air. We had somebody who did a tabulation of everything that was played. It was called music clearance. All of this information went directly into ASCAP. Payments were made by the show for all the music performed. I didn't understand the accounting mechanics, but I understood what a check meant, and I knew how to cash it and how to spend it.

I gave "Leave It To Me" to an actor/lyric writer by the name of Dick Gautier and he wrote words for it. I don't believe it was ever recorded lyrically, but the Three Sounds with Gene Harris recorded it as an instrumental on an album with Anita O'Day. I didn't even know it had been recorded until my secretary got a call while we were taping a show. She said, "Somebody called and wanted to know about that song that we do… ?" and she went on singing it. "Is that your song, and what's the name of it?" I replied, and she said, "It was just recorded by the Three Sounds." The song is a twelve-bar blues with an eight-bar bridge. I don't think they knew the bridge of the tune. They did it as a straight ahead blues because they knew it from what we played on the air. We hardly ever played it all the way through.

The show was rewarding in so many ways, financially rewarding because we made quite a bit of money for that time. This enabled me to build my home in Woodland Hills. In addition to our salaries, we made extra money for doing the sketches. After we got enough shows in "the bank," we were syndicated. They started to show re-runs, which we were paid for, as well. Then we discovered how we could do two shows a day, so it was down to a four-day workweek. We did a show on Monday and another on Tuesday. On Wednesday we did the third and fourth show. Eventually we got it down to two days a week for the orchestra. We'd come in on Monday and do two shows, two again on Tuesday, and then they would pull a re-run. Still five shows, but the band only went in two days a week.

We did a lot of comedy sketches that were really fun. We did a takeoff on *Mutiny on the Bounty*. I was up on a mast as Captain Bligh. We had WW I fights with actual planes that they would bring in from Paramount property lots. We hung airplanes out on the street and staged battles between Steve and the band. On other nights, we used to do these little thirty-second vignettes. We had one with a ticker tape machine. The set was a stock room with an old conventional ticker tape machine that had a glass dome on it. We shot close to the glass dome and a little piece of paper came out of the ticker tape, and it was Frank Rosolino's face with the ticker tape coming out of his mouth. One night we had him dressed in a diaper. Another night I was standing out on Vine Street dressed in a hip

The band performing in a sketch.

1940s zoot suit. I'm leaning against a telephone poll and some guy comes over and says, "This is a stick up." He pulled on my shirt, and right on cue my clothes fell off down to my shorts. A lot of crazy things happened on the show.

Once, the band dressed up in army fatigues and carried rifles with bayonets. We walked out of the stage door, marched over to the Hollywood Ranch Market, which was next to the studio, and launched a stabbing attack on all the cabbage in the produce section. Of course all of this is being filmed and on the air. On the initial opening show the band was outside. We got permission to take a sewer cap off, and for the opening shot Steve and his wife, Jayne, came out of the sewer on Vine Street. We used to do those kinds of bits all the time.

There are many wonderful characters who became "the regulars" on *The Steve Allen Show*: Pat Harrington Jr. as the Italian golf-pro Guido Ponzini, Bill Dana as José Jiménez, Gabe Dell as Bela Lugosi, Louis Nye as the precocious Gordon Hathaway, terminally on edge Don Knotts, and terminally expressionless Tom Poston.

It was such a creative group of people who pulled the show together. We actually had a staff of people, whose job it was to find unusual people and book them on the show. We referred to them as the "kook guests." Many of them had extraordinary jobs or talents. Gypsy Boots lived in a tree with his family and sold vitamins. He was a "fitness nut," who concocted fruit health drinks he referred to as a "smoothie," and he got Steve to drink one on the show. We had a Miss Something, like Miss Tomato of the Week, or Miss Mattress. For Miss Mattress, we brought in a company that made mattresses and they described how the mattresses were made. We'd have some girl in a scant bathing suit lying down showing the mattress to everyone. We had all these girls like Georgia Peach on the show that demonstrated a product or something silly.

There were a lot of peculiar situations on the show. An animal trainer from the Knott's Berry Farm brought on some alligators. They entered the stage two feet behind where I sat at the piano. Of course we were all on alert. Sure enough, one of those alligators leapt up and clamped onto the trainer's arm and pulled him down to the floor. We went to a commercial immediately. The other trainer got on the alligator's back and jabbed his fingers into the alligator's eyes then put his hand over the nose and pried its mouth open to release the trainer's arm. Another time, they let a hundred cats into the audience. Not realizing or remembering that Steve was allergic to cats, they let them out backstage and they all ran through the audience. He started sneezing, and we were in a lot of trouble. We had to cancel the rest of that show.

It was so much fun and musically great because of the guests who came on the show. Miles Davis was one of them. The wife of our Executive Director had done some recording as a singer. I never heard her, but knew that was part of her earlier career. She was a good friend of Miles, who visited them at their home when in California. Rumor had it that maybe he was going to do our television show. We thought that Miles had never done a TV show before, so we got a little bit excited about it, but we didn't hear anything more about it.

It came time for us to go on a "hiatus period," which was a two week vacation, and I chose to go to Hawaii. I checked into the Royal Hawaiian Hotel, and as I was up at the desk registering, Milt Hoffman, who was the producer of the show, came up to me and said, "How would you like to meet Miles Davis? He and his wife are outside. I think he is probably going to do the show." So he took me outside. They were sitting at an outdoor patio restaurant. Milt introduced me. Miles was really beautifully dressed. I said hello and didn't stay long. I always like to be on the under-side of staying too long. So, that was that.

The hiatus period was over and I came back to work. I noticed on the schedule that Miles Davis was going to be coming in on a certain date and we were all excited. The day arrived, and Miles was there with his group, so being the musical director, I went up and said, "Hello Mr. Davis. You may not remember, but I met you a couple of weeks ago in Hawaii. I'm musical director of the show and I just want to tell you how thrilled we are to have you here."

He looked at me and said in his gruff voice, "Dat ain't no big deal."

That was my total conversation with Miles Davis, and to this day I don't know what it really meant. I couldn't tell whether it was a put down, or if he felt I was taking too long to say welcome to the show, or if the whole thing that I said was superfluous to him.

We heard a rumor that comedian Lenny Bruce was going to be a guest. When it came time to do the show, the lawyers representing Lenny were there, because he had just been in a lot of trouble for some of his routines. He was doing some far-out and rank material for his nightclub show. Everybody was a little uptight because he was totally unpredictable. The day came and we had lawyers representing Westinghouse and he had his lawyers representing him so there wouldn't be any problems.

Fortunately, at that point, we were on a one-week or two-week tape delay because we were the first syndicated show. This meant the show was sold to as many television markets as wanted to buy it. The show aired in many, many, major cities, but some would televise the show a week before the others. There was enough time that if anything did go wrong we could eliminate it, or edit it, or do whatever was needed to make it work.

Lenny Bruce had arrived, and Steve, who really admired him, gave him a long introduction, and we played him on. He walked out and up to the microphone and said, "Well, I guess you know what's expected of me. You probably expect a lot of four letter words. I don't want to let you down so I'm going to start out with a four letter word. It's so bad I can't even tell you, I'm going to turn around and tell the band." He turned around like he's telling us and said, "Okay, it's a four letter word that starts with S and ends with T. The word is snot." He did a seven-minute or eight-minute dissertation on "snot," which I really don't want to discuss, but it included quirks like, "You can't get it off of suede jackets." Of course, the whole routine was scrapped. It started out well, but it went too long and wasn't at all funny.

Rose Marie, famous for her role on *The Dick Van Dyke Show*, called me one day and said, "I've got a tape of somebody that I'd like Steve to see. He's from Cleveland and he's very funny." I told her to bring it down to my office and she gave it to my secretary while I was gone. She called me a couple of months later and asked, "Did Steve view the tape?"

I said, "I don't think so. Let me go and take care of it and I'll call you back."

So I went to Steve and said, "Okay, we have to look at this tape right now." It was a tape of Tom Conway, who was at that point undiscovered. His name was changed to Tim as to not be confused with prominent actor named Tom Conway. Steve booked Tim Conway for a couple of shows and that started his career.

All the famous Italian crooners were on the show: Julius LaRosa, Jerry Vale, Al Martino, Sergio Franci and Tony Bennett, who did the show several times. Frank Sinatra did not do the show, but Frank Sinatra Jr. did. Singers Rosemary Clooney, Jenny Smith, Eydie Gormé, and Fran Jeffries were wonderful. We also had many of actresses that were appearing in many of the major motion pictures and television sitcoms, like Rose Marie, who became a lifelong friend.

The celebrity piano duo of Ferrante and Teicher was on. On another occasion, we also brought two grand pianos onto the set for Roger Williams. He was known as a popular music artist with a classical bent. The nose of each piano was in opposing directions so the two keyboards were available for him from one stool. He played an arpeggio that started on one piano, turned on the stool, and finished on the other. This was one of his tricks of the trade. I'd never seen anything like that before. He's a fine pianist and a unique musician. His playing was flowery and technically brilliant. Roger had a cheerful approach to music and his personal style was consistent with his playing style. I was a fan of the atmosphere he created and he was easy to work with.

The innovative twentieth century composer, Frank Zappa, came on and gave us a taste of the avant-garde. This was among his first national television appearances. Frank brought two bicycles and stood one upside down. He and Steve played the bikes with a violin bow and drumsticks. The band provided an ensemble of free improvisation where I strummed the piano strings with my right hand.

When the shows were really good, the whole form of the show was stellar. When we had a musical theme, like when Dizzy was on the show, it was particularly memorable for me and for the rest of the orchestra. Dizzy and Charlie Parker were the originators of the jazz style that came to be known as bebop. He was harmonically inventive and a superlative trumpet player with a spirited sense of humor in his playing. Harmonically-skilled musicians are able to create chord substitutions that are intended to be an enhancement beyond the original standard harmonic structure of the composition, and Dizzy was the master of this. The band was in awe of him and he was most respectful of them. One of my fondest memories was driving back to Los Angeles with Dizzy after we all spent Thanksgiving at Herb Ellis' home. Dizzy was as generous and gracious personally as he was as a musician.

The great jazz pianist Bill Evans did the show. His style was a unique approach to jazz that utilized his classical background. It gave him the facility to play rapid progressions and melodies with ease, but Bill was not constrained by his classical training. His inventive harmonic sensibility permeated his style. At that time, no one played like Bill Evans. There was a sadness connected to his appearance on the show, because, when we filmed him playing the piano, we had to use diffusion on the lenses because he, unfortunately at that point, was actually shooting up in his hands. It was getting close to the end of his life. He was wonderful, but it was a great sadness to see that, particularly from such a brilliant musician. He was an intellectual person, so you wonder, when there is capacity for brilliance in more aspects than one, why a person can't use that intelligence to realize the inevitability of their own self-destruction. But intellect loses governance over addiction. I remember so many people saying to me, "If you try it once, that's it. If you try it and you like it, that's all it takes." Fortunately, I never got there. Heroin does not facilitate creativity. The creativity, the talent, and the ability are already there. I think drug use, whether it's alcohol, heroin, or other drugs, creates a temporary loss of inhibition, and can lead to sad consequences.

We had the famous Beverly Hills hairstylist, Jay Sebring, on the show. Jay Sebring owned an exclusive men's barber shop that a lot of well-known people in the business went to. We invited him on the show and he cut Steve's hair while we were on the air. After meeting him he said, "Why don't you come on over and we'll do your hair for you."

I said, "Next time it needs a cut I will."

He had several barbers working there and he placed me with Bob Cox. Later on that year, Jay Sebring was murdered, along with Sharon Tate and Abigail Folger, by Charles Manson. Bob Cox was questioned several times by the police. After that, Bob opened a shop of his own.

That barber's chair was a gift from Burt Reynolds. He still gives haircuts to a lot of people. Bob became a good friend. I still go to California for my haircut, and to find out what's going on.

For the most part Steve and I had a really nice association. I saw a great deal of honest humility in him, particularly in the beginning. As time went on, and as he became more famous and successful, he had, as many of us do, deep-seeded insecurities that sometimes got the best of him. I remember one night Groucho Marx was on the show. I was sitting at the piano with the orchestra, as I always did, with my headset on. I was able to talk to the director or the assistant director, if need be, by pressing a button, sometimes even while I was playing or conducting. The night that Groucho was on, he was getting a lot of laughs and that became a little difficult for Steve to handle. Steve came over behind me and lifted my headset off and said, "Tell the director to go to a commercial, this is enough already."

Steve was an interesting and multi-talented man. He, for not having had any formal training, played piano surprisingly well. He wasn't a great pianist, but it was amazing that he could play as well as he did. And he wrote hundreds of songs. I notated them for him because he did not read music. I used to go to his house and write out four or five of them at a time. He scribbled on a paper napkin the letter C and the next letter G above and the next letter D below, which would mean the song would start on C and go up to the G and down to the D, and so on. That's how he could remember what he had composed. Then he would play it for me.

Sometimes he called me and I transcribed his songs over the phone. Generally, they were truly his tunes and I didn't have to do too much to repair them. Occasionally, he would get into some harmonic or melodic trap that created a problem, and together we would correct it. I'd finish them up and then give him completed lead sheets with the lyric on onion skin, which was a method of printable duplication at that time. I used to do these tunes for him for $5.00 a piece. I tried to have somebody else do it while I was out of town and they said, "I'm not doing that much work for $5.00 a piece. Are you kidding me?"

Steve was amazing in a creative sense. He was always writing a book. He wrote many books and gave numerous lectures. He was a brilliant man, but I found him highly opinionated in a way that would make the interview turn negative sometimes. In contrast, Johnny Carson had a thoughtful way about him and did not project a personal slant when talking with his guest. Johnny could take a neutral position, representing both sides of an issue, and never develop a bias. Steve's interviews often reflected his own personal views.

Some things that Steve did bother me, even to this day. When Dizzy Gillespie was on the show, Steve was sitting over at what we called "home base," which is the area that he does his interviews from, and while Dizzy was performing Steve picked up a trumpet and mocked playing it. He did the same thing on clarinet with Buddy DeFranco was a guest. As I said, Steve had many talents but he was neither a trumpet player nor a clarinetist. When these things happened, it made me, and the rest of the musicians, very uncomfortable.

He had a keen ability to recognize talent and was helpful in getting many careers started and in promoting rising stars, including Eydie Gormé, Steve Lawrence, Tim Conway, Gypsy Boots, singer Jenny Smith, the comic Pete Barbutti, and so many more.

In his own peculiar way, Steve was also generous in giving recognition. When he played the role of Benny Goodman in the movie, *The Benny Goodman Story*, he was coached by the well-known clarinetist Gus Bivona, who became a close friend of Steve's. Steve frequently used the name Gus Bivona in comedy sketches on the air. He often teased me during the shows with a litany of fictitious names using my initials. "That was the piano styling of Dire Tramplings."

Belle Montrose was Steve's mother, a woman that Milton Berle once said was the funniest woman in Vaudeville and could steal the show. She was part of our early Las Vegas engagements, but never seen on the nightly television show. As famous, and as successful as Steve was, it was difficult for him when his mother used some of his own material and got a stronger audience response, but there were some funny moments with the two of them on stage.

One time, my mother called me wanting to know if I was getting along with Steve.

I replied, "Yes, sure I am, there's not a problem. Why did you feel that?" And she said, "Well, we watch you and sometimes your face sort of tells me that you're not totally comfortable."

Actually, that observation was pretty accurate. It had to do with musical challenges, not with Steve personally. If we were playing piano together, he could stay on the same chord for four measures and perhaps my face reflected a need to change the chord. When Andre Previn was on the show, we played as a trio of pianists, using three pianos aligned in a tight triangle. We were on the air live playing and we got to one of those

Steve Allen and his mother, Belle Montrose.

traps where Steve got stuck on a chord for a long time. While on camera, I leaned over and whispered to Andre out of the corner of my mouth, "Just hang on, it will change any moment."

Regis Philbin was brought in as a guest host for about a week, when Steve and Jayne traveled to China, where Jayne had been born to missionary parents. Regis, who had become well-known for hosting talk shows in San Diego and Los Angeles, was a natural choice at that point. He actually gave me a solo piano feature, which is something Steve would never have done. I remember playing the Gershwin tune "But Not for Me," including the little-known verse. During the week, Regis expressed to me that he felt like he might be in a little over his head with this show, but he did a fine job. It was great having him, with his easy-going, uncomplicated, and warm style. I loved working with Regis. He is funny, a great interviewer, and wonderfully spontaneous without any noticeable ego. To this day, what you see on-air is who he is, a truly genuine person.

From comedian Buddy Hackett to White House Press Secretary Pierre Salinger, we had just about every noteworthy celebrity on the show for that time period. With five, hour and forty-five minute shows per week, it becomes a talent incinerator. We burned up so much so fast that all of sudden we were faced with what else we could put on the show that's different and new. We seemed to be able to do it, but it became more and more difficult. As a result, the energy of the show gradually waned and just sort of came to an end, after almost three years. Another factor contributing to this decline was that Steve had become deeply involved with a young singer who had been appearing on the show. His wife, Jayne, had learned about this and was absolutely opposed to a divorce. Steve was going through a great deal of emotional turmoil.

Steve went back on the air again later and called me, but by that time I was doing another television show in New York called *ABC's Nightlife* and wasn't able to go back. Steve hired Terry Gibbs, who he always loved. They had a good relationship. Terry was a straight-ahead jazz vibraphone player with a lot of fire, but it was not his style to be a musical director, which required orchestrating and conducting. Terry and Steve developed a vibes-playing bit, where Steve would go to the left side of Terry and play the bottom octave, then go around his back and come up to play the top octave, and they continued to rotate around and around. Typically, Steve was again able to show his invaluable prowess at many things.

I remember John F. Kennedy's assassination vividly. It was a Friday and I was at home in Woodland Hills because we had finished taping *The Steve Allen Show* for that week. I stood outside in front of the house in a complete haze. I just couldn't believe it. I watched as other people started coming out of their front doors. We sort of spoke loudly back and forth about what had just happened because it had come over the air in a news bulletin. The aura that came over everybody was as if everyone's best friend had just been killed.

11

Fantastick

SHORTLY AFTER THE *STEVE ALLEN SHOW*, I relocated to New York to do *ABC's Nightlife*. They called offering me the position of musical director. This was a turning point in my life. I met Betty Jean Ward.

At the time, there was a show in New York hosted by the pioneering late night interactive talk radio host, Les Crane. The audience was seated around a circular stage, and they used something that was new to the electronic world, a shotgun microphone. The microphone was on a long poll and they extended it out into the audience so people could ask or answer questions.

The musical group on The *Les Crane Show* was The Cy Coleman Trio. Cy Coleman was a successful Broadway composer, who wrote several musicals. Later on, Cy and I collaborated to create Shirley MacLaine's first nightclub show. *The Les Crane Show* was the first network show to compete with *The Tonight Show* with Johnny Carson, and unfortunately it did what lots of shows do: it failed. The new show, *ABC's Nightlife*, was developed to fill that timeslot. The format was not unlike *The Steve Allen Show*, we had many different guest entertainers, except it was designed to have a new host every week or two. The co-host of the show was a well-known radio personality, William B. Williams, who used to have a jazz show in New York on WNEW. I had a nine-piece or ten piece orchestra that was similar to what I had with Steve, but I added a percussionist. The *Les Crane Show* went off the air on Friday, and on Monday *ABC's Nightlife* premiered.

I had some interesting players in that band. A few were ABC staff musicians, such as Toots Thielemans, who was perhaps better known as a harmonica player, yet was on guitar. Mel Lewis or Don Lamond was on drums. I used to get one of the drummers for two days a week and the other for three. It's amazing how differently the band played with each drummer. The band played much tighter and more musically with Mel Lewis, yet Don Lamond was a wonderful drummer, but he was primarily a big band drummer and more often he worked with sixteen-eighteen piece orchestras. I feel funny even saying anything negative about Don Lamond because he was so fantastic in the period he played with Woody Herman's band, but I couldn't believe the difference in the band when Mel played. A drummer who is musical doesn't just play rhythm. Mel had a certain sensitivity to melody and harmony and was aware of textural changes. He shades the volume, anticipates subtle changes and phrases with the band. It's a matter of perception. A musical drummer feels the whole scope of the music instead of just playing his part. He adapts to the changing dynamics in the arrangement and that permeates throughout the band. It wasn't so much that you heard Mel as much as you felt him. He was a quiet driving force. The subtleties of his playing made the experience and the music so much richer. It always felt right. They used to call him "Mel the Tailor." It was like he tailored everything he played like a custom fit suit.

We started out with comedian Shelly Berman as host, then singer Pat Boone, and after that comic Jack Carter, who has a well-earned reputation for being difficult, coarse, and abusive. Some years later, he was booked for a show in Las Vegas and he asked me to work on it. I didn't want to do it, but I agreed to help him rehearse and opened the show with him. He came to my studio bringing all his arrangements. As we spread them out on the floor, we both noticed it was covered in less than flattering graffiti about Jack. I had never seen musicians let loose that way. It was hard not to chuckle at some of the statements. Jack was furious. There's another name in this business that, when I hear it, makes my blood pressure rise, and that's Milton Berle—not as talents go, but for the abusive way he treated people.

After we did two weeks with Shelly, Pat came in. Unfortunately he was not able to throw a party, as many of the hosts did at the end of their stint. So, Pat made arrangements with a famous New York delicatessen, the Stage Deli, to have a big spread sent over to the theater on Monday, which was when we would come back to start the new week with Jack

Carter. Our offices were in the Park Central Hotel. We had the tower, and the new host had his office. I went in to introduce myself to Jack, who was reading a newspaper, and he would not even recognize the fact that I was standing there. I went in a second time and got the same response. I finally went in a third time and whacked his newspaper with the back of my hand. "Listen, you're going to be here for a week and you're going to want some support from me. So we'd better say hello and communicate. My name is Donn Trenner and I'm the musical director."

He said, "Okay, okay." So that's how we met, which set up a really bad feeling for me.

Later that day, we went from our offices several blocks away to the theater, where we shot the show. When we got there, Carter had all his writers there. I heard him downstairs yelling at them with the worst profanity I've heard in my life. He was really putting them down. I don't know what for, but after I got to know him, I realized that this was his modus operandi. He saw all the stage hands eating sandwiches, potato salad, coleslaw, and everything. This was the spread that Pat Boone had sent over with a thank you note telling everybody how much he appreciated their efforts. Jack was appalled. He couldn't believe that they were doing this. We did the week with Jack Carter, which was interesting. He had his own guests on the show. Then we learned that he had been held over for another week on the show and we all went, "Oh, my God." But, there was one consolation: we got a ten percent break. Out of ten possible days, he only did nine because in the second week, for some reason, they preempted one of the shows, so we only had to do four days that next week. At the end of his stint, Jack Carter threw a party at Danny's Hideaway, which was a famous show biz hangout, where all the comics would go. We all went. The party was on the second floor and I was sitting right at the top of the stairs talking with someone. All of a sudden, Jack found this wonderful moment when the din level of all these people talking lowered enough for him to get a sarcastic line in. "Well, I guess this cuts the Pat Boone Sandwiches." Jack was telling everybody his party was far better than Pat's. Milton Berle was there and was walking toward the stairs after Carter had made this embarrassing remark. I didn't think he would remember me, so I said, "Hi Milton, Donn Trenner."

Milton said, "I know who you are. Are you kidding me? Remember when I used to be that way?"

Not that Milton had really changed, but it was more a momentary recognition of his own abrasive personality.

Milton could be terrible to the people he was working with. I had played on a *Milton Berle Special*. This was a pre-recorded television production, and Les Brown was selected to be the orchestra. Lena Horne was on it along with Burt Lancaster, and many others, all big stars. This is when I got a little insight into Milton Berle's personality. The crew had a pool going about when we would finish taping the show. We were supposed to start taping at 7:30 that night. There were numbers in a hat predicting times we would probably get out of there. I picked 3:30 a.m. and they said, "Oh, it will be much later than that." We usually finished taping variety shows around 11 p.m., so I didn't believe the crew. Somebody said to me, "You just watch and wait. During the show at some point Milton will go up and push Les Brown off the stand and conduct the orchestra." Sure as hell, at one point, as Les was accompanying him, he went up and embarrassed Les, "That's not the way it goes. Let me have it. Let me take the band." So he attempted to conduct the orchestra.

Another time, I saw him climb up this twelve-foot step ladder after yelling at the lighting man, telling him it wasn't set the way he wanted it. He went up the ladder and did it himself. He truly knew a lot because of his early involvement with variety television, but he was dealing with professionals, and offered no professional respect or courtesy. Milton just didn't have any manners and, at times, could be offensive.

My 3:30 a.m. drawing from the pool didn't hit the mark by a long shot. We left at 5:45 in the morning because Milton just kept going over and over things, not liking anything someone else did, but we were paid well for it. It was revealing to see how Milton operated.

I worked another date with Milton at the Friars Club. He was the president of the club at that time. We were using a mild-mannered, wonderful drummer named Jerry McKenzie. He used to be with The Stan Kenton Orchestra. He did something for Milton Berle, that Jack Carter expects every time he opens his mouth, percussion embellishments called "periods" and "rum-pums." Jerry did a little rum-pum at the end of one of Milton's jokes. Berle turned and scolded him through the microphone, "I don't want any of that. I'll tell you if I need it. I don't need any help from you." He did it in this really intense, personal way. It wasn't funny. He must have turned around three or four times during the show needlessly bringing up that situation again, pointing his finger at the drummer. Jack Carter had that same abrasive style of personality.

One might think of Don Rickles as being much the same way, but in fact he is very different. He doesn't attack the people he works with. He pokes fun at a variety of entertainers and well-known personalities. Personally, I don't care for the style of Milton, Jack, or Don, but what differentiates Don is that his persona on stage is not Don the person, whereas I always felt Jack and Milton's style reflected their true personalities.

Don was working the Sahara Hotel in the lounge, while I was at the Flamingo Hotel with Steve. It was early in his career. He wasn't a mainroom act yet, but he was so popular in the lounge that there was a line that went all the way from the lounge through the casino and sometimes out to the front door. Steve and I went down to see him one night. We were sitting there and he made a couple of Steve Allen remarks and then he got to me and said, "Big deal piano player up there, he waves his arms, big deal conductor for Steve Allen, big deal." I couldn't figure out how in the world he knew me. I didn't even know who he was. Maybe he's doing some research or something. Another time, I went in to see him and I was by myself. It was getting pretty late, and I'm not a hanger-outer, but I went in to watch him. I was trying to be discrete, but I glanced at my watch to see what time it was and he nailed me from the stage. I couldn't believe it. I tried hard not to be noticed.

When I saw Don Rickles a third time he knew that I had worked with Bob Hope. He called me over and we sat down in a booth. He knew that Bob had been in to see his act. He asked me, "What did Bob Hope think of me? Did he say anything? Did he like me?" The insecurities can really show up in these performers. I've never seen more insecure people than comics, seemingly more so than actors.

Mort Sahl was a funny intellectual comedian. He always walks out with a newspaper under his arm and does political satire. We were shooting *ABC's Nightlife* and William B. Williams and Mort Sahl were on stage together for one segment. They had their backs to me the way we were situated. All of a sudden, he turned toward me and then back to William and said, "Do you know who you've got back there?"

Williams replied, "What do you mean?"

Mort said, "Do you know who Donn Trenner is?"

He went on with some embarrassing accolades, but I thought that was a really sweet thing to do and it meant a lot to me. Mort has a great regard for musicians, particularly jazz musicians. In the late 1960s, there were still a lot of name big bands on the scene, such as the Dorsey Brothers, The Glenn Miller Orchestra, Les Brown, Woody Herman, Buddy Rich, and The Stan Kenton Orchestra. Sahl was especially close to Kenton; he knew the managers and everyone connected with that organization.

A good friend, Jack Riley, known as Mr. Carlin on The *Bob Ne-whart Show*, brought Mort out to my house one day. Several weeks prior to this, I was going out for an evening walk. My pool in Woodland Hills was in front of the house overlooking the whole San Fernando Valley. As I walked outside, I saw something I couldn't quite believe. There were two ducks in the pool. Two days later, they came back again and they started coming every day. So, Mort Sahl was over visiting, and as he was leaving, I said, "Gee it's too bad you can't wait a little while because my ducks should be arriving any moment."

As if on cue, they made a splash landing. He couldn't believe it.

I said, "How's that Mort? How's that for color?"

Mort's on-stage persona comes across as self-assured, even snarky sometimes, but he was quick-witted, well-informed, and a true gentleman.

One of the most memorable nights of my life was when Shelly Berman was hosting the show. Doing my advance work from my office, as I always did, I contacted the guests who were scheduled to do a musical number. One of the guests for that week was a young lady starring in *The Fantasticks*. Her name was B. J. Ward—Betty Jean—but everyone called her B. J.

B. J. was booked as a guest because, in addition to doing the Broadway musical, she was working in the New York Playboy Club as a playboy bunny. She had a press agent and had done some negative press about the whole Playboy enterprise and how demeaning it was. She had talked about the exploitation and that the waitresses were not allowed to date or even talk to the costumers. There was a great deal of press about her, so it was another reason to book her on the show.

The Fantasticks was a wonderful piece of theater and also contains some very nice music written by Tom Jones and Harvey Schmidt. "Soon It's Going to Rain" and "Try to Remember" are pretty tunes. In preparation for the show, I called B. J. and asked her about her charts.

She said, "Charts?"

I said, "You know, your arrangements, the musical arrangements. What you're going to sing?"

She said, "Oh, okay," and kind of bluffed her way around that.

When it came the day of the show, Joe Williams was on, and this petite young woman, who was wearing knee socks and a plaid skirt, was sitting on what looked like an orange crate, waiting to rehearse. It came time for me to do her music. I said, "May I have your charts?"

She had a piece of paper that she had gotten from somewhere, crumpled up in her fist. Handing it to me she said, "Here are my charts."

I opened it up and all it had were some chords symbols for a song.

Later, she often told the story, "There I was. I'd never done anything like this before and I'm sitting there very nervous about giving my charts to this musical director. I watch Joe Williams, the great singer with the Count Basie Orchestra, go up before me. On the way by he says, 'Hey Baby, how are you?' Reaching the bandstand he counts off, one-two-ding-ding a ding,' and all this music comes out. And here I am, sitting with my crumpled piece of paper wondering what's going to happen now."

BJ was twenty years old at the time. She celebrated her twenty-first birthday in the living room of my parent's home. We had fallen in love and the relationship really felt right to both of us. We got married in Connecticut with both her parents and my parents present.

ABC's Nightlife didn't last long, around a year, and the show went down the tubes. They changed the format of it again and decided to bring Les Crane back. They dressed him up in some new kind of a personality and went back on with The Elliott Lawrence Orchestra. That show was not able to compete with *The Tonight Show* either.

12 Dire Tramplings

AFTER *ABC'S NIGHTLIFE*, BJ and I returned to California to live in the Woodland Hills home. For the next few years, I continued to do a variety of jazz engagements and a fair amount of studio recording in Los Angeles, working mostly on albums with various artists. It was an active time. I've forgotten about most of these dates, but I occasionally get a small royalty check for pieces of music, cues, songs, and sometimes television shows that are replayed. I did only a few movie calls. As a musician, you don't normally get royalties from the movie sessions. Depending on the contract, royalties can be paid to the composer and musical director, but orchestra players are generally compensated for studio time.

I did get a call to play for *Finian's Rainbow*. I was having trouble with muscle spasms in my back, so my doctor gave me a muscle relaxant. Being leery of pills, I generally didn't take them. The prescription said to "take two in the evening before going to bed." I was afraid to take two, so only took one. Even so, I woke up the next morning and could hardly see the newspaper. It had gotten to my optic nerves and really laid me out. I went down to the studio, but couldn't focus on the music. It was impossible for me to clearly see and I felt terrible. I had to find somebody else to come in for me.

At an earlier point in my career, I met Rose Marie, while doing one of the television shows or specials. She called one day and asked if I would go to Sydney, Australia for a three-week engagement. She said, "I need somebody that can do what I need musically, and can also be my friend."

103

Her husband, Bobby Guy, had recently passed away. He was an important trumpet player on staff at NBC studios in Burbank. Bobby was also a great laugher and we used him for sweetening sessions on The Bob Hope Show. After we did the kinescope, another audience was brought in to augment the laughs. Some of the material was played back, overdubbing extra laughter. We always had Bobby in the audience for the laugh sessions.

In Sydney, Rose Marie and I played at a showroom in the Chevron Hilton Hotel, which was booking a lot of variety show artists. Rose Marie was an interesting kind of act. She was well-known to so many people for her work on radio and television, especially *The Dick Van Dyke Show*. Most people don't know this, but Rose Marie started in the business when she was three years old. She always wore her identifiable trademark, the bow in her hair. Her nightclub act and persona was different from what she did on radio and TV, but she was nevertheless always charming. Occasionally, she did some bawdy material, not really risqué, but old English barroom songs and humor, and she did it masterfully. She was funny and sang with a great sense of rhythm.

We did a television show in Sydney called *The Don Lane Show*. Don Lane, who had been an American entertainer, became the host of this Australian night-time talk show with a format similar to *The Steve Allen Show*. We appeared with Rose Marie singing a couple of numbers. The producer of the show was John Collins. When I first met him, I said something quite silly, "Pleased to meet you, I've been drinking you for years," and he politely laughed at my off-target reference to a popular cocktail. Anyway, he contacted me wanting to know if I would be interested in spending time with him developing a pilot for what could be my own show there. I wasn't sure if he was serious and nothing happened on that first trip.

While I was at the Chevron Hilton, a woman called me, said she was an author, and asked if I could introduce her to Rose Marie. People usually can't meet with a famous entertainer unless they go through someone closely associated with that person or group. I was frequently approached by strangers who wanted to get in touch with a celebrity, whether it was Bob Hope, Steve Allen, or in this case, Rose Marie. I felt especially protective of Rose Marie because of Bobby's recent passing, so I thought it best to meet this woman in the lobby before going forward.

Elizabeth Kata was an elegant lady with a thick Australian accent. I got to talking with her and found out that she wrote a book titled, *Be Ready with Bells and Drums* (1961), which was produced as a movie

Elizabeth Kata and Rose Marie in Sydney 1966.

called, *A Patch of Blue* (1965). It is a wonderful film with Sidney Poitier, Elizabeth Hartmann, and Shelly Winters. In fact, Shelly won the Academy Award for Best Supporting Actress.

Elizabeth had another project she wanted to discuss with Rose Marie. After our initial meeting, I put the two of them in touch. Elizabeth was kind and sweet to me. After she met with Rose Marie, she rented a small theater and arranged a private showing of her film. It just knocked me out. I don't think anything came of her meeting with Rose Marie, but Elizabeth became a friend. Over the years BJ and I stayed in touch with her, trading visits between California and Sydney.

Singer Frankie Randall got booked in Sydney at the same hotel and asked me if I would work with him as his pianist and conductor. This became my second trip to Australia and I took BJ. Since we had recently married, this was more or less our honeymoon. Frankie Randall, originally known as Chico Randall, was a wonderful talent and a gentleman. He was an accomplished pianist in his own right, and a great vocalist who used to work at Jilly's, a famous late-night club in New York on 52nd Street. I became involved with Frankie in California years before. RCA called me to work with him on a couple of albums when they were launching his singing career.

While we were in Sydney, I got another call from John Collins, saying he wanted to do the pilot show with me. He proposed that I would host an entertaining, humorous variety show that included a monologue, a guest interview, and music. He had a monologist write an opening for me. It was dreadfully unfunny, so BJ and I went down to the hotel desk, rented a typewriter, and wrote our own monologue. We shot the pilot and it was a lot of fun.

My guest was a vocalist named Matt Monro. He did quite well with records for a while. Matt was from England and his story was that he used to deliver milk until somebody found out that he had some talent as a singer. During the interview I threw lines at him like, "I've known about you for years. I even knew your sister Marilyn." Which I thought was funny, but it didn't really go over well. He only kind of chuckled. I sang, "I Left My Nose in San Francisco," which was one of Steve's songs. I played piano and had my own musical director. I also did a couple of sketches that they had written. I was offered the possibility of coming over there for a full year, but the deal fell apart during negotiations. There was only one television channel in Sydney at that time and they had two weekly variety shows already, both hosted by Americans. One was *The Bob Crosby Show* with Bob Crosby and The Bobcats. He got into some kind of trouble there. As a result, they decided it was not the right time for another American host.

Frankie and I became good friends. Later on, he asked me to do a promotional tour with him. We took a quartet on the road for four weeks and worked about five cities a week promoting his new album. It was a lot of fun. We had too much fun actually. Frankie would often stand in the curve of the grand piano and inside the piano he'd leave a glass of water. Every so often, while he was singing, his right hand would come back behind him. He'd stick his fingers in the glass and flick water in my face while I was playing. We were doing one of the big clubs up at Lake Tahoe and upon closing I decided that I was going to get back at him for weeks of this kind of torture. I went out and bought water guns for the guys in the band. When he did this to me again, we attacked him with the squirt guns and chased him off the stage.

Frankie had a habit of calling me names that began with D and T. This all came from Steve Allen's show. Steve used to do a segment imitating the old radio announcers, sounding like they do when they did a remote broadcast. "And now ladies and gentlemen, from downtown west of the Mississippi we're bringing you the music of Dire Tramplings and his orchestra." Steve also made up all kinds of names that began with my initials. Dump Truck was my favorite. The gentleman that ran the teleprompter during the show was situated right in front of the stage telephone. If a call came through that was for me, Steve would say, "Dump, it's for you."

Frankie would call me in the middle of the night from almost anywhere when he came up with a new name. He'd say, "Hi, Diph Theria" or "Damp Tongue" or "Dirty Toilet," anything he could think of. One night he called me, "Donald Trump." I'd call Frankie, "Frankly Rundown." It became an ongoing gag with the two of us. His favorite name for me was "Tractor."

Frankie did an engagement out in Mineola, New York, at a place called the San Su San, back when I was still doing *ABC's Nightlife*. It was apparently home to some underworld characters. Each night, Frankie had a limousine waiting to pick me up as soon as I got off the air, and he would wait until I got to the San Su San to play the show. One particular night, he was singing the verse of this beautifully sensitive song "When the World Was Young," and some people were making a lot of noise. I was sitting up there at the piano with a full orchestra, sort of profiling the audience as I often did from the piano. The chairs were set up banquet style like they do in Las Vegas, perpendicular to the stage. One table in particular was noisy and, as far as I was concerned, downright rude. So I turned around toward the noisy table, which I couldn't even see because of the lights, and gave a progressively louder, "shush, shush- shuussh!" I looked over to the other side of the stage and there was a waiter standing there. He was looking at me giving me a negative head shake with his hand pushing on his nose and his ear flapped over. I didn't know what that meant. When we got off the stage, the waiter came over and advised me, "You better go upstairs and stay in your dressing room. Do you know who you just shushed? That was Philly Da Hat." I went upstairs and stayed there. About twenty minutes later, the waiter came up and knocked on the door. He said, "It's okay, the coast is clear, Philly didn't say anything." I will never forget the San Su San. Now I know the secret signal for Mafia.

These were the Rat Pack years. The Sands Hotel was famous for presenting comedians like Corbett Monica, who was part of that whole group, and of course Frank Sinatra and his cronies. Las Vegas went through two distinct personalities. There was the Mafia period. In the early days, the Mafia was in charge of Vegas, and there was no petty crime because they wouldn't allow it. These were the Bugsy Siegal days and there was a lot of talk about what the Mafia was doing, but I didn't pay any attention to it. I wasn't a gambler and I didn't hang out. I was perennially naïve and it just didn't interest me. I was there to play music.

I was never called directly by Sinatra because I avoided it. On three separate occasions, I was called by someone in the orchestra who said they are talking about calling me to become Sinatra's musical director. Each time I said, "Tell him not to call. Do it diplomatically, but I'm really not interested." The last time was when Joe Parnello was conducting for him. I knew how Joe's health had been seriously impaired. He had been with Vic Damone for years and that was another strenuous association. Some singers are excessively steeped in their own self-image. As a result, they can be difficult to be with. I have to be careful about the way I speak of this. I don't want to say a lot of negative things.

I knew a lot of good people, who played with Sinatra, and I knew it was an honor to be asked, but as much as I respected his talent and the quality of the musicians he had in his band, I just didn't want to be part of the Sinatra camp. I also didn't much care for his attorney Mickey Rudin, who was also one of Sinatra's henchmen. There was always something going on that just seemed not quite right. Sinatra was involved with the notorious Cal Neva nightclub and gambling resort in Lake Tahoe. As well as he sang, and nobody can get away from the fact that a Sinatra sound is preeminent, he still felt like an underworld character to me. I also remembered when my friend ,Vince Falcone, was conducting for Sinatra and how poorly he was treated. On opening night at Carnegie Hall, Vince was fired by Mickey Rudin. If Sinatra didn't do it himself, he always had Mickey do it. I heard so many stories and I had seen many uncomfortable moments. Although I stand up for myself and for my musicians, I generally try to avoid confrontational situations. It just didn't feel right to work with Sinatra and his group.

Even though I never worked for him directly, I'd been on stage with Sinatra on several occasions. One time in particular, I felt his brand of power. I was playing piano with the orchestra for a show in a big auditorium at a Catholic University. Sinatra was very generous with funding charities, particularly Catholic charities. He gave a lot of money to them. That night there were three acts, the famous pantomime duo of Shields and Yarnell, Sarah Vaughan, and Sinatra was the closing act. Vinny Falcone was conducting for him. Sarah Vaughan went on first, and Shields and Yarnell followed. We were behind a scrim on stage and I remember Sinatra, who was now apparently eager to go on, loudly insisting, "Get them off the stage. Get 'em off! I want to go on now!" Situations like this were difficult for me to witness. I didn't take them personally because they didn't affect me directly, but I just felt very uncomfortable. He was so angry he didn't even acknowledge the orchestra at the end of the performance, which was unusual because he was almost always gracious enough to do so.

The first call came from within Sinatra's band when I was doing a lot of studio recording in Los Angeles. Bill Miller, who had been with him for years as his pianist, was unmercifully fired. There was a flood in Los Angeles, and a mudslide came down an embankment. Bill's wife was caught in a car and killed in the mudslide. Everybody talked about what a terrible time for Sinatra to let him go. I was called shortly after this happened.

I don't know what happened exactly, but Bill continued to work for Sinatra on and off right up toward the end of Sinatra's career, but only as a pianist. He just didn't handle the conducting chores well. I was called by someone saying that I was in line as the conductor. And I said, "I'd like to get out of line please." As wonderful a job as it probably was, it was too predictably anxious for me. Normally I'm mild mannered, but if I feel negative pressure and get uncomfortable, I'm not so mild mannered anymore and I get more outspoken than I should be, or what might be defensible.

The last tip off came from his bass player at the time, Don Baldini. He called me one night and said, "It's going to happen, they're ready to call you."

And again I said, "Please tell them no."

That was when Joe Parnello was working with him. The circumstances were quite similar. Don told me that Joe was having a lot of trouble conducting, or at least Sinatra and Parnello were having trouble with interpretation and communication. Joe wasn't following Frank, or Frank wasn't going with Joe. Whatever the case, it was disconcerted in rubato passages when it was necessary for Joe to control the orchestra in following Frank. A rubato passage is an "out of tempo" musical interpretation that requires conducting to necessitate the orchestra's need to accompany the singer's phrasing. Listening to Sinatra recordings, you'll hear this is part of his signature style; one of the things that tell you it's a Sinatra arrangement.

When Howard Hughes bought the Desert Inn, there were some changes. He resided there for part of the year, but no one ever saw him because he was so reclusive. Hughes was entrepreneurial and represented the outer-world, not the underworld. Through his enterprise, called the Summa Corporation, he changed Las Vegas for the better. The cement shoe business was ruined, but petty crime increased.

Many of the Las Vegas hotels name suites after the stars that play there regularly. Caesar's Palace has the Frank Sinatra Suite and the Ann-Margret Suite. They have two or three bedrooms and a huge round room with an enormous Jacuzzi that looks out on the lights over all of Las Vegas.

Once, when I was playing at Tahoe with Shirley MacLaine, Sammy Davis was across the street at Harrah's, where of course he was staying in the Sammy Davis Jr. Suite. Sammy was having a party and I had been invited. After our show, I walked across the street. He is famous for taking dozens of pieces of luggage with him, including suitcases filled with audio and videotapes. He was playing the Woody Herman "Early Autumn," recording and I went over to him and said, "I hate to do this to you, but can you back up this tape? I want to sing something in your ear." So he did and I sang him the Stan Getz solo with the Red Kelly lyric. "Oh, good morning. How the fuck are you..." Sammy broke up.

At the party that night, there were a lot of provocatively-dressed ladies. Outside of Lake Tahoe was a place called the Mustang Ranch, a well-known brothel. Joe Conforte, an infamous Mafia figure, was the owner and brought a bunch of his girls over from this place. At one point in the party, somebody said to me, "Why don't you go upstairs? There's a nice room up there." I wasn't really thinking about what he meant, and so I went. Two women came after me. One opened her suitcase and took out a big battery operated vibrator. I couldn't believe it and I quickly got out of that situation, but I stayed at the party and had a couple of drinks. After a short while, I decided to leave. When I got in the elevator Joe Conforte entered with two women. He started slapping one of them around. He was yelling at her and physically abusing her face. I was completely shocked and frightened. As we got down to the lower floor, he looked at me and he said, "You know, I don't usually do this, but there's a reason for it." I looked at him, but didn't know what to say. Apparently the two were fighting during the party. One had taken a lit cigarette and stuck it into the other's face. Joe had heard about that and was punishing her in his own way. To witness this kind of violent abuse exemplified all that I found reprehensible in the world of Las Vegas.

In the entertainment business, there were the hanger-outers, the people who drank, caroused, and stayed up long after the shows. The entertainment business is filled with people who do everything to excess. The stars make so much money that their whole value structure can be easily changed. Although some people manage, for others it becomes hard to maintain perspective. I was not interested in the after-show activities and usually went back to my room with my Heath Kits and the soldering iron.

Some years later, Sinatra called Frankie Randall and told him he would not be performing anymore and that he wanted to give Frankie some of his original arrangements. Sinatra had always surrounded himself with really talented people, so that was a real honor he had bestowed on Frankie. Frankie was doing a tribute to Sinatra and asked me if I would like to do it with him. Frankie had been musically influenced by Sinatra's singing, so much so that at times he sounded like Sinatra, though Frankie certainly has his own wonderful style. Strangely, it was the week in May of 1998 that Sinatra died, and I drove from my new home in Connecticut down to Atlantic City on a Thursday to met with Frankie. We talked over what his show was going to be. Then on Friday we rehearsed a really fine orchestra and appeared Friday, Saturday, and Sunday. Our opening act was Tom Dreesen, who was Sinatra's opening act for thirteen years. Tom was a pallbearer and the funeral had just been the day before he came in to do our show.

That was a horrendous week. Following that weekend, I drove home from Atlantic City, which took about four hours, repacked my clothes and went to New Haven to catch the limousine service, which was a bus, and rode to JFK airport, got on an airplane for London, where I changed planes and flew to Istanbul, Turkey. There I boarded a ship to do four shows with Rita Moreno, while on route to Venice, where I got off the boat and came home.

13

Guess Who I Saw Today

NCY WILSON WAS HANDLED at that time by an attorney named Jay Cooper, who was also a musician. He later became a lecturer and taught show business law, recording contracts, motion picture contracts, and publishing. Jay knew me from other musical activities and called to ask if I would be interested in doing a fifteen-day engagement with Nancy Wilson. I did that engagement and stayed on as her musical director for five years.

A little later on, John Levy became Nancy's manager. I had met John some years prior, when he was playing bass with the George Shearing Quintet. When George first settled in New York, he had a quintet with John on bass, Denzel Best on drums, Marjorie Hyams playing vibraphone, and guitarist Chuck Wayne. What a great group. John Levy went on and became a manager. Two of his important and strongest accounts were Joe Williams and Nancy Wilson. He also established a publishing company. Joe Zawinul's "Mercy, Mercy, Mercy" is one of his copyrights.

Nancy sang many standards and also did a lot of special material. She used a group of arrangers that were important to her. Jimmy Jones wrote some arrangements and conducted on her album titled, *Lush Life*. Billy May did a several charts for her. Oliver Nelson, who was a great musical talent, wrote some things for her. Oliver lived very near Nancy and I spent a lot of time at his house with her. Lyricist and director, Martin Charnin, who, since this time, wrote the Broadway show, *Annie*, was a special material writer. Martin came to Los Angeles, where we put together a show for Nancy, the theme of which was "Black Is Beautiful."

Part of my job as musical director was filling in the orchestra with capable players at every tour stop. It was different when we did a television show. There was a fixed orchestra, where the musicians were part of the show's staff. The instrumentation with Nancy was always eight brass, with four trumpets doubling on flugelhorns, and four trombones. We had five saxophones doubling on various woodwinds and usually at least twelve strings, comprised of eight violins, two violas, two cellos, plus harp. I was able to take care of the conducting from the piano as needed. When we went on the road, we would carry just our rhythm section, which is a common practice for tours that required larger orchestras. I was on piano, and for a time Nancy's husband, Kenny Dennis, was on drums. We always brought our own drummer and bass player with us on the road. The rhythm section is the motor of the orchestra, the basis for the whole sound. We could also rehearse new material with the artist and rhythm section, without the rest of the orchestra, and still provide enough background so it would sound and feel more complete than just piano.

The music was always great, and we played wonderful engagements. At some point along the way, Kenny was replaced on drums by Mickey Roker. Buster Williams or Bob Cranshaw played bass. Mickey worked with many great artists including Dizzy Gillespie, Ella Fitzgerald and Joe Williams. Buster Williams recorded with Betty Carter, Sarah Vaughan and Herbie Hancock, among others. Bob Cranshaw, known for his association with Sonny Rollins, worked with numerous legendary figures as well. That's as good as it gets.

Working with Nancy Wilson was interesting both musically and socially. At that time, Buster was kind of a rebellious soul and could be confrontational. He seemed to me to be unhappy with his life. There were a couple of incidences where he seemed to show a problem with race. He stayed in his room a lot and didn't want to come down to coffee shops with us because he might have felt out of place. We had disagreements over this issue. One day, when I went up to his room, he pointed his finger to his own face and said, "Don't you ever tell me that you don't think of me as a Black man when you look at me."

I was taken aback, "Hold on a minute. What does that mean? I think of you as Buster Williams when I talk to you. My brain only correlates that I'm talking to a person. I'm sorry if you have a bad feeling, but it's your problem, not mine, and I will not become a part of it." I hadn't been in this kind of situation before.

Nancy loved to travel with an entourage. She had many friends and she liked to be surrounded by them, and that was great. We were in Cleveland, and there was a local baseball hero, Jim Mudcat Grant, who was a major league pitcher for the Cleveland Indians and a friend of Nancy's. One day she asked me, "How would you like to go horseback riding?" She had three limousines come to the hotel and we headed out to some remote part of Cleveland. The group that day included Mudcat Grant and his wife, Nancy and Kenny, Buster, my dear friend Sparky Tavares, and me. Sparky, who resembled Billy Strayhorn, spent eighteen years as Nat Cole's personal assistant, and then twenty years with Nancy Wilson. Sparky was the sweetest man alive.

We drove out to the stables and were brought around to pick out our horses. As it turned out, I got the only black horse in the stables. The horse's name was Rochester, named after Jack Benny's sidekick on his television show, who was a Black man. So, here's the White guy in the company riding Rochester. They take us to this little inside arena so that we can become familiar with our horses. Buster's horse immediately became aggressive and reared up on his hind legs and then jumped on another horse. He continued bucking and it scared us. Buster got another horse. I was riding Rochester and they led us out into a field to get on the bridle path. Rochester was hanging way behind and everyone else was already ahead of us. Nancy turned around and said, "Come on Trenner."

I said, "Rochester doesn't want to go too fast."

She said, "Come on Trenner, kick him."

I said, "I'm not going to kick Rochester." She was more insistent, "Kick him!" I gently gave him a little jab. He turned around and gave me his horse snorts. I looked into his face and realized that was about as far as he and I were going. They got further ahead of me.

Nancy was still yelling, "Come on Trenner; really kick him!"

So I kicked him a little harder and he moved a little bit more, but he was too busy smelling the flowers. Finally, they waited for me and we reconvened at a place along the path. Nancy said, "Give me that horse. Give me Rochester. I'll show you how to ride him." She got on and gave him a real jab with her heels and they took off into heaven.

Nancy is an outstanding musician. I don't think I ever heard Nancy sing a wrong note, or even close to an out of tune note. It is so natural for her to sing. Accompanying her was an incredible joy that I will never forget. One of the songs she became well-known for is "Guess Who I Saw Today," written by Murray Grand. If you listen carefully to the lyrics, they have a sophisticated and subtle humor. No one else can touch that song; it belongs to her. Nancy is a remarkable singer, but didn't really look the audience in the eye. As a result, she could appear to be a bit aloof. It was just part of her personal style on stage.

While it was awesome to conduct and play for her, she would call me on the phone and do one of my least favorite things. "Hello, Trenner?" I hated to be addressed this way because it reminds me of my time in the service, but I knew that coming from her, it was meant to be endearing. "Trenner, I'll be coming into Vegas late so I want you to just pick out a show for me and do the rehearsal." I was not entirely comfortable with being placed in this position, but flattered that she had that much confidence in my ability to put a show together for her. There was a professional trust in our working relationship and I was grateful for that. On one of our tour dates someone told Nancy that the Hebrew origin of the word "Trenner" was a slang word akin to the English slang, "bugger." From then on, Nancy introduced me with great emphasis on my family name, and it became a longstanding joke between us.

Nancy and Kenny had a son named Casey. The three of them together looked like a magazine cover photo. We brought the new show, *Black Is Beautiful,* to the Cocoanut Grove, which was in the famous Ambassador

Conducting for Nancy during a nightclub performance.

A moment with Nancy, almost anywhere.

Hotel in Los Angeles, before Robert Kennedy's assassination there. In the final segment of the show, there was a big screen on stage where a picture of her young son, Casey, was projected and Nancy sang to the screen. She did all these lovely little tunes dedicated to him. The closing number for the show was "Black Is Beautiful." On this particular night, when Nancy approached the end, where the lyric invokes the title, "Black Is Beautiful," some lady in the audience yelled out, "Never!" The room went quiet. It was a frightening moment to deal with. Nancy was devastated. She didn't know what to do and walked off stage. After a few moments, she came back out in tears, but composed herself and said, "Madam, I was singing that song to my son, not you." She finished the song and we closed the show.

Nancy also did a series of programs in many of the high schools. There were a lot of drop outs, particularly in the inner city schools. We would do assemblies with a trio, where she sang a few tunes and then she would talk to the students about the importance of education and staying in school. When we got back to New York we did an assembly at one of the public schools in Harlem.

The Joey Bishop Show ran for a while. It wasn't spectacular, but it was another of those that we called "strip shows." It was on the air five nights a week and had many guests. Joey would bring on people from all different walks of life and certainly people in the entertainment field. On this particular evening we were scheduled to appear, along with Wayne Newton. They ended up canceling all the music. Martin Luther King Jr. had been assassinated that day.

Our schedule called for us to open at the Apollo Theater, and it was just two days after King had been assassinated. You could feel the emotional tension throughout the country, and in Harlem it was palpable. Our opening act was Flip Wilson, who was not well-known at that point. I remember somebody from the theater coming up and saying, "Here's your dressing room and we advise you to stay in it. If you are going to get something to eat, we'd prefer that you send out for it. If not, go out with a group of people." They were being exceptionally protective. I did go outside with a gathering of people associated with the show. We were on our way, walking to a restaurant, and I noticed what appeared to be a plainclothes officer talking to a division of Black and White rookie policemen not in full uniform. He seemed to be instructing them for whatever situation they might be encountering.

It was a privilege to perform at the Apollo Theater. It was also an educational experience. I was one among the few White people and, for the first time in my life, felt self-conscious about the color of my skin. There was an air of hostility that night that was new to me.

I was working with Nancy Wilson at the Sahara Hotel in Las Vegas, when BJ called to inform me that my father had died. I knew my dad was ill with pancreatic cancer and I had just flown my parents out to California where we had a nice visit. I could see my dad was perishing; his body was getting smaller all the time. When I drove them around, taking them to various places, I would look in the rearview mirror and see him with hands clasped over his head, which I realized I did a lot, too, and I saw all this loose flesh, and that he was in a quandary as to what was going on. He had been getting thinner and thinner and we knew that he had limited time. He died shortly after they got back home in Connecticut. I had spoken to him by phone during that last week when he was in the hospital. The cause of death was pneumonia, which often is the case. It was the night before closing and we had to bring somebody in to finish the show for me. BJ and I flew back east.

My mother died two weeks less than two years after that. I was just starting to build my recording studio at the house. BJ was sitting out on the deck getting some sun and she cautioned me several times, "Don't wear soft shoes out there. There are a lot of nails and stuff around." We were knocking a wall out and the phone rang. It was my cousin Stanley, who used to go over on Wednesdays to take my mother shopping because she didn't drive. BJ answered, she came to me and said, "It's your cousin Stanley and he isn't making any sense. You'd better take this." Sure enough, as I stepped off of the ladder to take the call, I put a nail right through my foot. I stumbled to the phone and cousin Stanley said, "You know I come to pick your mother up every Wednesday, and I came here today and… ." He was starting to stammer, "The police are here now and they found your mother sprawled on the floor in the kitchen and… ." She had experienced a massive heart attack. I got a tetanus shot and we boarded an airplane. BJ and I went back to Connecticut and took care of everything. We drove the effects that I wanted to keep down to Florida where BJ 's parents lived.

Nancy Wilson did major events in England, France, Holland, Sweden, and Denmark. They loved her wherever we went. We did many European television shows that were all memorable. On our first European trip, I met many people who have become lifelong friends.

Gilbert Bécaud was a famous French variety entertainer, who did a show from a television studio in Saarbrücken. At the time, Saarbrücken was a little city in France right on the German border. Since then, the border was moved and it has become a German city. Nancy was a guest artist on the show. They interviewed her in English and she sang a few songs. The staff orchestra was good and very kind to me. We had a wonderful time.

In Amsterdam, we did the Grand Gala du Disque, which is the Grand Performance of Records for the Benelux countries. The Benelux countries are Belgium, Luxemburg and the Netherlands. The event is a fantastic party that occurs each year and showcases the important artists whose records have sold well throughout the year, and Nancy was to perform. It took over about seven stories of an enormous downtown building.

I had made specific phone calls to Nancy's manager, John Levy, to make sure that I would have all the music I needed. When I got there, the orchestra was much larger than John had let me know. Quite coincidently, upon arrival, I met a Capitol representative named Joop Visser. He said, "It's simple man, it's like an American name, it is Joe Fisher to you." He later became part owner of Charly Records in England. Joop and I spent a lot of time at the Xerox machine copying parts, so that I would have enough music for the entire orchestra. I ran into Vicki Carr, who had done *The Steve Allen Show*. Vicki was thoughtful and arranged for me to have dinner with her back at the hotel.

Through Joop, I became familiar with Amsterdam and Holland. He brought me into his home and we became good friends. He was an incredible man and important to jazz as a producer. He put artists together, got record contracts, and recorded them. Joop produced Ben Webster's last album. He found some excellent jazz recordings at Capitol that hadn't sold well, repackaged them, and released them through Charly Records. Joop took me to see the Royal Concertgebouw and I was absolutely amazed. The concert hall is built like an oval with seats going all the way around the back of the concert stage. Inscribed in the facade on the front of the balcony are over forty classical composers' names.

Two years later, I was on that same stage with Rod McKuen, who was known at the time as America's favorite poet. Rod had become popular in Holland and was set to appear at the Concertgebouw when his conductor, Arthur Greenslade, had to drop out. On short notice I made it to Amsterdam. We recorded a live double album there. I was on stage with Rod and a barrage of microphones. We had a three-hour on-stage rehearsal with the orchestra. There was a lot of music and it was not at all organized. He had three arrangements of the same tune, others were only written for a small band. I had little time to figure it out. The performance went well, but I had serious doubts up until a minute before we went on. I looked around the hall and felt like such a fraud standing on that stage with that orchestra, looking at all the great composers' names etched into the wood over the years. The concert was sold out and Rod gave an impressive performance that night.

With Nancy, we did thirty days at Tivoli Gardens in Copenhagen, which is a famous and elegant amusement park in the center of the city. There are numerous restaurants, a variety hall, a symphonic hall, and a couple of jazz clubs interspersed among the beautiful gardens, and all that make up this extraordinary park.

The band in Copenhagen was great. I worked with a trombone player there named Torrolf Mulgaard. When he heard that Frank Rosolino had been in my band, it was like I had known God personally. I would tell him about the things Frank did, such as when he'd pick up his horn and play the National Anthem, straight at first. And then would go into some tailgating or Dixieland on it, and then he'd play bebop on it. Frank did this thing where he played a riff on his horn and, at the highest note of the lick he would release his embouchure from the mouthpiece and sing the note through the horn. I told this to Torrolf, who had a very deep voice. He came in two days later and said in his Danish accent, "Donn listen to this." He had worked out Frank's bit, but when it came to the high note he sang it down three octaves.

While in Copenhagen, I stayed at the Royal Hotel. Standing in line at the registration desk, I saw David Rose, an important musician and conductor, who wrote "Holiday for Strings" and "The Stripper," among others. He had been a staff musician for NBC, and later became music director for many television productions, including the Michael Landon shows, such as *Bonanza* (1959) and *Little House on the Prairie* (1974) David collected model trains, but not the little ones. He had a train that ran around his whole estate. He used to go all over the world to buy units and parts for it, and that's why he was in Copenhagen. I had done some work for him several years before as a pianist.

Years later, I caught an episode of *Touched by an Angel* and the music knocked me out. It was emotionally wonderful. I called David's home and his wife answered. I said, "May I please speak to David?"

She said, "Well that's impossible. David passed away two years ago."

I said, "If he's possibly hearing this conversation, I called for only one reason, to tell him how wonderful the music was that he wrote."

European orchestras are great to work with. To a certain extent, the European musicians may have interpreted the music a little differently than the players in the U.S. Sometimes the jazz figures were articulated in a manner that made them seem a little too clean or straight-up perhaps. They were not quite as laid back as a good American jazz band would be, such as Basie or the Thad Jones and Mel Lewis' band. It's a difficult concept to explain. When a large orchestra is playing a big ensemble portion of an arrangement, a European orchestra's interpretation may not swing as naturally as the American conception. Then again, I've heard many wonderful European jazz musicians. I worked with some incredible players in Stockholm, such as pianist, Benght Hallberg and alto saxophonist, Arne Domnérus. There are talented jazz musicians everywhere in the world. Maybe we thought at this time, because it is an American art form, that jazz isn't going to be happening anywhere else, but our indigenous music has been an enormously successful cultural export.

I think jazz eventually became as natural to Europeans as it has for us because we shared the same influences. American jazz musicians have always traveled to Europe and they worked with European musicians. Many decided to stay there. Don Byas took up residence in the Netherlands and Denmark. Dexter Gordon lived in Copenhagen all those years. Kenny Clarke lived in Paris and formed a band with the Belgian pianist and arranger Francy Boland. The Clarke-Boland Big Band included American expatriates and European players. Herb Geller recorded with the Clarke-Boland Big Band. I hired Herb frequently in Germany when I was there with Nancy. I also brought him in later when I was with Shirley MacLaine. He is a wonderful alto saxophone player, and a great woodwind doubler, who became a member of Norddeutche Rundfunk Orchestra. If you landed a staff position with one of the German radio orchestras, you're there for a lifetime. They can't fire you unless something really dramatic happens. Herb had a lengthy career there. He came from the period in Los Angeles when Lenny Bruce was out there and Chetty Baker, and that entire clique of East LA jazz musicians, so I had known him from several years prior.

The European audiences appeared to be much more enthusiastic about jazz than American audiences. It is more respected here now that it's in the schools. Today, it's no longer a liability to say, "I am a jazz musician," because now more people believe in the cultural value of the genre. There was a time, when I first came into jazz, when it was as if you were creating some worthless. "Jazz" had such a negative connotation. As a "jazz musician" you were suspect.

I learned early in my life when I was filling out credit applications to never put "musician" on the form. I wrote in "musical director" or "orchestrator" or something that took off the unfortunate stigma that went with being a musician in this country. Among creditors, musicians had the reputation for being delinquent on their bills. Playing club dates can be dicey, because it was, and still is, largely unregulated and players are not paid adequately or appropriately for their work. Financially, it is extremely difficult to make a living from playing clubs. But in Europe, the art form of music, and especially jazz, is widely respected and honored. Jazz clubs are generally better supported there. This is why many American musicians have enjoyed greater success in Europe.

Televised jazz festivals were an important part of European culture. I met Lennart Wetterholm when we shot the television special with Nancy in Sweden. Lennart and his assistant, Marina Bennett, gave me a tour of Stockholm our first days there and they are responsible for my longstanding love for that city. Lennart loved jazz and he could film a big band and actually make it exciting. In America, directors are not particularly interested in shooting a big band or even a whole band number. They think it is monotonous. They know when the trumpets play and they know when the saxophones play so they shoot back and forth a couple of times, but to them that's boring. Lennart is the first director I ever saw who was so enthusiastic in the booth that I thought he would jump out of his own trousers.

On one of my later trips to Sweden, Lennart took me down to the studio and said, "Let's go in, I want you to see this program that I did." He had shot one of the last interviews done with Stan Getz and Chetty Baker. This was shortly before Chetty died. He's the one who put me in touch with several musicians in Sweden, such as Benght Hallberg, Sweden's leading jazz pianist, and Arne Domnérus, the highly respected studio sax player.

On this particular trip, we didn't have Mickey and Buster with us. It was just Nancy and me. I ended up running into a drummer in Stockholm, Alex Riel, from Copenhagen, who did the television special with us. Somebody told me that he didn't read very well. I spoke with him on the phone before we got there and decided to take a chance and go with him. He turned out to be one of the most exciting drummers that I have ever played with. He heard the chart once and that was it, it was his. Rolf Ericson, a jazz trumpet player who had played with Les' band when he was in America, was back there in the brass section. He couldn't wait to introduce me to a Turkish trumpet player by the name of Muvvah Fukkah.

Over the years, Lennart and his wife Ulla-Britta became dear friends. A few years later in 1980, Lennart called me, "How would you like to be a co-host on our first jazz festival?" The Stockholm Jazz Festival was sponsored by Channel One Swedish Broadcasting, and the entire three days would be televised. I was so honored. He told me the musicians in Sweden talked about the show I had done with Nancy Wilson and that was one of the reasons he called. The money was not significant, but that aspect was not important to me.

A Swedish variety show host, Gunilla Marcus, was to be my co-host. She was a household name in Sweden. Gunilla was a warm lovely lady and she loved America. Lennart's idea for hosting was to have the American who loved Sweden and the Swede who loved America. We did about forty hours of television over a three-day period on the little island of Skeppsholmen, one of the many islands adjoining Stockholm. We had many fine musicians at the festival, including Dizzy Gillespie, Stan Getz, James Moody, Toots Thielemans, Clark Terry, Kai Winding, and some Swedish players. Gerry Mulligan came over, but didn't have a pianist so I played the set with Gerry. They created many different shows out of that filming and the segments played all over Europe.

With Dizzy Gillespie at the Stockholm Jazz Festival in1980.

On another occasion with Nancy Wilson, we were staying at a hotel outside of Copenhagen, in a town called Rødovre. I went back and forth by cab; it was a thirty-minute drive out of Copenhagen. I got into the cab and said, "I need to go to the Continental Hotel in Road-over."

They said, "What?"

"Road-over" and I'd have to spell it. I could never say it properly.

One night at that hotel, I became quite ill. I was in intense pain and didn't know what was going on. Alan Jackson, our bass player and his girlfriend, were there at the hotel. I called them and said I wasn't feeling well. They called a doctor for me and got an immediate response. During the night, the doctor visited me several times.

The next morning, the maid came in to make up the room and there were three or four empty hypodermic needles on the coffee table. She looked at me like I was some kind of a junkie. It was morphine he had been giving me. The pain persisted and finally I went to the hospital and stayed overnight. They decided that it was kidney stones, or kidney sand, which it turned out to be. I received the best care possible and the hospital bill was really extravagant, $2.90. They apologized because I wasn't Danish, or there would not have been any charge at all. They recommended that I drink beer with my food to avoid future kidney stones.

I had made arrangements to buy a new Volvo at the factory in Gothenburg, which is a lengthy drive from Copenhagen. The day came and I took the train up to Gothenburg to pick up my new car. I took delivery and drove back with my elbow pushing into my stomach because it was so painful. When I got back, I had to go to work. I was on stage with

Nancy's acknowledgement during final bows.

Nancy conducting when, all of a sudden, I got another piercing attack and then it just got unbearable. I went back to the hospital and they put me in the same ward, on the same floor, in the same bed, and the same people took care of me. I was there overnight. There wasn't much they could do except to give me more morphine. When I checked out this time, the bill was $3.40. Again, they apologized. It cost more than that to get the Volvo washed five days later.

Unfortunately, that was my last engagement as Nancy Wilson's Musical Director. The Black press was not happy that she had a White musical director, which was understandable in some ways. There were so few Black musical directors, and I think there was a feeling that she should have made the role available to a qualified director from within the Black community. There was a need for her to make a change, especially given the level of talent that was available. I was told that Kirk Stuart, a pianist, singer, conductor, and arranger, who worked with Della Reese, Sarah Vaughan, and Joe Williams, was going to replace me.

There was a little bit of bitterness at the end with Nancy Wilson. The change was supposed to take place before the next engagement in Copenhagen. This angered me, and I got in touch with her manager, stating that I had a contract which included that engagement and I intended to do it. It worked out that we both went. I conducted and Dr. Stuart played piano. In the world of jazz, skilled musicians are simply skilled musicians, whatever their race or cultural background. Among musicians, I have never seen or felt racist attitudes impact relationships within an orchestra.

Back home in California, I taught Buster Williams and Mickey Roker how to swim in my pool. Buster's father had died from drowning and he was therefore deathly afraid of the water, but I got him to swim and they enjoyed it. Some members of the Thad Jones and Mel Lewis Jazz Orchestra came out to the house as well. We had worked with Mel and Thad's band a couple of times. This was a wonderful chapter in my life. I loved working with Nancy Wilson. Musically, it was a superb experience. Nancy and Kenny treated me exceedingly well and always invited BJ to come along. On one occasion they called us to go on a shopping trip. They had first class tickets for us to go to Paris with them, just to hang out and shop.

14

Balances and Clicks

THE JOB OF THE MUSICAL DIRECTOR can be multifaceted. Often during rehearsals, I went up to the control booth to work with the sound engineer, helping him to balance the orchestra because I knew the charts and how they were going to be played. I could let them know if it was going to be heavy in the brass, or the woodwinds were doubling a lot so dig in for flutes, or if there was an oboe, or bass clarinet, or if mutes were being used. Knowing these aspects of the scoring gave him an advantage. For me, it was a fun addition to playing with the orchestra. This was another area that out of necessity became a facet of my responsibilities.

It was important for me to develop some expertise in the sound engineering of a show. I became engrossed in trying to achieve the best sound. Balance is so important. I hated to hear radio or television where the band was not presented properly. I knew it couldn't be perfect because we weren't working in a recording studio environment. Television stages are generally designed to accommodate visual elements and to maximize shooting angles, so acoustics are secondary. I learned how to work with what tools were available in the sound booth to maximize the quality and balance. In later years, acoustic deficiencies were overcome by pre-recording in a sound studio.

It starts with the players. On one occasion, I was playing in the orchestra for an Academy Award show. Andre Previn was conducting. We were pre-recording at United Western Recorders in Hollywood and a sound engineer was conversing with him from the booth. Andre said,

"Just hold it there. Let's get the sound balance correct here in the room first, then I'll come inside and we'll work on making it sound right in the control booth. It's important that we make it sound right acoustically first." In other words, balance out the orchestra so that there isn't any overshadowing. That was a lesson for me because it confirmed my feelings about orchestra dynamics and balance. Musicians, even great ones, can play well individually, but they are not necessarily aware of how their playing is affecting the dynamics on the whole.

When I start working with an orchestra, often I hear everyone playing at a single level. Sometimes the player interprets the dynamic markings in the music they're reading as simply "loud" and "soft," but they're not thinking about balancing the role of their part. They may not be aware they are playing a nice well-written background behind a saxophone solo, or a vocalist, and that the whole level should come down to enhance rather than be in the foreground. I've spent a lot of time working with musicians on dynamics and balance. It is absolutely essential to creating a well-rounded sound.

Sometimes the room feels too loud because of bad acoustics. The player doesn't always perceive that, being immersed in the ensemble sound itself. There are ways to overcome it and improve the experience. Listen and try to understand the room, understand the dynamics of what you're doing, and understand what it is you're playing. In music notation, B means background for a solo. It's rewarding to hear and feel the improvement. Some, but not all, musicians can hear the difference. This is one of the advantages of conducting. You try to make adjustments as diplomatically as possible without ever making anyone uptight. If people are tense or upset, the sound is adversely affected.

Regarding orchestration, balance is again the central issue in my mind. Balance should be inherent in the writing, but the integrity of balance also comes from careful acoustic listening on the part of the player, and the conductor. In scoring the music, consideration is given to ensemble size and instrumentation, not mutually exclusive to balance is the spectrum of loud and soft. Dynamic effect has been so important in my work and is always an important consideration in orchestration.

The writer should be careful not to get caught up with creating excitement by using weight to the extent that clarity and delicacy are lost. The quality of the music can suffer if it is over-scored. Excitement comes from the energy inherent in the music itself, clearly perceived by the listener. Central themes do not work if they are buried. Delicacy comes from thinning things out and choosing instrumental colors that create intimacy, and draw the listener in.

Good dynamic control by the player, which is also inherent in the writing, results in a natural acoustic balance. I think so often dynamic markings are overlooked, but many arrangers and directors have a tendency to want to create a really big ensemble sound. This can promote overblowing. High trumpet parts can be laborious to play with any delicacy. Often it's necessary to just scream. This can be effectively successful if the writing supports it well. Otherwise, balance becomes distorted and the ensemble sonority can turn ugly. Often, when those full ensembles are written, they are screaming and cooking, but the bottom of the orchestra is not strong enough to support the top.

I don't really care for electric pianos but for the fact that, through amplification, I can support a low line in the ensemble. Many years ago, when we weren't into amplification to the extent that we are now, bass players played acoustic bass and didn't carry an amplifier, and pianists played real pianos. I liked adding a bottom line because it enhanced the sound of the group, and often it doubled what the baritone sax was playing. Good balance starts from the bottom up. I think the listening skills of a fine musician, for the purposes of playing in tune with a good dynamic concept and an awareness of balance, stem from hearing the bottom.

Again, many of the musicality issues can be accomplished through the writing itself. Some of the best arrangers in the business have been trombone players and there's a reason for it. Again, it's weights and balances. I think it's because of where they sit in the orchestra. In the middle of a traditional set-up, they get a better feeling for the trumpets that are behind them and the woodwinds in front of them, so they are in a better position acoustically to feel and determine balance. As a result, they write accordingly. Nelson Riddle, Sammy Nestico, Bill Byers, Bob Brookmeyer, Johnny Mandel are great examples and the list can go on and on.

I feel bebop contributed to overwriting. I've heard ensemble writing that sounded as though it were a saxophone, trumpet, or piano solo. There are many important and influential musicians who came out of that period in jazz, but when writers have tried to orchestrate bebop lines in the style of Bird or Dizzy, it can compromise playing dexterity and clarity, along with ensemble sonority and, as a result, general listener accessibility.

There are a lot of wonderful arrangers, but it is a matter of taste. It can be performed masterfully and still lacking in aesthetic concept, especially if it is too busy. This style of writing can be challenging to rehearse. A

Making an on the spot repair.

musician feels as if in a sweat box, learning how to play figures that are not comfortable and don't come off well. I've heard musicians complain about the fact that some arrangements are just not fun. It may be intellectual in concept because they can write some slick harmonized sixteenth note phrases with a lot of counterpoint but that doesn't make it good. It can be exceedingly difficult to play this kind of writing. It takes incredible technicians. To these kinds of writers I want to say, "What's wrong with Count Basie?" It's important to honor simplicity.

As discussed earlier, most often the orchestration for a big production number resulted from the amalgamated creativity coming out of the choreographer and pianist. Frequently, the choreographer will take maybe eight measures and get some steps together, doing some combinations with the dancers. They will literally stand there, mid-pose on one leg, trying to think of what to do next. At which point, an awful lot comes directly out of the creativity of the pianist, who is also responsible for getting the music orchestrated. In some cases, the star may come with a specific song to build on, perhaps from one of their recent motion pictures. With others it may be just a matter of what they can sing with consideration for their range and their capabilities. My goal is to bring out the best in someone and showcase their talent and make that person feels comfortable in the performance.

Often the production occupies more orchestrated or arranged time in the chart than just the star singing. We may have an artist who is going to sing and dance, so there are going to be additional dancers and singers all supported by an orchestra. Given the context of the music, we begin with creating an idea of when the artist will sing and when the dancers will do interludes. Through the orchestration, the music has to manage what's going on all of the time. The music needs to be embellished and be supportive and events need to flow seamlessly. The dancers are going to do pronounced punctuation and they need to have that punctuation, as we say, "caught" within the orchestration. Most often, it is highly syncopated because of what they are dancing. It becomes a real task, to write an orchestration that maintains fluency with events that can be interruptive, if you don't somehow bury them or cloak them with something else musically.

An entertainer with a weaker musical talent can usually be helped by writing a prominently available melody in the orchestration, so they have some kind of paralleling guide for their musical thoughts. Again, simplicity is also important. Complicated figures, or syncopated figures that feel good to you as a musician, can be disconcerting to the person you're writing for. You're satisfying yourself in a way, but you're not helping this non-musical person be musical. On the other hand, for entertainers who have time problems, it may be necessary to actually over-write in a space to keep them from coming in too early for their next entrance.

Sometimes I get frustrated when people do not have the ability to feel some basic meter, but it can be an inherent deficiency that will never be overcome. Eddie Fisher, who possesses a really wonderful voice, had absolutely no metric sense whatsoever. You almost have to write World War IV in between phrases so he wouldn't step into a hole. I remember one of the most amazing things I've ever seen. Eddie was doing a Bob Hope Show that I was working on, and Eddie Samuels, his pianist, stood like a traffic cop next to the lens of the camera that was shooting Eddie Fisher as he sang. He would put his hand up vertically, as if to tell traffic to stop, then point a finger to go. He did that between every phrase, so Eddie would sing in the right place. To go a step further, I was working for Nelson Riddle on an Eddie Fisher album, and Samuels was in the isolation booth with Fisher mouthing the words to keep him in the correct place.

Something needs to be said about "talent" as a word. Some musicians are experienced and competent instrumentalists, but sometimes I find it difficult to say that they are talented. I think talent is first the ability to portray emotion, and second the ability play by ear or improvise. Many instrumentalists can develop a great stylistic concept but can't play "Happy Birthday" unless it's written out. So, if someone is an accomplished player in a symphony orchestra, they can be a proficient instrumentalist, but not necessarily talented. There are two credentials and the finest musicians are adept at both.

Through conducting, I can transfer the feeling of a pianist's accompaniment to orchestral accompaniment. There is a great joy in being the one who has been selected to analyze the music and find ways to deliver a performance that is musically fulfilling. From a technical standpoint, it can be a frightening responsibility, certainly for large live productions, but conducting not only gives me the opportunity to guide the pulse and rhythm, it offers me expressive control through shaping the contours of dynamics, the pace of accelerando, rallentando, rubato, and fermatas that sometimes crescendo or diminuendo. I think this comes from my love of accompanying.

I appreciate the art of supporting and embellishing a singer's performance. This is not the case for all pianists. Some don't honestly want to be accompanists; they need to be out in front. When I'm playing piano, I'm singularly in control of what I'm going to do in support of the artist. Should the interpretation change, I have the flexibility to shift and align myself more closely with the singer. The pianist can be nimble and move in ways that a full orchestra cannot. As a conductor, I have to interpret the written orchestration and direct the musicians to bring out the nuances of the performance. I've been privileged to accompany many wonderful singers, which helped me to become a better writer and a better conductor. Much of this is in the sense of orchestration I feel when I'm playing for someone. BJ used to say to me, "When you're playing piano it's a complete orchestration. You don't have to come up with another thing. Just listen to what you play and write it on a score pad."

It's imperative to be able to anticipate what the singer is feeling in each moment of their performance. It's an intimate relationship and I get into their heads when they're singing. I hear their breathing and their thinking. You do have an advantage when you have worked with somebody for a while. After a period of time, you know generally how they are going to interpret the music. There is a certain amount of liberty that they can take and you are prepared for that. You develop a concept for how they are going to handle the lyric, and the emotionality of that lyric. You have a pretty good shot at it if you've played with someone many times. Playing for Shirley MacLaine was intense because she's very interpretive and spontaneous. She would change her direction a great deal from night to night. I found it challenging and exciting to play and conduct for her.

For me, conducting is to guide an orchestra to play together. It is a bit tricky conducting a large orchestra on stage because it can be so spread out. The conductor is positioned physically in the middle. On the right, facing the stage, there is a full jazz ensemble with five saxophones, four trombones, and four trumpets. On the left, you have strings, harp, and sometimes some synthesizers. With Ann-Margret, we had two percussionists and two guitars so the music was written bigger, to accommodate the additional percussion and guitar. Having the added musicians brings more color to the orchestrations. The rhythm section was in the center in front of the conductor's podium right next to the nose of the piano so that I could sneak over to the bench. The other pianist had a chair next to me, so that he could slide over and cover certain things for the artist when I needed to be at the podium.

My job requires me to be a stickler for detail, rehearsing passages until they were clean and together, until it made sense, until it became comfortable. If you find a failure within a musical passage or orchestrated phrase, then it's necessary to go back over those figures and try and make them work, so that the essence of that figure is realized. In most cases, if you get good lead players, you can communicate this and then they can guide their section players with a good concept of the figure, or the passage, or the whole chart for that matter, but often it has to be worked out.

I've been fortunate to work with high-level musicians, and I know how complicated passages in music can be sometimes. After you get over that point of figuring out the notation, figuring out the spelling, figuring out the phrasing and the dynamics, then it all comes together and the passage is your friend. One of the things I will do with the orchestra if we have a rough spot, and I've done it many times to the point where they either laughed or become annoyed, is to play the passage repeatedly. I'd say, "Okay, let's practice this spot." I'd count it off and have them play it a few times in a row. I wouldn't waste any time discussing it in between. We would just keep it going, letting the players work it out themselves. Maybe on the fourth time it was perfect. Then I'd say, "That's it, nailed. That's where we want it." Here the old saying I would use, "until that passage becomes your friend."

To me, it seems jazz musicians prefer a conducting style where the stroke of the pulse remains in the bottom of the beat pattern. Which is to say, when conducting a four pattern you raise your right hand in preparation, indicating a tempo, and come down to a center point representing beat one, then go straight, with little lift, to the left marking beat two, likewise to the further right for beat three and up for beat four. There is a degree of lift, or upbeat, in the stroke that rebounds off the strength of the ictus and this is where the pulse is felt. A legitimate conducting style is not necessarily as strict that way. When I say legitimate, I'm loosely referring to the mindset of classical violinists, violists, and cellists. I wound up learning how to conduct two ways. My left hand conducted with a more subdividing upstroke, so the strings wouldn't play behind the beat, and my right hand strictly represented the beat pattern.

As a conductor, when I'm standing in front of twenty or thirty new people, I have a choice to make. Do I want them to be my friend, or my enemy? Am I going to be able to do my job with them, or without them? I always let the orchestra know that I'm completely dependent on them. The most important thing I need to do is create an atmosphere in which they feel like they want to do what they can to help me do my job. It's essential to foster a creative and supportive atmosphere. If you're rough on them, you're going to get less out of the orchestra. As we talked about earlier, Lenny Hayton had a tendency to be a strict, angry, cold and non-communicative conductor. He just frightened me. He was so sweet around his wife Lena, but so different around the orchestra.

While I was with Les Brown, I learned a lot from Butch Stone about handling orchestras and handling people in a leader capacity. Maybe one of the reasons I liked him right away is that his real name was Henry, like my dad. In a way, I saw Butch as a mentor. Butch had a wonderful sense of humor. He handled every difficult situation and made it look effortless. He is responsible for a lot of the devices I use to keep things calm and productive while I'm working with an orchestra. I admired Butch and he was a tremendous influence on me.

I can't work with stress. I don't like it. I don't like to create it. I don't like to make an orchestra uptight when I'm in front of it. Maybe I get corny sometimes, but I'm just trying to avoid confrontation. Even so, there can always be some musician that will push a situation until there's a standoff. When you come into town as a guest conductor, you can occasionally find a musician who is just not paying any attention; one, who has a negative attitude, or authoritarian complex, who just doesn't want to hear what you need to convey. "Who is this guest conductor coming in here and telling me how to play?" That's not what I do. I don't tell anybody how to play. I am going to tell them, if possible, about some of the traps in the charts. "Let's look at letter B, measures 75 through 79, there is a difficult change in tempo there. Let me talk that down with you now so that when we get there it will be a little easier and we'll sail through it. If it doesn't work we'll go over it again." I know the music better than those who are playing for the first time. My job is to anticipate the musical challenges and address them. Hopefully it's a working partnership. That's what I try to achieve with every orchestra.

When I bring an act out to a new city, I'm mindful that the locally hired musicians have never played this music before. Rehearsal time can be limited, so I need to work expeditiously. The music is important and I'm a stickler for accuracy. It is very important for me to be able to transfer my knowledge to them without sounding like an ogre. I cannot alienate my players if I am going to be successful. Many directors don't know how to communicate. As with most people, you have to show respect to get respect.

I don't look at someone when they make a mistake because I don't want to embarrass anyone. I've been with many bands where the leader would turn around and stare at a musician for making an error, like play-

Conducting for Shirley MacLaine in a live television special.

ing a wrong note. What does that accomplish? It intensifies the embarrassment of the person who makes the mistake, and nobody feels worse than the player who made it. I'd rather look at an orchestra when it's really cooking. Turn around and look at them then, when everything is going well. That's when you look at the orchestra and smile.

Managing rehearsal time can be tricky because it's all about money. Musicians are paid by the hour, and there are a certain number of hours they can work before they are paid overtime rates. I know how producers were about that and I know what our contracts allowed. Production budgets provide a limited amount of rehearsal time, so we had better get it done in that given period. This is especially true when you get into studio recording projects and live concerts with studio orchestras. Usually we got the job done because of the high caliber of musicianship. The orchestras were generally wonderful. For the most part, I've been lucky to be surrounded by highly skilled musicians. Even in my earlier life, I was working with what we used to call "name bands." The outstanding musicianship of the players allowed me to earn a reputation for being on time and avoiding overtime billing.

In Las Vegas, we did have a fair amount of rehearsal time, about ten hours. We had rehearsal for three or four hours the day before, and then we have a long on-stage tech rehearsal before the opening show. When we did run overtime, it was not the orchestra's fault. It was technical staff people who had to work out the sound and the lights, so everything ran correctly. Sometimes there were hours where the musicians sat and waited, but they were paid for it. Generally, I got the orchestra together with the music in that first day of rehearsal. The advantage of the next day's tech rehearsal was being able to polish the music and rehearse with the synchronized performance of click-tracks. The orchestra had more opportunity to play the show and get more familiar with the music.

During that time period, and for many years to follow, Las Vegas was a seven-night-a-week performance run for the star of the show and for me. I had to be there because I represented the star. It was a demanding schedule, often with fourteen shows a week. We did two shows a night. For me, in a typical four week engagement, there would be fifty-six shows and several rehearsals, including the relief band.

The orchestra played six nights and then had one night off every week. This was a musician's union requirement. The star performer and their singers and dancers worked seven nights a week. As musical director, I did, as well. On the seventh night, the relief orchestra came in. There were two relief orchestras that played all the Vegas shows. They would rehearse and play a different show every night. Some of the best musicians were in those orchestras because they could learn new music quickly.

Out of a four-week engagement, the relief orchestra played the show four times. Consequently, I had to rehearse another orchestra once a week. A lot of the players wouldn't like to rehearse more than the first week. They would have preferred to just come in do what they called a "talk-over." It's basically just discussing any musical changes in the show that might have taken place during the previous week. There was a time in Las Vegas that some of the musicians in the relief orchestras may have felt I was a taskmaster, but I did not have shows that lent themselves to simple changes, and I'm a firm believer in getting it right. These shows were tightly choreographed and had pre-records with click-tracks, which add to the complexity.

I'm sure my early interest in Heathkits and subsequent hobby in electronics equipped, gave me with an understanding of the studio engineering, and certainly helped when I constructed my own studio. An example might be the ability to properly record instruments and voices so that you get the best possible natural acoustical effect. It also provided the technical skills that became required in my job.

Click-tracking is a process that had existed in the recording world. The first use of clicks was to deliver metronomic pulses to musicians in a large studio space. A time-lag occurs from one side of a large recording room to the other, so that musicians on opposite sides of the room are not rhythmically coordinated. The sound engineer provides a metronomic pulse to the players through headsets. This is used in studio recording, as well as for, motion pictures and television recording.

There's another process called looping, which is when an artist has spoken or sung lines and they didn't come out clearly enough. Then they bring the artist, or somebody else, back in to match the pace of their mouth as they talk, re-recording whatever was not originally discernable. Additional Dialog Recording or ADR, also referred to as "over dubbing," is still done today. Using similar processes, musicians are brought in to replace a passage or even a single note if one is off.

I was first involved with this doing for Bob Hope Shows. We had to pre-record people in order to be able to do a performance where dance choreography was necessary at the same time as singing. If you put dancers on stage, it doesn't really matter how many, and hand them a microphone, that takes one limb away from a choreographer. They really don't want that. The radio microphone that a dancer can wear is a transmitter with a receiver off stage, which takes a signal to the console, where it can be adjusted, and then sends it back out into the house. Radio microphones can be difficult to use, but they solve the artistic issue.

I developed click-tracks in my own studio at home for many people including Ann-Margret, Shirley MacLaine, Charo, and Rita Moreno. Click-tracks are used when a big production number may have eight or twelve dancers on the stage and they're all going to sing. Dancers don't usually sing that well, and I'm being kind. To enhance the quality, we recorded vocal tracks with additional studio singers and use it during the performance to sweeten the dancers' singing. These pre-recorded vocals will be balanced in the hall and heard by the audience. The tape also contains a track of corresponding metronomic clicks to measure time. The clicks are heard only in headphones at the conductor's podium. Once in awhile, the drummer also has a headset.

Let us suppose a large production number has 400 measures and there is no singing in the first half. 200 measures go by then all of a sudden the singers open their mouths. If it's in 4/4 time, that's 200 measures with four beats a piece, that's 800 clicks. With eight in front, four as a start, and four to mark the count off. In other words, click-click-click-click, then the conductor indicates 1-2-3-4, and now you're starting at the top of the chart. 800 clicks later, the dancers open their mouths and the vocals appear.

In the studio, the pianist usually sits down with the drummer, plays the whole chart, and records a scratch track. Then the studio singers lay down their tracks. The dancers come in and actually sing with the pre-recorded studio singers because we try to keep it authentic. After the pre-record is finished, the sound engineer finalizes the recording and it becomes part of each show. The finished stereo tape has clicks in one channel and vocals on the other. Using this approach a choreographer doesn't have to give up an arm to hold a microphone. Radio mikes were not that dependable and we want the dancers' singing to be blended with the professional singers. The tape is started at the very beginning of the number. I control that from the conductor's stool. I have a whole network of equipment up there and hear everything through my headphones, which I put on and take off as needed. I have a push button to start the tape, because it might need to begin in the middle of a certain number.

Sometimes we play a ballad that comes suddenly to a point where we get to a big fermata. A fermata is a note that the musicians and singers hold until the conductor directs them to continue. On that fermata, I can push the button starting the tape, click-click-click-click. I hear those start marks, then after the count 1-2-3-4, I start the orchestra. When two hundred measures go by, the vocals drop in singing "Hello Dolly," or whatever, and it's in place with the orchestra. As far as the audience is concerned, they're looking up there and seeing all these dancers dancing around and they hear them singing. They are really singing, but they're not using microphones. Their singing is actually coming from the supplement of click-tracks that we prepared.

I heard something once in Vegas that really bothered me. I listening to a show that my friend from the service, Billy Byers, had written for the MGM Grand. This show was an epic. It was like watching the farthest-out motion picture you can imagine. They had a girl who jumped into a fish tank with two dolphins and some big show girls standing up in the background that were—well, you can't be a little bit bare breasted, can you? The show was great, but the orchestra played in a remote room downstairs. The musicians who played that show didn't even have to wear tuxedoes. They didn't have to come dressed in any fancy fashion. It was all done from the basement with click-tracks, and it was intensely out of tune. It might not have bothered other people as much, but the vocal pre-records were almost a 1/4 of a tone away from where the orchestra was. It really irritated me, kind of like dragging your fingernails down a chalkboard.

I devised a plan where that would never happen with us. I recorded two minutes of A440 on the front of the pre-record tape. With this, we could tune the tape recorder every night before the show. I would call the sound booth and press the remote start button I had right there at the conductor's podium. First of all, this let us make sure that the start button was working, that somebody hadn't pulled the wire, or had messed with the tape recorder during the day and secondly, it allowed us to listen to the pitch. I played the A on the piano to match them. I could tell the sound engineer to bring it up or down a little bit and hold it right there. We would be accurate, the tape, the singers and the orchestra were together. With this tuning method, we didn't have to take any chances.

Las Vegas and Lake Tahoe run on a clock that is absolutely accurate. They maintain strict schedules and they know if the show runs five minutes longer than it should, it translates to how much money they would have lost in the casino. They did not want the show to run all that long. Around an hour and twenty minutes was satisfactory. A major artist would do fifty-five to sixty minutes and an opening act would do around twenty minutes. Usually, the headliner would do about an hour nonstop, packed with really good music, backed by a really good orchestra with everything just driving. Wayne Newton disregarded it totally. He's a great entertainer, but the casino doesn't appreciate him if they lose too much revenue. He would do up to two hours and the band members got furious, but the audiences love him. He's truly a great showman.

We were up in Lake Tahoe and I had a drummer named Tony Marillo that I inherited with Ann-Margret. Tony's a little wiry fellow, who is so non-conforming that it's hard to believe. He used to drive me crazy. It would come time for the show and he'd wander into Ann-Margret's dressing room, which she didn't lock most of the time. He'd come in all the time for water or something. The show is supposed to go up at 8:00 and Tony would show up six minutes before show time not even dressed. I'd say, "Tony come on, the show goes up not at 8:01, it goes up at 8:00." So, he runs up to the stage and gets dressed behind the drums. He was a constant worry. I'd have my hands up ready for a downbeat for the orchestra and I'd look over to the drum set, but I couldn't see Tony. He was still bent down buttoning his shirt or putting his pants on. He'd pop up and say, "Okay, I'm ready." He also had a bottle there that he occasionally urinated into while the show was on. He is just one of those "out" people, as "far-out" as you can imagine. He would have me on edge all the time. In total support of Tony's talents, he is a marvelous drummer and a fabulously fun person, just "out there."

It only happened to me twice that I had to let a player go. We had a situation on a Vegas engagement where we needed a really strong acoustic bass player and this musician played Fender electric. He couldn't do the acoustic thing well enough and I had to gently explain to him that's what we needed primarily. He was pretty angry that he had to be let go. The other case was in Lake Tahoe with a trumpet player that worked with me on Sandy Duncan's show.

Sandy Duncan is another one of the genuinely wonderful people in our business. Sandy is one of those very talented variety artists. She's a warm person and is a talented singer and dancer. Peter Matz, a well-known musician, used to have the orchestra on *The Carol Burnett Show* and wrote the theme Carol used. Peter wrote a show for Sandy and they called and asked me if I would be musical director. We took the show to Lake Tahoe for a few engagements. It wasn't to be a longstanding involvement because Sandy was doing so many other things. She later married one of the dancers from the Shirley MacLaine Show, Don Correia.

I used to call Lake Tahoe the "heavy hanging hill." Being a pilot, I knew the statistics of alcohol is that one ounce of alcohol at 5,000 feet has the effect of three ounces of alcohol at sea level. A person who has only two drinks up in Tahoe is feeling the effect of six ounces of alcohol. The musicians who used to drink quite a bit up there were known to drive home and run into things.

One night while working with Sandy, I was following her singing through a rubato passage, conducting the orchestra accordingly. Suddenly, from the background I heard, "Jesus, how slow can we get? Are we going to come to a complete stop?" This remark could easily have been heard by Sandy and everyone on the stage, if not the audience. I knew who the source was, and realized that I was dealing with a serious drinker. It was my lead trumpet player. As the show continued, I heard more and more remarks, but I couldn't do anything during the show.

Afterwards, I called him over to the side. "Let me tell you something. The first thing that bothers me more than anything is that you're one of my favorite lead trumpet players in the business. I've done this for a long time and worked with many, many orchestras. And I find it almost impossible to believe that you did what you just did. That behavior was uncouth, uncaring and certainly unprofessional, and something I never would have expected from a musician like you. If she chooses to sing it slower than you like, and I follow her, I'm right, and you're wrong." I understand that he went back into the dressing room and threw his horn against the wall. Some years later, he worked for me again with Shirley MacLaine. At that point, he was able to bring up the incident with me and apologize. Alcohol does it better up there than anywhere else. In the interim, in other situations, I heard that his drinking was causing problems.

It is enormously difficult for me to let anyone go, whether it is professionally or personally. I think my commitment to communicate with people, the need to analyze the person, and the circumstances, became exceedingly important when dealing with artists, orchestras, and my relationships. Maybe this is a good attribute for a musical director, but maybe this has also caused difficulty in my personal life.

15 The Joint Is Jumpin'

WHEN I GOT THE CALL TO GO with Ann-Margret, it was from Marvin Hamlisch. I found out later that he was a good friend of hers. I had worked an Academy Awards Show with Marvin, doing some writing and some playing for the show. He called to inquire if I would be interested in going with Ann-Margret as her musical director. We discussed financial terms. I think he offered me an amount, and it wasn't sufficient for me to go out on the road. After some friendly negotiations he said, "I have a peculiar question to ask you. When you led the band on *The Steve Allen Show*, who was the piano player?"

"That would be me."

He agreed to the terms and said, "You've got the job."

I started working with Ann-Margret in 1973 and with Shirley MacLaine a year later. Shirley went to Ann-Margret and Roger Smith, Ann-Margret's husband, to pick their collective brain about me and the various technical aspects of Ann-Margret's show, which Shirley adopted for her nightclub production. Their schedules dovetailed nicely for me during the three-year period that I was working with Shirley. There were remarkably few conflicts. It was helpful that both women also had other projects in their lives, like movies. Work was intermittent with Ann-Margret. Some years, we might have only ten weeks, other years, twenty or more, with some international travel. It depended on her film schedule and the many events going on in her life. With Shirley MacLaine, engagements were more frequent. She booked longer and harder tours that were almost all one-nighters. Shirley had a big show to set up, but not nearly as complicated as Ann-Margret's.

Ann-Margret's show was an epic production and it was a Herculean task to book it because only few venues could accommodate all of its requirements. More than nearly all other shows, we needed a substantially greater amount of fly area, dressing rooms, stage depth, and physical space. The company included a thirty-six piece orchestra, singers, a troupe of dancers, sound equipment with extra sound personnel, and carpenters. Laser lights were used on some of the numbers, so we traveled with a special lighting company. It was also a hugely expensive show and at times had to be shaved a bit because of financial necessity and available stage size. We needed great depth in the staging for the dancers to be able to dance in front of the orchestra because Ann-Margret would not have the orchestra anywhere else except on stage with her. The musicians really felt like they were part of the production. Her inclusive approach to the show is emblematic of how she treated the people who work with her.

Roger designed and built what became known as the band-cart. It was a motorized stage platform big enough to carry the entire orchestra across the stage, providing for scenery changes and space for the dancers. His concept came out of old style musical theater and film extravaganzas. It traveled from any point on the back of stage right up to the front edge and then back up for certain numbers. It was incredibly effective. The musicians used to wonder about it and I would say, "Well, tonight we're going right up to the front row, make a left, and drive this bandstand right down Las Vegas Boulevard."

Directly in the center of the band-cart was a separate satellite rostrum that could carry the piano independently. I would travel out sitting at the piano while Ann-Margret came out from off stage to do numbers together. She would get up on the piano to dance and sing. It was really fun. All of this apparatus had to be assembled every time we went anywhere. The accouterments were unbelievable. The show traveled with two tractor-trailer trucks filled with everything from the storage warehouse.

I first went into rehearsal with Ann-Margret at a place called Paul DeRolf Studios in Studio City, which is in the San Fernando Valley. A lot of entertainers, who were doing TV shows with production numbers, would rehearse there because it wasn't too far from NBC studios. They had brought in a rehearsal pianist and I realized how nice everything was going to be. The rehearsal pianist is the unsung hero who often had the arduous responsibility of repetitive rehearsing. Roger Smith, who produced and directed his wife's show, never expected me to play rehearsal piano and never asked me to. On the other hand, there were times I needed to write something or add something musically, and would familiarize the rehearsal pianist with how it was supposed to go, or what was taking place. I spent hours and hours in the rehearsal hall watching the numbers being prepared, which can be a tedious process.

Again, the big production numbers came out of the creative effort that went into the rehearsal hall with the choreographer. A choreographer can take five days to do one number if they're slow creatively. There are others who work fast and can do a whole show in ten days. The rehearsals were exhaustive, but allowed me to become thoroughly familiar with the music. There were vocal click-tracks that had to be produced so they could have the dancers sing. The dancers sang in a mediocre fashion, but it didn't become a rip-off because, when they were on stage, they actually sang. We supplemented them with pre-recorded studio singers and BJ was one of the important singers in that phase. I brought her in to do all of the pre-recording. I engineered the click tracks at my studio because I didn't like the way the existing clicks had been constructed. They were inaccurate and they were not marked properly for my needs. The singing dancers needed to be absolutely synchronized and in tune with the orchestra at all times. I had to work out the music with the choreographer so there would be a pinpoint to begin that tape. I started and stopped the pre-records at every juncture it was necessary from my conductor's podium.

The entire show was predicated on accuracy, particularly with Ann-Margret because Roger was a stickler for precise detail. I had a great deal of respect for Roger's work ethic and attention to detail. And, like everyone else on the show, Roger and I had a good professional and personal relationship. When we worked together he was always there and if he couldn't be, that's when something would go wrong. Almost invariably, if he had to leave to go back to Los Angeles, something went wrong technically.

The male dancers formed a group called Raw Satin. They intentionally picked the name using Roger's initials because they were so fond of him. The dancers were like a family to her. Ann-Margret's choreographer, Lester Wilson, traveled with us for many years. He was great fun to work with because he was so jazz-based in his musical concept and feeling. Whenever I hear Whoopi Goldberg, the intonation of her voice and her vocal timbre, reminds me of Lester. He was funny and enormously talented. He did the dance segments for John Travolta in *Saturday Night Fever*. Lester did a lot of work with a lot of people.

We had a great time together creating arrangements that had a strong swing jazz feel. We did some old style Harlem-like dance segments. The orchestra played roaring tempos for roaring dancing numbers based on tunes like Count Basie's "Jumpin' at the Woodside" and Fats Waller's "The Joint Is Jumpin.'" There were never any of the metric problems that often happened with choreographers who weren't as musically inclined. The music, and everything generating from what Lester perceived visually, and what I perceived musically, would develop in the rehearsal hall and wonderfully become whatever it was going to become. I did another chart on "Kid From Red Bank," which almost wrote itself, building on a dynamic crescendo that culminated in an exciting climax. Lester's choreography for that was ferocious. The show was always great and always got standing ovations.

There needs to be a balance between what the audience sees and what the audience hears. Sometimes it was too much of an impediment for a choreographer to let Ann-Margret give up one limb so she could hold a microphone. When this occurred, we would pre-record her doing her own vocals. A segment would be pre-recorded, maybe sixteen bars, and the next sixteen would be live, depending upon the situation. We had that coordinated with seamless accuracy.

Ann-Margret did a lot of the dance segments and, at times, she would have to run off stage during the dancing so she could make a costume change. Roger wanted to be sure every aspect of an Ann-Margret show was the best it could be, and wardrobe was no exception. Her costumes were done by the very best. Bob Mackie, who was one of Hollywood's best designers, did her gowns. Her gowns cost a fortune, $15,000 to $20,000 apiece. Roger really is the "consummate producer." He wanted the show it to be the best it could be and never cut corners.

Roger was a stickler for what he believed could make or break the show, and that is good audio. If he didn't think the sound is right, whether it was Ann-Margret, the other singers, with the orchestra, or with the room, he did something about it. He was totally supportive in this regard. If you went to him and pitched, "Look, I just invented this contraption. It will enhance the voice and make it sound twenty-five percent broader." Roger would say, "Okay, show me." So you'd hook the device up and if he thought it worked, he'd buy it at once, anything to make the show better.

There was a point in the show when the piano satellite would leave the band cart and slowly roll forward toward the audience by itself with me sitting at the piano. I played a number that featured me with back-up singers who did background vocals. Ann-Margret called them The Tren-

With Ann-Margret at Caesars Palace in Las Vegas.

nettes, "Ladies and gentlemen, the Trennettes." Then, after I finished my number, the lights came down and she came out to sing a ballad. She made her way to the back of the piano where there was a little step ladder and she climbed up to get on top of the piano. She would lie down and put her forehead against mine while singing a ballad. On another show, for my piano feature, I had written an arrangement for strings on "Moonglow" and "Picnic" using each tune as a counter-melody for the other. When I finished playing this, we segued into a hard swing introduction and suddenly she appeared standing on the piano where she sang "Teach Me Tonight."

If you were not familiar with her stage shows, you wouldn't be familiar with the musicality that she is capable of. Ann-Margret is a talented singer with an innate musical concept and a natural jazz feel. As a persuasive ballad singer, she has a good sense of time and pitch. She often sang as a Broadway-style performer with a Gwenn Verdon type of vibrato, which is a little wider than I like, but that's part of the style that is represented in Broadway and something that she knowingly, or maybe unknowingly, emulated. Especially for the big production numbers, it was the genre that she wanted to model. In a more intimate setting, she sang without that vibrato. I think Ann-Margret worked diligently on everything she pursued, and it worked out exceptionally well for her. She was stunningly beautiful and sensuous in her persona. Yet, that's an on-stage personality. In reality, when the show's over, she is modest, quiet, refined, and unassuming. She could be inconspicuous in the green room or rehearsal hall.

I used to say to her, "Let's get a trio together and go out on the road. Come on let's just do it for a week. Come on Margret-Ann." Playfully I called her, "Margret-Ann." This came about after we were invited to entertain at the White House when Gerald Ford was president. I was working for Shirley MacLaine during this month, so Roger wrote a letter asking Shirley to release me for this engagement, which she agreed to. We used the Marine Orchestra and I remember playing a Steinway piano with a lot of gold inlay, which had been given to Harry Truman. The event was held in the Blue Room, after a formal head of state dinner. Gerald Ford's guest was the Shah of Iran who had actually requested Ann-Margret, so we brought a mini-show.

When we went through the White House, and we all had a White House tour, you could hear a group of people outside repetitively chanting, "Down with the Shah. The Shah is a murderer." I said to the person who was showing us around, "This must be difficult to listen to." He said, "That's nothing, you should have been around when Nixon was here." In fact, we noticed there was no Nixon memorabilia whatsoever. All of the other presidents were represented.

After the dinner, it came time for the performance and the Shah, along with everybody else, entered the Blue Room. Gerald Ford got up to introduce Ann-Margret and talked about how wonderful she was and mentioned things like entertaining the troops at Christmas time. After bestowing all these accolades he said, "Now ladies and gentleman, Margret-Ann." This seemed so typical of his bumbling style, a nice man, but could trip over dust. After that, I would teasingly address her as Margret-Ann.

Also in attendance that evening, as a member of the White House social agenda, was Pearl Bailey. An international incident had taken place just a couple of days prior. The American container ship, *SS Mayaguez*, had been seized by the Cambodian Khmer Rouge Navy while steaming in an international shipping lane. Ford exercised his authority as commander-in-chief, and the ship was successfully retaken. After the show was over, we went over to the Rotunda, where there was a small group playing for dancing. Pearl Bailey had gotten hold of a microphone and wouldn't stop singing.

Roger Smith went to President Ford and said, "If you can settle the Mayaguez incident, you certainly can get her off the floor."

Gerald Ford sauntered over to her, "Come on Pearly Mae, let's you and I dance." The President danced her away.

After work in Las Vegas, I would go back to my room and plug in the soldering iron to build the electronics kits. When my whole day was over, I'd have a couple of hits of grass. I didn't want to get too far out there because I wanted to be able to answer the telephone and do business, and be totally cognizant of what was going on. I guess it was like a cocktail for me; it was the drink that I didn't have. Marijuana had a funny effect on me. It seemed to help sort out twenty things that I had on my mind. It seemed to center me on things I was doing, either with the soldering iron, listening to music or whatever. It didn't create this tangential feeling of drifting away. It also energized me. Most people get totally laid out, but I wanted to go paint the house or something.

During my first engagement with Ann-Margret at the Tropicana in Las Vegas, I had a twenty-five-inch color television kit sent to the Hotel. I had already built a black and white TV, so I knew that I could do it. You had to build everything right from the beginning. You can't believe how many parts, literally thousands. It would take a full evening just to sort everything out, getting the condensers, the ¼-watt, ½-watt, and 2-watt resistors, and all the other hardware in order. There I was in my hotel room with all of these parts laid out ready to go, and I was building a color television set. One morning, there was a knock at the door. I opened the door and there stood two rather stout maids. They walked into the room, and I said, "I really don't want to be a lot of trouble, but do you see that side of the room where all those parts are lying? I would really appreciate it if you could kind of stay away from there because I'm building something."

They said, "Oh, don't worry," and started backing away. Their body language was revealing as they were backing up from where all the electronic parts were placed.

One of them said, "Tell me something. Will it 'splode?"

Roger Smith loved this story because he was fascinated with all things related to electronics and everything people did along those lines. So, on my first engagement, I made a hit and established an early affinity.

I started taking flying lessons in Las Vegas, which BJ had given me as a Christmas present. I built a Heathkit aircraft receiver that would bring in the towers and any communications between ground and air. We were back working at the Tropicana Hotel again and Ed McMahon was our opening act. He did a kind of W. C. Fields song and dance bit where he put on a top hat and told a few funny stories. He had become pretty popular because of his exposure on *The Tonight Show*. Ed had a wonderful musical director named George Hernandez. George was Ed's pianist and conductor, and also his personal pilot. George would fly Ed every night after Johnny Carson finished the show in Burbank. He would get out to the airport, where George was waiting to take him to Vegas. I think they finished taping around 6:30 p.m. The first show in Vegas was 8:00 p.m. and it's a forty-five-minute run from Van Nuys. I had finally finished the aircraft receiver and just turned it on. The first voice I heard was George Hernandez calling the tower saying, "I've got Ed McMahon here. We're coming in. We're on final approach for one-niner right." I just about fell out. That's how I heard my aircraft receiver working for the first time. I couldn't believe how close they were cutting it with a performance in less than fifteen minutes.

As a pilot, you have to do a biennial flight review with a licensed flight instructor. Years later, when I was with Jack Jones in Atlantic City, I needed my biennial review. George was a licensed instructor and coincidentally had the orchestra at the hotel where we were staying. So we went up together and he signed me off on my flight skills.

We'll revisit Ann-Margret later.

16 Gypsy In My Soul

SONGWRITER, ROBERT WELLS, was producing the Shirley Ma-cLaine show. I had known Bob because of work I did conducting shows for his wife, Lisa Kirk, who was a fairly well-known Broadway style singer. He called me to be the musical director for Shirley's new nightclub show and what would become a television special. The choreographer would be Alan Johnson, who was renowned for his work with Mel Brooks. I was able to bring my drummer, Tommy Duckworth, into the scene. From there, Shirley, Alan, Tommy and I put the whole show together in a rehearsal hall in Los Angeles.

Shirley loved Cy Coleman's music, and he was responsible for many of the songs that went into the production. Cy was the intellectual jazz musician, who wrote some magnificent music for the theater. "If My Friends Could See Me Now," from the Broadway show *Sweet Charity*, also recognized as "If They Could See Me Now," was a significant piece for her. Shirley's admirers closely associated that song with her and we used it twice in the performance. The intrinsic energy of the melody and rhythm, with the aggrandizing nature of its lyric, makes that song exceptional. Shirley also incorporated thematic material from the romantic comedy *Irma La Douce*.

Cy and I wrote orchestrations adapting his compositions for her show. In the opening, we did "If They Could See Me Now" as a big production number with full orchestra. For the closing we used it again, but brought it down to be a dramatically intimate moment with the audience.

The melody was played as an oboe solo, at a slow tempo, supported by strings. After that, the number would build again to create a grand finale. Oboe is a tricky instrument for a saxophone player to double on. If the saxophonist hasn't played oboe as an important part of his life, truly understanding the instrument, and all of a sudden he's got a solo on it, he could be in big trouble, particularly after having played the show for an hour on saxophone. I've heard some oboe sounds that you would not believe. Tommy kept a rubber chicken under his drum set and threatened to throw it at the reed section player with the oboe part. He tossed that rubber chicken many times because it sounded so awful. Sometimes we had to give it up and play the solo on soprano sax, which did not achieve the intended intimacy.

As part of her dialogue, Shirley referred to "ladies of the evening," saying, "I've done thirty-seven films and I've been a hooker in fourteen of them." She said alarming things like that to the audience and they acknowledged her humor and candor. During the show, she told of how she actually spent time working with a prostitute in studying for the part of *Irma La Douce.* She used these mannerisms and style she had learned particularly for "Big Spender." Shirley and Alan Johnson incorporated a lot of Burlesque moves into the choreography and her costumes were consistent with the theme for that segment of the show. Her dancers were dressed in similarly risqué fashion and the costuming helped create the atmosphere.

Shirley was a perfectionist and a stickler for details. She never cut corners, and put in an extraordinary amount of time and effort to make sure everything was authentic, from the orchestration and choreography, to the costumes, and the way she sang each song. Indicative of a great performer, when on stage, she made it all look easy.

Besides the Burlesque numbers, Shirley did some other things in the show that were wonderfully theatric. Cy wrote a piece of special material called "I'm A Person Too." It contained a poignant moment, and she delivered it well. Musically, it was orchestrated with sensitive string playing, where I played piano with my left hand and with my right hand conducted the strings over my left shoulder. Sometimes, just trying to keep it all together, I also conducted with my head because she was quite unpredictable in the rubato passages. Shirley enjoys performing in the moment, which, from the audience perspective, is great, but as her band director it could be an adventure. On long passages, she would take great liberties with the tempo and lyrics. It was a challenge, and having Tommy there made life much easier.

Each performance had its uniquely special moments and was indeed "live." She would sing some funny songs, such as "If There's A Wrong Way to Do It." We did a song called "Change Partners and Dance with Me," where we had a doorway on the stage. Shirley would go out to do a routine with one of the dancers, and as she's doing so, her costume would start coming apart. At first, to the audience, it looked like; "Oh my God, that's not supposed to happen." As the song continued, more and more falls off until finally she danced off and into the doorway that also fell apart. One day, she missed the part of the prop that was supposed to give way, and danced right into the stationary doorframe and hurt herself. The audience never knew because, true to her professionalism, she went right on with the show.

Cy would show up intermittently, like when we came to New York to do a television special for CBS titled *Gypsy In My Soul*. That show was the only time I worked directly with him, and we were honored with an Emmy nomination in the spring of 1976. Much of the orchestration for *Gypsy in My Soul* came out of the rehearsal hall. We adapted the music as needed by adding and extending the material.

Cy was a fine pianist and had specific musical ideas he wished to convey, which, as they developed, became difficult for a pianist to play. He wrote a musical figure for the title song that had a syncopated theme moving around with constantly shifting accented eighth-notes and these punctuations needed to be in precise locations. I played it for several weeks in a rehearsal hall for the dancers. It became a chore to orchestrate because the pulse and accents had to be retained without interfering with the melody when performed by the vocalist. With all that was going on in the music, it could get crazy and disconcerting for the audience. Finally, it went into click-tracks for the singers to do, and I had another pianist play it because I needed to conduct. It was all about maintaining textures and balance. It turned out to be effective and given the results, it was well worth the effort.

Shirley invited dancers, many of whom had since retired, to the show. At one point, they were all summoned from the audience to come up on stage and dance. It was ethereal and was remarkably effective. None of them were necessarily dressed up for the occasion. They looked like every day folks and all of a sudden they came to life on the stage. It had that spontaneous electric feeling that people now experience with "flash mobs." Lucille Ball was a guest on the show and there was some tension between Shirley and Lucille. I can't recall what caused the stress, but you could feel it. Together they performed, "Bring Back Those Good Old Days," as a choreographed musical sketch. In spite of their strained relationship, the segment came off well.

Shirley is a fascinating lady and has a reputation for being a taskmaster. Again, I've always respected her work ethic. She expects a tremendous amount from the people around her, but is exemplary in that she never gives any less than her absolute best. It was always about making sure the audience didn't just like the show, but that they really loved it. On rare occasions, the audience would not be as enthusiastic as she always expected. This is not uncommon in show business. Every now and then, you have an audience that seems like they just aren't there. After those rare occasions, she would call a rehearsal with me and the choreographer. To be honest, I would come to dread those calls, but we always worked it out, and looked for every opportunity to make the show better.

With each performance, she was concerned about getting every detail exact. We had a lot of click-tracks, which I had done at my studio, and a lot of components that required technical backup. We went to Norfolk, Virginia to play a theater for what was supposed to be a week-long engagement. On the opening night, there were twenty-two sound failures with microphones and clicks not working. Shirley was not happy, to say the least.

The next day, I went into town to buy some greeting cards and headed back to the hotel. I found Shirley standing in the lobby with Bob Wells. She called me over and spoke quietly and directly, "Bob and I are on an airplane in about an hour. The kids are over at the theater packing up and I want you and Tommy to go over and get the music."

As usual with a touring show, we hired local musicians to fill out the orchestral requirements. For this particular production, the saxophonists also doubled on other woodwinds. They had asked if they could take their books home so they could practice their parts. This presented a problem because they weren't expected back at the theater until the thirty minute call time. Tommy Duckworth and I went to the stage area to gather our things. We packed up the station wagon with costumes and most of the music. Tommy and I waited there all day, getting more nervous by the hour, while watching the stagehands strike the set. When the musicians showed up, we had to tell them that there wasn't going to be a show that night, or for the rest of the week. We saw Shirley MacLaine fans arriving for that evening's performance. As soon as we collected the rest of the music, we left town driving north to Washington D.C., and caught up with the rest of the cast and crew.

I felt like we were betraying the audience. I could see all those people who were excited about coming to see her. But, there were just too many sound failures and the producers weren't returning Shirley's calls, so there was no way to fix the sound problems. On the one hand, it felt like we were sneaking out of town. On the other, it was entirely consistent with Shirley's work ethic. If we couldn't do the show properly, we would be disrespecting the audience with a production that wasn't professional. Sound is something you can't second-guess. It needs to be consistently correct.

My working relationship with Shirley was always good and over the years our friendship has remained cordial. I recall only one slight altercation with when we were in Mexico City. We needed to straighten out a problem. It was an internal matter involving a new road manager who was not taking care of business. There were problems with sound set-ups, which I was involved with because, again, my job was predicted on perfection. I had told him, like an airplane pilot, he needed to run a complete "checklist" before each show. There was some tangling of personalities within the company over this and Shirley intervened. She and I worked matters out quickly. That particular road manager didn't stay with us much longer.

Shirley had a real fascination with Amelia Earhart's life. She did a great deal of research and was interested in finding a way to tell her story. I had decided this was a good occasion to give Shirley a special gift. I arranged for Shirley's first flying lesson with my instructor, Gary Koenig, a remarkable young man who already had thousands of flight hours. I not only trusted him with my life, I trusted him with Shirley's. Like all introductory flight lessons, it included some ground school time, followed by air time. Shirley climbed in the left side and piloted the plane. I talked with her afterwards and she was thrilled by the experience. For an artist who had so many wonderful life experiences, and who had given me the opportunity to share in her entertainment, I was glad to be able give something special in return.

I was with Shirley at the time she wrote her book, *You Can Get There from Here*. We were at the MGM Grand Hotel in Las Vegas. The book created even more things for her to do during the day with signings and additional interviews. The book brought out more dimensions of the already multi-dimensional Shirley MacLaine. She was ambitious, and I saw her as someone who was always seeking the next plateau, whatever it was. I don't know if she ever saw herself that way, but I did. Just when she seemed to be getting closer to that next stratum, and knew she was about to achieve it, she had her next attainment planned. She is a remarkable multifaceted talent.

For a few years, Shirley dated the popular New York journalist, Peter Hamill. She was also friendly with social activist, Bella Abzug. The show was booked at the Palace Theater in New York. It was the first time Shirley had played New York in many years and she was really excited about her home coming. New York was climbing out of its financial crisis, things had been really bad. We rehearsed at the theater and prepared the show for opening. The first night was quite a show. Shirley was more "adrenalized" than usual. The orchestra was set-up on the stage nicely and presented in a good visual fashion. That evening, in addition to its normal appearance, there were many extra microphones on stage because we were doing a live album to be titled, *Shirley MacLaine Live at the Palace.* We played a long overture. When we finished, I took my customary bow and immediately went into the music that brought her out. The theater was filled with electricity and the applause was almost frightening. When she came out, I turned away from the orchestra for a moment and could see her silhouette from the back. As the audience cheered her entrance, she was literally quivering with excitement. She ran to her microphone and said, "Oh, I'm so glad to be back in New York." She went on and on about how wonderful the city is and you can't get New York down, all in reference to its financial difficulties. "Nothing can get it down. New York is the Karen Quinlan of American cities." The audience gasped. Everyone was thinking, why did she say that? Karen Quinlan was a young woman being kept alive on a life support system and had become a national story because of the controversy. I don't know how she came up with this statement, but it occurred to me that Peter Hamill may have said something like this to her in passing. She had to apologize on television to the Quinlan family. A couple of months prior to this we had been in London where she was hailed for her triumphant appearance at the Palladium. A week later it was in the press there, as well.

I was the musical director for the first *People's Choice Awards* show. The director of the show, Bob Stivers, called and asked me to do the second annual show, but there was a scheduling conflict. He was on a strict schedule, but I had a commitment to Shirley. We were in London and Shirley was going on to do two nights in Paris, but I had to fly back home from London to prepare all the pre-records for this show. Thankfully, she agreed to let me off as long as I brought someone in who could handle her performances in Paris.

It's difficult to have someone else step in, and I appreciated her willingness to be flexible. Given her kindness, I wanted to make the transition as smooth as possible. Having been involved from the creation, I felt that Shirley's show was a big load for somebody to come in and take over. Jack French was the only one I knew that could handle it. Jack was a strong pianist and a skilled conductor. He had a lot of experience, having been with Liza Minelli and many other talented performers.

This show included a lot of click-tracks, a lot of starting of pre-records, and a lot of conducting that needed to be done from the piano. I had worked it out in one section of a song, where I wrote a ritardando coming to a fermata; at that point, I played an ascending arpeggio going up the keyboard hand over hand to a button on the piano that I pushed to start the tape. I continued conducting the orchestra playing through a series of clicks that lead to pre-recorded vocal tracks for Shirley and the singing dancers. Of course, she and the dancers also sang live, but we didn't want one of her hands, or the dancers' hands, taken up with a microphone during certain dance segments. Jack came over and we went through the orchestra parts. I showed him all the synchronization with the clicks and how to play for her on certain passages. He sat next to me each concert for a week and learned the show.

I had forty-eight hours to get everything done for Bob Stivers and rejoin Shirley in Düsseldorf. Bob was displeased because I couldn't stay an extra day to do the mix-down so, after recording all the cues; we stayed in the studio that night to get it finished. Later, when the show was to actually take place, the pre-records would be finished and I would be back to conduct the orchestra. Jack did the two days in Paris with Shirley and I made it back to join her in Germany.

We did a concert in Hamburg and there is a famous street there named, Reeperbahn, which was the red-light district. The venues are all lit up. Shirley wanted to see a live sex show. She actually had somebody arrange for her and an entourage to attend one of these shows. Presumably, it was all set for this club to open and present a special performance for Shirley and she invited me along. When we got there, the club was locked up and there was nobody around. Shirley became angry. We all started walking down the street and there was Derek Healy, our trumpet player from London. He was falling out the door of another nightclub nearby. Fortunately, we were able to get a laugh out of that. Derek drank a lot and used to wear a little red trick nose. He would wear the red nose at the airport and take his horn out of the case and start playing. Another time, on the road with him in England, we couldn't find him because he had fallen asleep on a public bench with his red nose on.

Shirley seemed to always have contacts with high-level politicians. We did a concert in Stockholm. After the show, she was gracious about signing autographs for my friend Lennart Wetterholm and his whole family. She was a little anxious that night because she had a date planned with Olof Palme, the Prime Minister of Sweden. Well, he never showed up. She became so furious that she threw all her clothes out of the dressing room window onto the street. Whenever I asked about her date that evening, the usually forthright Shirley became rather reserved.

Shirley and I had a funny bit that we used to share. I'd been having this inkling, probably because I love chocolate ice cream, while walking down the street and seeing somebody coming toward me with a chocolate ice cream cone, I'd stick my hand out and say, "Give me that," take the cone right out of their hand and continue on. I never thought I could actually do such a thing. One night at the MGM Grand, Tommy and I were over at the newsstand where he was looking at magazines. There was an escalator that came up from the downstairs floor where among the shops there was a Swenson's Ice Cream store. Sure enough, a gentleman was coming up the escalator with this big chocolate ice cream cone. I felt compelled. When he got to the top of the escalator I reached out and said, "Give me that."

He started to hand me the ice cream cone.

Quickly I said, "No, I'm just kidding. I've just wanted to do that for some time now."

He said, "No, please have the cone."

I said, "No, I really don't want it, honestly."

He continued, "Have the cone."

I said, "No, it's okay."

When Shirley heard about it, she broke up. After that, if we were all eating together, she'd sneak up behind me, "Give me that," pulling my plate away.

We've shared many inside jokes over the years. One night, as Shirley was doing a dance number with a cane, she was close to the orchestra and had accidentally dropped it right in front of me. As she bent down to pick it up, I whispered, "As long as you're down there...." She maintained her composure, but I could see her almost lose it. We had a lot of fun on stage.

I decided to leave the show because of my developing scheduling difficulties, and also because Tommy had left. Shirley chose to bring in Jack French as my replacement. Jack came out to Sparks, Nevada, and was sitting in my dressing room as I was getting ready for my last show. I had

With Shirley and Tommy Duckworth.

a brown velvet tuxedo and a blue velvet tuxedo, and two matching pairs of shoes. Jack said, "Why don't you wear one of each?" So I did, I went on stage with one brown shoe and one blue shoe. Shirley noticed it. During her goodnight speech she said, "Isn't that strange? This is Donn Trenner's last night with me and he has two different colored shoes on. That's because he has two heads. I can tell you that because no matter what I do, he's inside my head knowing what I'll do before I do it." She talked about the magic that comes from not knowing exactly where you may be going musically in performance, and having a director that has tuned into you.

It has never been about me delivering the magic. I try to give something to people that is a few more percentage points than just playing the notes. It has always been about bringing the highest level of sensibility to the process. Shirley continued to do "I'm a Person Too." The personal accompaniment I provided for that song was not a written arrangement, but Jack listened to the tape and learned what I played. I felt flattered that he and Shirley continued to use something I created.

I call Shirley from time to time and have her laughing because we share a lot of wonderful memories. She has always been generous with her thoughtful gifts and open about her life experiences. In her early performing days, Shirley was a Rat Pack girl and they adored her, for good reason. She's talented, smart, charismatic, well-informed, quizzical, and just fun to be around. She gave me a piece of jewelry to give to BJ, telling me it had been a gift from Robert Mitchum. At the time our European tour finished in Germany, she presented a unique art rendering of the city of Berlin and signed it: "It's not where we started, it's where we finished," which was the title of a song Cy had written for the show.

17 Happy Birthday, Bob

ANOTHER INTERESTING CALL CAME from Alan Copeland. Alan made quite a splash in the music business many years prior as a choir boy in the famous Robert Mitchell Boys Choir that performed in many hit movies. He recreated The Modernaires, whom he sang with while associated with the Glenn Miller organization. Alan is well-known as an outstanding vocal writer and composed some beautiful arrangements for renowned singer, Dick Haymes.

Dick enjoyed great celebrity as a vocalist and film actor. He had many hit records, such as "You'll Never Know" and starred in many motion pictures including *State Fair*. James Fitzgerald was an artist manager who wanted to get Dick's career going again. I guess Jim put up a lot of money and brought Dick back to the States after living in Spain for several years. Alan wrote a musical act for Dick to reignite his American career. I had done a couple of television shows with Alan, and he called to ask me if I would be interested in doing a few dates with him. I wound up being Dick's Haymes' Musical Director.

Alan's orchestral colors are also wonderful and imaginative, but they are difficult to play and demand a great deal from strong musicians. Actually, they are downright treacherous for brass players. Case in point: "Flea" Campbell was playing lead trumpet on a gig, and his upper lip literally split after playing one of Alan's more demanding charts. We had to take him to the emergency room after the show. Trumpet players all over the country, who have felt "hung out to dry" by Alan's writing, are still

161

looking for him. I call this "risk writing" because if it comes off really well, it's beautiful, but requires extraordinary skill. There is no in-between. A player can't fake their way through an Alan Copeland arrangement.

Dick and I traveled on the road together for about a year and it was quite an experience. The music was good and fun to conduct, but we appeared in many places where the orchestras were not good enough to play some of those charts. Being just Dick and me, it was problematic because we didn't carry any other players with us. When you have to hire an entirely new orchestra for each location, and you don't have at least your own drummer, it always makes things dicey. You do not know what kind of players you'll get.

It was ideal for me when I traveled with Ann-Margret because I ended up carrying five musicians; drums, bass, guitar, a percussionist, and a lead trumpet player. It made traveling so much better musically. The rehearsals went by quickly and easily, with much more clarity, because the new players coming in got so much support from the people who knew the charts, particularly from the lead trumpet player. We carried Don Smith, who was with Les Brown for years. Don did most of the road work with Ann-Margret and Shirley MacLaine. He was a wonderful player, who played right up to the time he died, which is how any musician would want it. With Shirley MacLaine, all she wanted to travel with in the beginning was a drummer and me. This is because we wrote her whole show, and put it together, in the rehearsal hall with just piano and drums. Therefore, we were the two that would be living with the show, but it wasn't enough. I finally had to tell Shirley, "We need to carry more than just the two of us. It's too much of a load. It's too hard to pull it all together in the limited amount of rehearsal time, and it creates too much of a gamble."

Dick Haymes was perhaps insecure personally, but enjoyed performing and liked to talk to the audience. He spoke well and was elegantly dressed. He loved our working association because it created stage references. He would talk to me from the microphone so there was a little bit of stage support from me, which he needed, and that was fine with me. After all, this is one of the things that I really enjoy about being a musical director. Accompanying someone means that you not only backing them musically, but that you accompany their lives in a lot of ways. You become, to a certain extent, their resident psychologist. I spent a lot of time listening to Dick go over parts of his life that were not so wonderful, crumbling periods actually. I also listened to him talk about using all these formulas for living. He did yoga before he went on stage; he felt that was important for him. His mother, Marguerite Haymes, was a renowned vocal coach and I think that's where much of it came from.

We did an album, *Live at the Cocoanut Grove.* The Cocoanut Grove was a famous nightclub in one of Los Angeles' well-known hotels, The Ambassador Hotel, and we used Les Brown's band. Alan Copeland conducted, and I played piano. While it showed quite a bit of Dick's ability to sing, it also showed some weakness that had developed over the years. If you had followed his career, you might detect a little more faltering in his voice than you would expect. In his earlier periods, when he sang with Harry James and Tommy Dorsey, his voice was perfection. While I was working with him, I would hear air checks or tapes that people did of him and it wasn't as strong as it could have been. I think maybe, over the years, it was the effect that alcohol has on the voice.

Dick was a lovely man, with an incredible volume of stories. He lived an involved and colorful life. He was married to actress, Rita Hayworth and later Fran Jeffries. Dick was married a few times, actually, and had gone through some turbulent relationships. He faced his first lengthy sobriety upon returning to the states from Spain. Dick was disciplined about his diet and exercise regimen and preached a clean life. He practiced, at least he talked about practicing, all these kinds of health seeking activities that would make him strong and overcome all the weakness of the past, but that all fell apart after we finished *The Dick Haymes Show.*

James Lipton called me to be the musical director for the *Gala Inaugural Eve*, celebrating Jimmy Carter's inauguration in 1977. Shirley MacLaine was to be in the show, which may have been a big part of why they called me. I've played venues all over the world, and I have to say the Kennedy Center is an exceptional space. The stage is well-equipped and it's designed to accommodate both a live performance and a television audience. There was a great feeling of optimism in the country during this period and it was certainly reflected among all involved in the production of *Gala Inaugural Eve.*

About a year later, I was glad to have a chance to work at the Kennedy Center again. This time the call was for a three hour television special, which is a lot of time on live television. *Happy Birthday Bob* would celebrate Bob Hope's 75th birthday.

As musical director of this show, I worked with a group of executives, producers, choreographers, engineers, contractors, other arrangers, the director, Bob Wynn, and all of the quest artists to creatively put together what this show would be. In addition to the staff that was already in place,

I brought copyists in from New York. I built an orchestra by working with a contractor in Washington D.C., letting him know what I needed. I called John Setar, who usually helped me put things together in California. Because of Les Brown's association with Bob Hope's shows, I felt strongly about trying to include some members from Les' band, and I also brought Butch Stone and Stumpy Brown, Les' brother who played bass trombone.

While we were in pre-production, I found out Les was upset that he was not asked to be musical director, because of his long association with Mr. Hope, but this was not a Bob Hope production, it was a show commemorating Bob's 75th birthday. We worked it out for Les to conduct one number for Bob's wife, Dolores, to sing. Dolores gave Les the usual hard time that she always did, and Les handled it well.

There were over fifty stars planned for the show and I was a thrilled to be involved. Acts, such as Shields and Yarnell, Ann-Margret, Elizabeth Taylor, Donny and Marie Osmond, Tony Orlando, Dorothy Lamour, John Wayne, Lucille Ball, George Burns, Don Rickles, Freddy Prinze, and many, many others would be performing. President Carter and members of Congress would be in attendance that evening.

There was a tremendous amount of writing that needed to be done and I had to look at all of the music that would be used by the guest artists. Will it fit the orchestra? Do we have to change the instrumentation? Do we have to change the voicing to accommodate the instrumentation? I did some of the writing, but I certainly couldn't do it all myself so I brought in Bob Alberti to work with me. His many accomplishments include working as the pianist for Steve Lawrence and Edyie Gormé. He also wrote for the weekly television show, *Name That Tune*. Bob was a speedy writer and was able to write a lot of cues. We had the Marine Band as part of our opening number, so we wrote an arrangement that combined our orchestra with the band.

Sammy Davis, Jr. was going to appear on the show, but he was not going to actually be there. They were videotaping him from a remote location on one of his tour stops. He was working with his group and had five or six people with him. We knew the music that he was going to do because it had been sent to us on audio tape. From the recording, I wrote an arrangement of his piece, and we sweetened the music with the orchestra live on the show in the moment. There was no opportunity to rehearse for this, but we got it coordinated and fortunately it worked.

Shows of this kind involved a lot of coordination and a lot of conducting. I had to direct it live, on the air, and even with careful planning a live performance will come out a little differently than expected, but as long as you're together visually and audibly, it will be acceptable to the viewer. For some numbers, there were too many things that could go wrong. It was necessary to pre-record certain things because they could not be coordinated live with all the other elements of the show. We engineered solutions for several technical challenges.

Carol Lawrence choreographed a dance routine and we had to create a pre-record for her. She did a tap dance as part of her number. In order to make it work, I recommended that we pre-record the taps, which none of us had ever done before. The stage crew built a three-sided plywood box with a floor that was resonant. We used a boom microphone close to her feet and recorded Carol's taps with just a rhythm section playing the tracks through headphones so she could hear it. When it came time for the live performance, we could get the sound of the taps directly and she was able to dance with the whole orchestra playing, all synchronized with her own pre-recording.

Pearl Bailey's performance was a challenge. When a producer chooses a specific song for a specific performer, it's called an assignment. She had to sing an assignment, which was a little difficult for her. She got nervous because we had to pre-record it. I went into the booth and worked with her. She was known to get bent out of shape sometimes and even a little volatile, but I helped her and she was gracious. We were staying at the Watergate Hotel, and over the next few evenings, when I got back to the hotel and went down stairs to check my mail box, each time there would be another autographed recipe book. Apparently, she had written a few of them.

One afternoon, the orchestra was rehearsing in the pit below the enormous stage at the Kennedy Center. We had paused for a moment and as I was standing at the conductor's podium someone said, "Take your headset off and turn around." The first row of orchestra seats is directly in front of the pit. I turned around and looked right at Leonard Bernstein. I had no idea he was sitting behind me. He had so much hair. He said hello to me and we shook hands. My heart sort of changed a little. I was humbled just by his presence. He said, "The orchestra sounds wonderful and you do a magnificent job." I didn't know why he was there. The Kennedy Center is divided into three different performance halls and he may have been doing something in another venue.

Redd Foxx was in a sketch where he appeared in full military regalia as the Chairman of the Joint Chiefs of Staff. In rehearsal, while doing camera blocking, Redd came out proclaiming, "It ain't easy being the head of the chief's joint." Everyone just fell apart and a break was called. We worked seriously hard on that show, but there were a lot of laughs along the way.

18

Your Love Is Good For Me

WHEN I FIRST STARTED WORKING with Raquel Welch, I was writing some things for her show and helping her get it together. At that time, she was married to producer Patrick Curtis. I brought a recent novel written by Elizabeth Kata to Patrick and he sent her $35,000 of option money for Elizabeth to come to America. She stayed with us in Woodland Hills, and then they went to England to look for a location. He was going to produce her story. I guess it never really reached fruition, but it was an opportunity for her to come to California. Eventually Patrick and Raquel ended their relationship.

I did a couple of engagements with Raquel and that was enough. We were at the MGM Grand in Las Vegas and shared the bill with Burt Bacharach. It was Burt's show, he was the headliner, but for the ending of the show, she came back out and they did a closing number together. Burt was completely smitten with Raquel. He couldn't even talk when she was around. Musically, Burt knows what he wants and can articulate it. He conducts well and gets what he needs out of an orchestra. He's an accomplished musician and writer, but one of musicians in the orchestra commented on his writing, "A Burt Bacharach melody sounds like a third alto sax part." Maybe that's not a fair characterization, but it's a humorous description of Burt's unique compositional style. He and lyricist, Hal David, contributed a substantial number of memorable songs to the repertory of American popular music.

Another time in Las Vegas, Bob Hope was in the audience. He came backstage to visit with Raquel and I took him to her dressing room. Bob and I were talking when Raquel came out from her inner dressing room, wearing a robe which was quite open in front. Well, it was more than just a little décolletage and I saw Bob Hope having difficulty keeping his eyes on her face.

Surprisingly, Raquel didn't always seem comfortable on stage. She was a sex symbol, a gorgeous-looking woman, but I was never attracted to her stage persona. At some point early in her career, a creative decision was made to emphasize her visual sexuality through choreography, wardrobe, and song selection. It worked well for her, but like many wonderful performers, Raquel had a pitch problems, meaning she couldn't find the center of a note. Her vocal quality was breathy and immersed in a lower chest register that was best for her style. I recommended that she have some backup singers because I felt it would help her sound. It turned out to be great for me, because BJ was hired as one of Raquel's singers. We had three backup singers, and, believe it or not, it helped Raquel center her sound and pitch. BJ and Raquel became close friends. BJ can be very funny and she made Raquel laugh. Their friendship continued long after my involvement with her show.

Raquel was demanding my advice. It became a difficult situation, and the only time I have ever been so bluntly critical and direct with anyone. She was going back to work in Las Vegas and had I turned down the engagement. Instead, she hired Chris Boardman, a successful arranger in Los Angeles. Chris had done some television work and is a good jazz orchestrator. Raquel wanted me to come down to the rehearsals to see how things were going. I think she was worried about Chris' young age and whether he had enough experience, but I liked Chris and knew he would be terrific. He was a fine pianist and easy to work with. I thought maybe all Raquel needed was a little reassurance that Chris could handle the musical direction.

For most productions in Las Vegas, when one show is closing, the new show comes in and rehearses on the closing day of the previous show. Raquel's new production was the next in line for the Circus Maximus room at Caesars Palace after Ann-Margret. Raquel called me in Vegas during our last week, and asked again if I would work with her. I said, "There's no way I can do that Raquel, I just can't. I'll try to help you though. I'll come to your rehearsal before opening and see how it's going."

I attended Raquel's rehearsal on the morning of our closing performance with Ann-Margret. Chris was doing a fine job and I thought Raquel was judging him unfairly. Again she said, "Will you please do the show?"

I said, "I can't. I can't do that. It's not fair to Chris. He knows the show, including the new production numbers I've never done before." I wanted to find a way to support Chris and smooth things over. So I said, "If you want, I'll be your 'Roger Smith' and go out front and listen. I'll stay here for a couple of more days and watch the first few performances. I'll take some notes and make some recommendations."

She agreed and asked how much it was going to cost her. I was taken aback by the way the conversation transpired. She wanted my help, but at the same time she talked to me as though I would have put some kind of premium rate on my offer. I suggested she just pay me a daily rate like she used to, or whatever she wanted. I promised to stay for a few days and get the job done.

It wasn't that I didn't have the time available to do Raquel's show. The truth is, I had difficult experiences with her in the past, and as much as I enjoyed many aspects of working with her, I didn't feel it was a good match for us. I just knew I couldn't work with her again. I remembered when we had rehearsed at Caesar's. She came over to me saying through her live microphone, "What's the matter with that trumpet player up there? That section sounds terrible." You could hear this through the PA.

I crushed my hand over her microphone and pulled it down. I stared her down and said, "Don't ever do that again or you won't have an orchestra to play for you."

That closing night, Ann-Margret made a little speech because she knew she wasn't going to be working for five or six months. Her speech to the audience and the company that night was pretty emotional, we all felt it. There was a lot of love on that stage, as always.

I went to see Raquel's opening performance and for the first time, I was seeing things from the front. I was used to seeing the show only from the position of being behind her, sitting at the piano with the orchestra. This new perspective changed everything. I saw a dance number where she rubbed up and down the dancer's leg. I had to cover my face. I was sitting in the booth alone, cringing. She opened with a number called, "Your Love Is Good for Me." It was some rock tune, and she finished saying to the audience with a heavy breath, "Your love is good. I feel vibrations in the air, your love is so good for me," now referring to the audience. It didn't come across in the sincere way she intended. I took a lot of notes.

Immediately after the opening show finished, she expected me to walk into her dressing room. André Weinfeld, her new husband was present, and some people were back there visiting. I could see all the focus was on me, and I was getting a little nervous.

Raquel asked, "What did you think?"

I tersely replied, "Well, Ms. Welch, I feel that I have some things that I would like to talk to you about privately. I'd rather not discuss this with you here."

The room emptied. In a moment everybody was out of there except André, Raquel, and me. I put my hand on her arm and said, "Maybe this is unfair. Maybe it's because I know you so well, and maybe it's because I sat on the other side of you for so long. Raquel, it's the worst piece of shit I've ever seen."

I had never ever said anything like that to anyone in my life, before or since that moment. I didn't walk in there expecting to say that at all. It was an emotional response. I honestly didn't think the whole show was terrible. There were just certain elements of it that didn't reflect Raquel's talent, or the talents and skills of her whole creative team.

Then I told her everything. "You need to work on pitch. You never should say hello to an audience after the first number. You don't tell them that their love is good for you because you haven't earned their love yet. It's too early to be thanking them for being so receptive to you because they haven't been. You have to get out there and work for it first."

She sang a song in the show that she had dedicated to her daughter. It is the first time in the show that everything gets a little bit more sensitive. The spot comes down to a pin spot on her face. It's a ballad and kind of pretty. Then the spot opens up and all of a sudden she goes whack-whack with her hips and all of the intimacy she's just created, that one moment she has finally gotten to, goes out the door. I had to tell her all these things. I also told her that Chris Boardman was doing a terrific job for her.

I offered to write some new dialogue for her, and gave her some more advice: "Don't talk after the first number. Don't talk after the second number. Don't talk after the third number. After the next number, you'll speak and you'll say, 'Thank you ladies and gentlemen, it's really wonderful to have you here tonight.' Then go straight into the next number. If you want to do some dialogue with them, wait until later. I can only tell you what my experience tells me and what works the best."

I went on to talk about her voice qualities. "I would like to work with you because you are speaking so breathy all the time. When you sing, you're expending so much air that your pitch suffers." I suggested she have a piano sent up to her room so we could work together. I continued, "You know, Raquel, you don't always have to be a sex kitten, you can be a woman. You don't have to be as obvious. That's who you are, everybody already knows that." I was nervous about stepping on the choreographer's creativity, because it wasn't their fault. The people working with her designed a show based on a persona that had been successful, and so heavily identified with Raquel.

Blane Savage, later known for his work on *A Chorus Line,* was a wonderful dancer in Raquel's show. I had to tell Raquel that her dancing up and down on his leg looked terrible. She used to do an entrance from way up on the top of the stage, and walked down through the orchestra. I said, "When you're walking down, it's got to be more elegant. You're already flaunting it and throwing it in their face. You talk about your daughter later in the show, so everybody knows that you're married and you've had a child. Your child isn't a baby any longer. You need to incorporate this part of your life. It's not a bad part of your life." I went through all of this with her and, in a quick ten minutes, I was out of there. It was a little rough for me to be that brash, but I was upset and couldn't do it any other way.

A good show requires the producer and star performer to invest significant time in pre-production, choosing material carefully that is commensurate with what the star of the show does best, and it has to be presented in a fashion that makes sense. The show should have continuity so it expresses a point of view, where thematically, something relates to something else. Not just random songs here and there, but subject matter that has segments with a connected feeling.

Every show needs a quality opening act. It was almost always a comic because singers usually don't want another singer. It's important to warm the audience up a little from the time they walk in. They've been seated, and maybe they don't like their seats, and they're waiting to order their drinks, or their food isn't good. Something's got to take that whole tension out and unify the audience. That's usually the job of the opening act.

Then, out comes the star attraction, and they have to make some friendship between the stage and that audience. You don't do it in one or two numbers. I can see occasionally, a short greeting after the second number, but quickly go into another number. You don't start talking about your life, or whatever, until you've earned some respect. That's what I was trying saying to Raquel.

A show must have a strong opening and a strong closing. Creating a large production can be viewed as identical to composing a musical orchestration. The constructs of the introduction, the head of the tune, the development, the shout chorus, and the finale are all crucial. You have to keep looking at the dynamic contouring of the whole performance. It can begin with a *forte*, then go down to a *mezzo piano*, then go up to a *fortissimo*, all by way of the musical material and devices that are employed. The moments where you slow it down and become quiet, can create intimacy with the audience. That's when Ann-Margret was able to talk personally. The approach and style can be contrasting. Ann-Margret went on stage to give. Shirley MacLaine performed to receive.

We planned for standing ovations. You can actually create them musically, through the arrangements. Wayne Newton is a perfect example. People stand up three or four times, and they usually can't wait to jump up. He will seem to be finishing a number and coming to the final cadence; it feels like the song is concluding and the audience is about to applaud, but he continues, modulating chromatically. He brings it to another peak where the music is just about to end, and they're all ready to rip into applause, and again he goes somewhere else with it. He keeps delaying the ending. He uses that device several times during the production numbers. These modulated emotional musicalities reach a peak and another peak and another. Just when you think it's over, they go for one more peak. By the time it finally ends, the audience is so anxious to clap they jump to their feet cheering. This technique worked effectively for him. We didn't do it quite the same way with Shirley, but we did link segments together. Shirley performed dramatic pieces from her movies. She is a phenomenal actor, even when she sings. The delivery of a lyric has always been important to her, because she recognizes and portrays the story elements of the song.

Raquel agreed to let me work with her for the next couple of days. In the afternoons, we got together and reorganized her show. We changed the placement of musical numbers and wrote some dialogue for her to speak at different points in the performance. I helped Chris put together what was needed for transitions. The show seemed better by everyone's standards. Raquel was grateful and wrote a letter thanking me. BJ was more skeptical, "You wait, and a week from now it won't be like this." Sure enough, after a short while it went back to resembling its previous form. Well, so much for my attempt at repair.

Between building Heathkits and chores at home, I was always carrying some kind of tool bag around with me. BJ used to do an impression of me around the house, "Donn is leaving for an important trip to Europe. He has to get out of here by 2:30, at the latest, to make that 4 o'clock plane. He's rushing around the house trying to get packed and he's also got to make it to the bank. Just as he is about to leave, he walks to the front door and jiggles a loose door knob and says, 'I've got just the right tool for that. Wait a minute, I'll fix it. Hold on, let me get my tool bag!'"

BJ and I had been married for over eleven years. During our marriage, she had set aside her own career and became a tremendous support in my professional life. We tried to have children, but it just didn't happen for us. BJ was dedicated to being super-wife. That's really kind of what she had planned, until the business bit back at her. I was traveling a lot and sometimes she didn't choose to come with me. I think that was more interruptive than what is needed for a healthy relationship.

I can relive the moment like yesterday. I had come home after a trip and we were sitting at the breakfast bar. She said, "I want to talk to you." She put her hand on my arm and said, "This is going to be very difficult, but I have to tell you that I don't want to be Mrs. Donn Trenner anymore. I don't want to be Mrs. Anybody anymore. I don't want to take care of dogs. I don't want to live in Woodland Hills. I want to take a shot and see if I've got anything left in show business. I love you very much, but I need to move on."

This was so difficult emotionally. I loved her deeply, but I also respected her great talent, and the fact that she had become unhappy in our marriage. I had to let her go. I helped her find a temporary apartment and then I helped her find a house.

BJ and I made a simple gentleman's agreement. When it came time for us to follow through with the divorce, which was not a lot of fun, I was working in Vegas and I ran across an ad in the paper, "Do It Yourself Divorce." This was rather ironic, me being "Mr. Do-it-yourself." What had attracted me to this company was the $39 fee to have all the paperwork prepared, and a few dollars extra to do the clerical work. Las Vegas required six weeks of residency, which I was able to prove through a friend there. I had talked to an attorney because I wanted to get a property settlement drawn up that was agreeable, as we had to present this. I told the attorney that I wanted to keep it simple. I didn't want documents, documents, and more documents. I knew what we had agreed upon and the attorney simply put it in writing and BJ signed it.

Being the close friends that we were, BJ flew down to Las Vegas. We went to the courthouse and filed the paperwork that we had completed. We were in the office with the clerk and BJ was sitting on my lap while we were filling out some forms. The clerk asked, "Are you sure you want to go through with this? Do you know what you are doing?"

Hesitantly I said, "We're reasonably sure that this is the right thing to do."

At the end of the day BJ asked, "How much did all of this cost you?"

I added everything up and she wrote me a check for half of it.

To this day, BJ is very dear to me. Even though we needed to go our separate ways, we never completely let go. She went on to successfully revive her career and continues to do many exciting things in her life. Years after our divorce, she married director, lyricist, and acting coach Gordon Hunt, who is a wonderful gentleman and is well-respected in the business. I've written music with Gordon for a few of his projects. BJ and I talk regularly and her friendship continues to be a cornerstone in my life.

19 My Very Own

WITH ANN-MARGRET, we made sure that we didn't keep the same program for more than a year, and for each booking the show featured something new. If there were two or three Las Vegas engagements, her loyal fans would return to see a different production each time. Most other shows didn't make any changes, even if they came back to Vegas frequently. Out of respect for the audience, we felt it necessary to keep it fresh.

The show always contained a dazzling production number. *Harlem Days* was a tribute to the legends that came out of New York during the swing era and included jazz classics like Duke Ellington's "Jump for Joy." We created a nautical theme, complete with a set piece designed as a large pirate ship. This incredible scenery would fly up and come in from the sides. Ann-Margret also presented a film segment employing video Roger shot of her in the region of Sweden where she lived as a child. They enjoyed motorcycles and she danced on a Harley Davidson, until Roger had an accident and wouldn't let her ride anymore.

Live shows are always an adventure. Things do go wrong, and every performer has to decide how they will handle the unexpected. I was impressed by Ann-Margret's ability to deal with breakdowns. Although Roger and his team were detail-oriented, on rare occasion, a major problem would occur. Ann-Margret was always apologetic to the audience, "Ladies and gentlemen, I'm sorry. I feel like you've spent a lot of money to see this show. I want you to see all of it, so we're just going to take this moment to talk to you and we'll do the number again from the beginning. That's what's so wonderful about doing things live."

Occasionally the pre-record tape broke. Ann-Margret didn't want anyone to know anything was pre-recorded. We tried to pull it off so no one ever knew. Sometimes the tape would get stuck and we would immediately relate that it was something else that went wrong. It might be a synchronization problem, but we would not indicate it was a pre-recorded tape failure. Sometimes the band cart didn't work, but we would continue to do the show anyway. There were sound failures when the microphones went out. Sometimes even the backups didn't work. We used a lot of radio frequency microphones, particularly for the kids dancing. In Las Vegas they would pick up taxi calls. In the middle of the show, "Send cab twenty-one to forty-seven 14th street."

More than once, I went to Ann-Margret after a show and said, "Wow, that's a peculiar audience, isn't it."

She would make excuses for the audience. "You know, Donn, they're probably here attending a convention and they probably don't get out very much. They're tired and probably more concerned with eating their dinner." She never got upset.

I didn't dare trust Ann-Margret during the first year. I figured nobody could be that wonderful; it had to be a façade. After getting to knowing her, I came to realize that she was truly a magnificent human being. Besides being thoughtful, kind, and caring, she is honest and not the least bit egocentric. This is unusual, particularly for show business, which is steeped in egocentricity. You'll never find anyone that ever worked with her say anything negative. The biggest confrontation I ever had with her was one day when she came up to me with her face scrunched up and said, "Donn, do you think maybe that number ought to be just a little bit slower?"

I said, "I think we can try it."

She was a joy to work with and didn't take those she was working with, or her fans, for granted. Many times, after the curtain finally closed, she came back out to compliment the orchestra, "You guys are so wonderful. You really make me want to work."

One night, Ann-Margret was not feeling well. Her heart was racing and they brought her to the hospital. We did some portion of the show without her and then she returned and we did the opening act. She was adamant about not letting anybody down. The opening of a show at the Golden Gate Theater in San Francisco, she had to leave the stage. Feeling a responsibility to her audience, she came back out. She sat next to me on the piano bench seeking comfort. From there, she rallied to do the entire show.

During the show, she often came over to sit next to me on the piano bench. I would be seated there quite properly, in position to play the next piece, and she'd start to push against me, playfully trying to knock me over. If I was standing next to her off stage, I'd have to be ready because she might just fall into my arms. I tried to say funny things to her. Kiddingly, when it was hot and sticky outside, I would say in Norm Crosby comedic style, "Boy, there's a lot of humility in the air." That became a phrase I used.

One night during the show she said, "Why is it so hot in here?"

I yelled from the back, "It's the heat."

It got a laugh from the audience and she, fond of musicians' humor, came back with, "Oh, you musician, you."

I said, "It takes one to know one." She got accustom to being playful this way because it was important toward building her confidence on the stage, and a level of trust between us.

Perhaps more than anyone, the musical director becomes the source of confidence for the artist. In front of the performer is their audience, this great fearful group of friend or foe. Behind them, is the musical director, who must to provide what they require, supplying self-assurance. This was a deeply personal matter for me. On or off stage, I developed some interesting affinities. In performance, I was together symbiotically, and off the stage, I gained an ability to talk personally. Ann-Margret spoke of matters that I could never have repeated to anyone at the time because they were private. I developed a rapport with her for a few reasons. I think one was that we were both only children. Also, that she wanted to have a child, but never did. She was exceptionally close to her mother Anna Olsson, who also became a dear friend to me. "When You're Smiling" was her most beloved song because it was her father's favorite. His death was particularly difficult for her. She always referred to her husband in the show. After each performance, Roger would be waiting for her in the wings. She would run back stage and jump into his arms and he carried her to the dressing room.

Roger had a rough time with an illness called Myasthenia Gravis, which is a debilitating and often a fatal disease. His was a milder strain than some, but frequently got quite fatigued. Roger's illness was scary for her. I produced a show every year for the Myasthenia Gravis Foundation.

It was a charitable event held at one of Beverly Hills hotels. Once in a while, if asked, Ann-Margret would reluctantly sing a number. She didn't like to perform unless it was in her own surroundings, where she and Roger could plan what number she was going to do, and how it would be presented. All of that preparation and planning made her feel comfortable on stage.

Roger has always loved the latest technologies and was an accomplished videographer. He hosted a lavish party for the entire company each week in their suite and would bring all of his video and audio gear. He would find clips from shows, performances, and events that were meaningful to different people in the company. When we were on break, the dancers had done a show with The Osmonds in Provo, Utah. Roger called the producer of the show and arranged to get a few out-takes from the filming. Roger put some excerpts together and played it at one of the weekly parties. The dancers were completely surprised. I had mentioned to Roger that I missed seeing the first space shuttle landing. At the next party, "This is for Donn Trenner." There it was and he made a copy for me. This was long before the days of YouTube and the Internet. It was difficult and time-consuming to get material and edit these pieces.

There were many ways that Roger and Ann-Margret showed us their appreciation. One night, I was up in the suite and he asked, "Do you listen to a lot of music on the road?"

I replied, "No, I've never done much of that really."

He said "Well you ought to. Do you have anything to play it on?"

I said, "Well yeah, I've got a little cassette player that I bring with me sometimes."

He said, "Come here a minute." He took me back into his room and he handed me this enormous stereo cassette deck with two speakers. He said it was a little extra Christmas present he thought I might like to have.

Christmas was always wonderful with them, not just for the gifts, but for the joy of having the company together. Roger treated everyone like family. I remember one night, after a few years of working with them, I was walking across stage with Roger and he had his arm around my shoulders. He said, "This is personal, but I have to tell you this because it's meaningful to me. Donn, I've never waited one minute for music since you've been with us. There's never been a delay and there's never been anything wrong with your work. Do you know how important that is? Don't you think it's time for a raise?"

I said, "Well that's your department."

He asked me to call him and I said, "I'm not going to call you."

Sure enough, he remembered and he gave me a substantial raise the next time we went back to work. Over the years, he nearly quadrupled my pay. Roger was most generous, but never present when people wish to show their appreciation. He had a way of being disappearing at just that moment.

The company was so tight, like a happy family. It is a commonly used term when you're traveling on the road, but this truly was a family. I had a cardiac episode and they immediately came to the hospital to be with me. Ann-Margret came to my room and actually fed me. I was a big hero in the hospital after that. The doctors came in and said, "Why didn't you tell us Ann-Margret was going to be here?"

One night, Earl Hughes, our stage manager, wasn't feeling well, and he came into my dressing room.

Ann-Margret came running in after him. "What's the matter Earl?"

He said, "I just don't feel very well."

She said, "Wait a minute." She ran back to her dressing room and got a banana. She thought bananas were the cure for everything. "First of all, eat this, you need some potassium." It's only minutes before the show is to go on and she said, "Listen Earl, you know how many times Roger has had to cancel the show for me. The show doesn't have to go on if you're not feeling well."

He said, "No, no, don't do that!"

She proclaimed, "Really and truly." After a couple of seconds, "You need a piece of beef." She ordered him a roast beef dinner and fed it to him.

When Ann-Margret greeted people, she brought them backstage and introduced them to everyone in the company. "This is my musical director, my very own Donn Trenner." "My very own" became her byline in reference to me, and she used that whenever she introduced me. When friends of mine came back stage to meet her, she always addressed the woman first. Most people were a bit nervous, but in less than five minutes they felt comfortable with her. She found some way of putting everyone at ease, either with a compliment or an endearing comment.

Often, Ann-Margret did some prepared dialogue telling the stories of her life while sitting on the piano bench with me. She liked to tell her George Burns stories. "Mr. Burns, how come you don't ever date any girls your own age?" She imitating his voice, "Annie, there aren't any." She continued, telling the story of when she went to audition for him, wearing

With Ann-Margret at Caesars Palace.

tight toreador pants and a little angora sweater. With that outfit she got the job. She was so excited that she went out on a spending spree at a Beverly Hills boutique.

At work that night he asked, "What's that you're wearing?"

She said, "Oh, it's my new outfit that I just bought. It's very stylish."

He paused and said, "What happened to the pants and sweater? People don't only want to hear you sing, they want to see where it's coming from."

Every time we did the show in Las Vegas, she would have another vignette related to Mr. Burns. Ann-Margret's real name is Ann-Margret Olsson Smith and Ann-Margret is not two words, it is a hyphenated Swedish name. She did not like to be called Ann, but George was one of the few allowances. He often said, "Hey, Annie... ." From the time they first met, George was a particular favorite of hers. He gave Ann-Margret her first big break.

Ann-Margret is actually shy and gets embarrassed. We went to Minneapolis to do a special performance for the King and Queen of Sweden because Minneapolis has a large Swedish population. We were discussing which would be the proper way to address royalty, saying Your Highness or Your Majesty, and she was getting nervous. After the show, we had a processional where we all greeted the King and Queen. A little later, I went up to Ann-Margret's suite. She didn't drink at all, but it was almost like she was a little tipsy. She said, "I can't believe what I was doing. Do you know what I was doing up there on that stage? I was up there going bam, bam, doing Burlesque bumps with my hips. I can't believe I did that in front of the King of Sweden!"

She came from a little town in Northern Sweden on the boarder of Norway called Valsjöbyn. I really wanted Ann Margret to go to Sweden because she is Swedish, and because I had so many friends there. I went to Roger and said, "I think I can pull off a television special for her. Just pay my transportation and let me go over to see what I can do." I went to Stockholm and stayed with Lennart Wetterholm. I asked him about going up to Ann-Margret's home town. He got a photographer from Channel One in Sweden and we boarded a plane. We landed at a military base and took a car from there. We got to Valsjöbyn and went into a little market to ask if anybody knew where Ann-Margret lived. Pointing and speaking in Swedish, "Right over there, that house." We knocked on the door and Ann-Margret's uncle answered. I was surprised that someone from her family still lived in the same house.

I returned to the States and went to Ann-Margret's and Roger's house with photographs from her hometown. I pulled them from my briefcase, and Ann-Margret got so excited when she saw the picture of her uncle that she ran to call her mother, speaking in Swedish, and Anna Olsson was there in just a few minutes.

What I had been able to work out was an opportunity to do the show in Stockholm's beautiful and well-known, China Theater. Roger, being the controlling businessman, was pessimistic. For me to be stepping out of my role as musical director, and all of a sudden trying to help with production, might not have appealed to him as much as I thought it might. Roger was the consummate manager. He didn't allow anybody to photograph her and was careful about protecting her image. He did not let anything go out without his prior approval. When I told them how successful the trip was and how much they would like to do a television show, he was concerned about who would own the rights.

In the fall, after being in South African, we brought the show to Sweden. The China Theater was really too small, but we were able to put together a plan where we could get the whole orchestra on stage. I went over with just my lead trumpet player and a percussionist, and hired a Swedish orchestra. Our show generally called for two percussionists, but our amazing percussionist, Richard Brown, could handle both parts. For most shows we had enough in the budget for two percussionists, but when the budget or space didn't allow, somehow Richard worked his magic and handled all the percussion parts, which is what he did at the China Theater.

I also needed to use a Swedish pianist because I couldn't play the whole show. I played all the personal things for Ann-Margret, but I would have to be up front to conduct tempo changes and run the click-tracks. We were able to devise a show that would work, but we had to stack the orchestra in such a manner that the trombone players were up on an elevation above me. The spit valves at the end of their trombone slides dripped on the top of my head. The trombone section presented me with an umbrella hat in the Swedish blue and yellow.

It was a successful production. Even though she had been gone since she was six years old, they were thrilled to have Ann-Margret because she was a Swedish star. This was an especially meaningful occasion for her and she did most of the show in Swedish, much to the delight of the audience. Ann-Margret's demeanor connected all of us together and we all felt like we were part of a large community event.

We ended up doing a lot of press interviews. Some of the press knew the background of the show and wanted to share the story with a broader audience. On our last show, the owner of the theater and another Swedish gentleman came up on stage with two little cannons and fired them in salute. They gave one to Ann-Margret and one to me. We returned to the China Theater again a year later. We had a little trouble that time because they did not allow laser lights into the country. They were apprehensive so we had to make a guarantee to the fire department, and get special insurance. We were the first production company allowed to bring lasers into Sweden.

Ann-Margret is a director's dream in motion pictures. I've never heard a film director; actually I've never seen anyone around her, that didn't just rave about what a joy she is to work with. She takes direction well and she is a consummate actress. Not only was she the sexy Elvis girlfriend, but she has done major films that have been dramatically compelling. She did a made-for-TV-movie titled, *Who Will Love My Children?* for which she received an Emmy nomination. The movie was a true story about Lucile Fray, played by Ann-Margret, who was an Iowa farm wife with ten children and stricken with cancer. She knew that she had a limited time left, and with a husband unable to care for their children, she was determined to place every one of them in a home before she died. Ann-Margret went to Iowa to meet the Fray children and learn about them as a family. Barbara Stanwyck actually won the Emmy that year for *The Thorn Birds*, but when she made her speech she said, "This really shouldn't have gone to me, it should have gone to Ann-Margret."

One night between shows, we were all invited up to Ann-Margret's suite at Caesar's and Roger showed the film. He also showed a before-airing tape of the television show, *That's Incredible!* It was an interview with Ann-Margret and the Lucile Fray children. They talked about how much she captured the essence of their mother and how close they all became during this project. It was a real tear-jerker for everyone. Then all of a sudden, Ann-Margret stood up and said, "Okay, let's go downstairs and do another show now."

The last show that we did was at the Radio City Music Hall. We presented the strongest segments from shows we had done over the years. It was a big production with a wonderful New York orchestra and an incredible stage situation. The orchestra went down to the archives and got on the band-cart, which was on an elevator. I will never forget that opening night. My knees were shaking, I couldn't believe it. This huge platform with the full orchestra rose up to overture level, where you can just see us a little bit from the audience, but the main stage was still above us. After the overture, the platform rose up further and went onto the stage and slightly back. Raw Satin came on and danced in front of it. At the end, it went all the way to the rear of the stage. We could see the Rockettes before they came on. Radio City is an incredible theater and it was quite a show.

Ann-Margret and Roger decided that she would not be performing with such a huge production any longer. A house choreographer for Radio City Music Hall put together a plan for a far less expensive production and sold this bill of goods to Roger. The choreographer decided that he and Don York, who was a capable pianist, could put together a package with a small band of five or six, a troop of five that could dance and sing a little. This marked the end for the large orchestra, all the dancers, laser lights, and all the other accouterments. Ann-Margret continued with a much smaller production and I was not included for that very reason. I certainly didn't take it personally because I was not about to dance and I don't sing all that well.

20 My Attorney Bernie

MY FATHER USED TO SAY, "Do me a favor. Why don't you date a Jewish girl sometime? What have you got to lose?"

I had been dabbling in real estate and invested in some apartment houses. One of the transactions didn't go well and I ended up in a legal disagreement with the seller. I was sued for Specific Performance and needed an attorney. The realtor I was working with recommended her brother, Ted Horton. Ted helped me get out of this situation somehow. Later on, someone called me to do sound production on a videotape for a company that was putting a studio together. I felt I needed an attorney to represent me on this, so I asked Ted. He said he didn't handle entertainment contracts. I explained that I just wanted to have an attorney present. It was sort of like the song, "My Attorney Bernie," which is a funny tune by Dave Frishberg, a jazz pianist, who has written the most obscure and wonderfully peculiar songs.

Ted and I drove out there and on the way he said, "My daughter is trying to buy a piano and she doesn't know much about them. Could she call you sometime?"

After a while, I did get that call and agreed to meet her at the piano showroom. As I walked in, the salesman took a look at me and said to her, "Do you know who this guy is?" I thought, Oh gee, here we go. He ran off a short resume on me. To this day, it surprises me when people do that, and I still get embarrassed. I looked at the piano. The deal was that she would take me out to lunch in return for my advice. She took me to lunch all right. Oh boy, did I pay for that lunch.

Susan and I started seeing each other. She was a nice person, quite attractive, and laughed a lot. She was a court-appointed criminal defense attorney for the city of Los Angeles. Susan made a lot of money, and money was important to her. We repeatedly broke up and reconciled. I had never been in a relationship like that before. It was always the same issue, her jealousy over my friendship with BJ. I should have known that jealousy was not something she would get over, but we both wanted to make it work.

Susan lived in Sherman Oaks, which was half way between where I lived and her office. One night she said, "I'm tired of going home from your house and having to dress for work." So she moved into the house in Woodland Hills, which I thought would make things easier for her and give her more confidence in our relationship. I wish it had been that simple.

Susan was not capable of handling the fact that I had a life before her, particularly that I had a life with BJ. This was the most psychotic situation I've ever been part of. I told her, from the beginning, all about BJ and that her family is like my family. They were there for me when my parents died and they would always be in my life. I didn't know what to do about it. We went to a psychologist once a week for three months. The psychologist looked at her and asked, "Susan, what do you want?"

She said, "I don't want him to talk about BJ anymore. I don't want to know about her. I don't want to know that she exists. I can't handle it." She got so upset you could see the color in her face change.

The psychologist then turned to me and asked, "What do you want Donn?"

I said, "I want Susan to know that I need to call BJ once in a while and need to feel free to have her call me. I want to call from my kitchen in front of Susan. I have nothing going on with her except for the past years of friendship and family. I cannot give that up. I don't want to have to sneak out of the house to call her, which is what I have had to do."

I would slink out of the house, go to a phone booth and call BJ to see how she was doing. Occasionally, BJ called me for professional reasons, talking about some musician that she wanted to use or to discuss upcoming projects. One day she called and said, "I've got an opportunity to record an album and I'd like you to do it with me." I thought about this and figured I'd better see the psychologist. She said to me, "This is your profession. You need to do this. Susan can learn to separate this." Still I could not see how it was possible. I would have to lie each day I went to the studio and could never bring the finished album into the house so I turned the project down. I'm sorry it turned out that way.

Throughout my relationship with Susan I was working with Ann-Margret and traveled quite a bit, including my first trip to Africa. Sun City is a resort in Bophuthatswana, located in the North West Province of South Africa, about a three hour drive from Johannesburg. As I understood it, the Republic of Bophuthatswana was supposedly independent of South Africa, which was under the restrictions of apartheid, but essentially landlocked by South Africa and non-apartheid. In just a fifteen minute drive from their homes, people lived by segregated rule. For many of the local people I met and got to know, Bophuthatswana represented hope for the future of South Africa, a step toward a more progressive existence. I saw Blacks and Whites working in the hotels together. People coexisted socially, going to the night clubs, mingling, dancing and they could intermarry. I didn't realize that it was much more complicated than that. Black people there were literally trapped within South Africa's larger borders. They couldn't get passports, because no country other than South Africa recognized Bophuthatswana's independence and its leadership was hand-picked by the South African government. It was believed; the money generated by Sun City resort supported, directly or indirectly, the apartheid government. Many major acts came through Sun City, including Frank Sinatra, who opened the theater, also Elton John, Shirley Bassey, Rod Stewart, and many others. Most of us did not understand the complexities of the situation.

While our show was in Sun City, I met Verity Lloyd, who was in charge of public relations for Sun City, and since became a good friend. Verity handled an extraordinary list of important details, including the building of a large stage to Roger's specifications so we could do the full production. She also arranged tours for all of us, including a trip to a platinum mine. The tour guide spoke guardedly about the conditions of segregation, but explained to us that while Blacks and Whites did the same work, Blacks were paid a fraction of the wages compared to Whites. After we got home, we had to be particularly careful because of the increasingly negative press for entertainers who performed there. Travelers had to journey through South Africa to get there, which also contributed to the negativity. We had been given souvenir jackets from Bophuthatswana and later, when we played Toronto, some of our crew wore those jackets to work. There was a boycott of the show.

After Southern Africa the show traveled directly to Sweden for Ann-Margret's national debut. When I returned home from this latest tour, Susan and I broke up once again. She moved out and bought a house about four inches away from me in Woodland Hills, and we continued to date.

Given my past, I had become reticent about marriage, but one evening, after having known each other for more than four years, I realized that if I wanted this relationship to progress, I needed to marry her. She accepted my proposal.

Susan told me several times that no one had ever asked her to get married. I made arrangements for a special wedding that would take place on Ann-Margret's second tour to Sweden. My friend, Peter Lundin helped me arrange for a ceremony on a touring boat that I chartered. I found a rabbi in Stockholm, Morton Narrow, who spoke English perfectly and was a dignified gentleman. He required certain things, which I arranged for in advance. I didn't know anything about conservative Jewish traditions, like conducting the ceremony under Chuppah. It's like a little trellis that I referred to as a hoola hoopa. Another is that you take a wine glass and wrap a napkin around it and break it by stepping on it. I didn't tell Susan anything about the wedding plans because I wanted everything to be a romantic surprise.

The night before we arrived in Stockholm she asked, "Will you tell me anything about the wedding?"

I replied, "No."

"Well, is it going to be indoors or outdoors?"

I quipped, "Yes."

I just didn't want to tell her. Peter picked her up the next day and drove her to the boat. We chugged out and married on the water near the Drottingholm Palace, which is where the king and queen live.

I had Susan all set to think that there wasn't going to be a reception. I had gone out and bought a couple of bottles of champagne and I put them in our room. We were standing there with Ann-Margret and I said, "Maybe some of the kids in the show will come up and have a drink." All the time I had this plan. After the ceremony, as the boat was docking, I told her we'd go back to the hotel, but I had arranged for us to get on another boat, the *Mäladrottningen*. It was Betty Hutton's luxurious yacht that had been docked at Riddarholmen Island and converted to a hotel and restaurant. I took Susan on-board and pretended to use the pay phone to call Peter. Peter suddenly showed up behind me and escorted us upstairs where we enjoyed our reception.

Susan talked about how she would need a lot of help if we had a child. She'd have to have somebody to take care of the child because she would be in court all the time. Given all of her apprehensions, I felt Susan would not have been a nurturing mother. Nevertheless, we attempted to have a child. Going through fertility treatments spoils a lot of the romance. Although I was deeply disappointed at the time, it was just as well we did not have a child. My life would turn out much better as a result.

Interestingly, Susan wasn't bothered by my friendships and working relationships with other women, but my friendship with BJ continued to be a hurdle in our marriage. Susan made an attempt to deal with her jealousy. We had dinner with BJ one evening and she even bought her a couple of Christmas gifts, but she just couldn't get over it.

We had German Wirehaired Pointers at that point and I had Sandy, the female, bred. I named all the pups, and there were eight of them. One pup was named More Brown and another one was, well, I couldn't call the dog Les Brown, so we named him Mr. Brown. I kept Mr. Brown. One day, Susan and I were sitting at the breakfast bar and she said, "Tell me something. How did you find a dog to breed Sandy with?" At that point my mind went, "Do I speak the truth, or do I do that thing about going around the circle and try to make some statement that is almost the truth." The truth was BJ found a breeder. Now, could I say BJ found a breeder? I could say someone found a breeder for me. So I took the chance and I said, "BJ found a breeder." I watched the color just go out of her face and she ran upstairs. My heart sank because I knew this was going to be another one of those really difficult emotional episodes. She was sobbing and I said "What are you crying about?"

She said, "You didn't have to say that to me."

I said, "Susan, I could have said what I said, which was the truth, or I could have done another one of those dances to avoid using those two letters that you don't even accept in the alphabet. I can't do that anymore."

At that point we made a decision. The relationship ended after nine years and I helped her look for a house.

Just prior to getting married, Susan thought it would be a good idea for us to have a prenuptial agreement, but we never followed through and it sort of became a joke between us. One night we had some friends over for dinner and she asked one of our guests, "Is there anything else I can get you?"

I piped in and said, "Yeah, where's my prenup? I want my prenup. Where's my prenup?" We both laughed.

She said it was too late for a prenup so I asked for a postnup. Well, she drew one up and we signed it.

I had purchased a washing machine and dryer for her. She had decorated the bedroom the way she wanted it done with wooden shutters and built-in furniture. Susan knew the house didn't belong to her and she didn't want any part of it. We bought a car together, a Volvo station wagon. When the car was running well, the back part of the station wagon was mine, and when it wasn't running well the front was mine. We added everything up; the washer and dryer, she charged me back for the shutters saying, "This enhances the value of your house."

I said, "Okay." We worked it out that I gave her my half of the car, in lieu of what I owed her for the shutters. In the end, there was no money exchanged. Thank goodness for the postnup.

Being around Ann-Margret and Roger, and my touring family, was especially helpful at this time. I was grateful to be busy.

21

Change In the Pockets

JACK FRENCH HAD A SCHEDULING CONFLICT. He was at the Desert Inn at Las Vegas conducting for Anthony Newly and asked me if I could come down and do the rest of the engagement for him. Jack had rescued me when I had a conflict while working for Shirley MacLaine, so it was my pleasure to return the favor.

I came in with one night to watch the show and figure out what had to be done while looking at some duplicate parts. In addition to conducting, there was a lot of personal playing for Mr. Newly. He sang a lot of the tunes he co-wrote with the English writer Leslie Bricusse, such as "Who Can I Turn To" and "What Kind of Fool Am I." Anthony was a dramatically strong performer on stage, with a peculiar singing voice that people made fun of at times because of his exceptionally wide vibrato, but it was distinctive and fit him well. His voice was a representation of his stage persona.

At that point in my life, I was just getting to where I needed glasses to read. For the most part, over the years, I had always known the music I was responsible for and did not have to read, unless the musical situation was new to me. It was the first night that I was with Mr. Newly, and that particular night was the first time I really needed to wear glasses on stage. When we did his song, "Candy Man," he brought out a wicker basket of candy and he started dancing around throwing candy out into the audience, and he threw some right at me. Well, I couldn't see it coming and it hit me square in the face, right on my glasses. We all broke up over that.

Anthony was actually wonderful to work with. He did the classiest bow I've ever seen in my life. This man's body would start from a rigidly upright position and just begin to fold down slowly, and when he got to the usual bow position, he would just continue his bow, going down until his head was almost at his ankles. It worked so well and prompted more applause.

The music for Mr. Newly's show was excellent. He worked with a British arranger and musical director, Ian Fraser, who had done many television specials. Ian was a good pianist and a versatile arranger. He used the styles and colors of a jazz musician, but was also able to complete a wide range of musical assignments. His chord changes were more creative than what you generally heard. He built harmonic sonorities into his orchestral writing that offered richer substance and textures. In the same way that Anthony had a distinctive vocal quality; Ian has a distinctive way of bringing more out of a composition.

A composer creates the melody with a corresponding harmonic structure. An arranger takes that melody and prepares it for orchestral performance. Without an arrangement, a song cannot be performed by the ensemble. All of the parts have to be written, based on the size of the orchestra, what instruments are to be featured, and what the harmonic background needs to be for a particular performer. The arranger can also take an original song and create a different feeling or mood. "Rhapsody in Blue" was originally written for orchestra, but jazz bands have also performed this same piece with a completely different concept, emanating from the talents of many different arrangers.

On ballads, Ian, like many good arrangers, heard and wrote enriched harmonies where the original composer had written only a basic harmonic framework. This created greater warmth. Songs are written with an inherent poetic nature. A creative musician can elaborate on that essence and fashion a rendition with an enhanced personality. Even the great composers of the American Songbook wrote wonderful melodies supported by a rather utilitarian harmonic concept, but a skilled arranger will employ a broader spectrum of tonal colors.

Mr. Newly was from England and had a great admiration for Charlie Chaplin. I think he was plagued by the feeling that he may have been a Chaplin reincarnate. Although he never spoke of this to me directly, it was indeed a supposition understood by many people who were associated with him. I believe that is where the dramatic physicality of his end-of-performance bow came from. Like Mr. Chaplin, he also had a great propensity for romantic interludes with younger girls, and he fell in love frequently. Mr. Newly wrote a show called "Chaplin," which went out on the road and failed. It cost him and his investors a lot of money. They re-wrote it and it failed again, and he went back to England. He also endured prolong illness.

Later on, I did a cruise with him, which was a lot of fun and I enjoyed his company. The cruise line flew us from Los Angeles to Hawaii where we stayed overnight, boarded the *SS Rotterdam*, and sailed back to San Francisco. This is one of several cruises that I did with various artists, and the old *SS Rotterdam* was my favorite ship. It was an elegant vessel appointed with beautiful wood. The entire voyage was about six days and they brought in entertainers to do different segments. Somebody mentioned to me that a Charles Barnet was on that cruise. I learned that it was, in fact, the real Charlie Barnet I had worked for years ago. He was retired and this was the second or third world cruise that he had done with his wife. That evening, I found out where he was seated and went over to his table and said, "Charlie?"

He turned around and in his normally gruff manner, saying, "Yeah."

I said, "It's Donn Trenner."

He said, "Wow! Sit down. Tell me why you're here."

I told him and he came to my rehearsal with Mr. Newly. We had a nice visit and it was fun to reminisce.

Another trip to South Africa came when Mr. Newly was invited to entertain at a million dollar golf tournament. Gary Player was the resident pro at the Sun City Resort. I went over and put a small band together for his show. I brought a couple of musicians because I needed at least a lead player for the woodwinds, and one for the trumpets. I ended up with two players with whom I had never worked with before. I found out the hard way that the reed player was a social misfit, but I didn't know this until we were literally on the plane. The hotel had sent me a first class ticket, which I did not request, but the two musicians were flying coach. Although it's common for musical directors to get preferential treatment, I never liked this kind of travel arrangement. It makes me feel like I should apologize. Shortly after take-off, the reed player snuck up and sat down at my feet because he wanted free drinks. On the way over, we made a landing in Monrovia, which is the capitol of Liberia on the west coast of Africa, and was a volatile area with political unrest. We were told before the airplane landed that it was a fuel stop, with some passengers boarding, and no one was allowed to leave the airplane. This musician decided that he wanted to take some pictures. He walked up to the front, out the door, and down the metal ramp they had brought up to the airplane. It was heavily guarded and his lack of respect for the situation caused us a two-hour delay. They took his camera apart, confiscated the film, and turned it into a political incident.

I received a call to work with José Feliciano, who is a remarkable and talented man with an impressive stage presence. He engages and directly connects with his audience on a personal level. I found José to be genuine and I really enjoyed working with him. Usually, he worked with just his own group that went on the road playing his yearly engagements. I was brought in to conduct on big events that used a large orchestra. One was with the Atlanta Symphony where he was booked as a celebrity artist on their subscription series. The first time I conducted for him was in Atlantic City at Resorts International. It was a joyous experience for me. I remember on that first night almost being distracted by José's genius ability to sit there and be funny, erudite, clever and exceptionally musical. He played a couple of encores that brought tears to my eyes.

When I got to Atlantic City, his scores and the parts were in serious disarray. The four or five musicians who worked with him all the time knew his music, but they were not familiar with the written expanded orchestral versions. They didn't know which part belonged to which chart, so we had to sort all of that out. We finally got through the rehearsal and it came time for the show. I went into José's dressing room, where his wife was helping him get dressed. He was really sweet and his wife was dressing him. Just before the show he was smoking the largest marijuana cigarette I've ever seen. It was rolled like a cigar.

Gesturing to me he said, "Here would you like some of this?"

I said, "No way, José."

It would have been a very different show if I had. I was not about to go out on that stage stoned and not know what the hell I was doing. He took several hits on this joint and went out and did a great show. I didn't know if José used marijuana regularly, because that was my first night with him, but he was able to perform exceedingly well.

Jack Jones hired me as his pianist and conductor because we had worked together on television shows. I went to his house and rehearsed some things with him and thought, "Oh boy, this is just going to be great." After rehearsal, Jack expressed how pleased he was. At the time he was a well-known jazz-pop singer, but he wanted to do tunes that nobody really wanted to hear. He sang a few songs that the audience expected, like "Lollipops and Roses" and other tunes he had made popular. However, he also performed other songs that the audience did not respond to and he appeared to be unaware of their disappointment. He opened with a song called, "I Am a Singer." That got old quick.

The first tour we did was in England. Jack brought his wife, Kim. I thought Jack did a lot of things just to please her. He made her the head of his corporation. It seemed like she had him figured out pretty well.

We left from Los Angeles International and I showed up with all the music cases. I had not done a date with him yet, but needed to let him know I could not carry them anymore because I had a bit of a back problem. I met up with Jack and Kim and, as we each started to walk through the security archway, the airport security person most politely spoke to Jack. "I'm sorry sir; you can't take that in with you." She was pointing to his camera.

He rudely snapped back, "I know, I know, what do you think, I've never traveled before?" As we were walking away, he said, "Can you believe the way they talk to you here?" I was embarrassed for him. That happened again when we were boarding a ship to go to Alaska. As we were making our way through security, he looked at me and said, "I can't believe the way they talk to you here." He just wouldn't let it go. When we got to London, Jack stayed in a flat that both he and Mel Tormé always used whenever either of them was in town. It was a lovely place and Jack had all the musicians over for a reception.

Jack's sometimes abrasive style was not just out of his own self- interest. If he felt anyone else was being slighted, he was equally mistrustful. We brought Jack's drummer and bass player with us and then hired the rest of the musicians in England. We had unusual instrumentation, four horns, a tuba, two trumpets, and one reed, plus the rhythm section. It worked okay; it wasn't marvelous, but it was all right. Jack was concerned about where the musicians were going to stay, so he came over to look at our accommodations. As we were checking in, he went up to the floor where we were going to be staying. He immediately came back down and said, "I'm sorry. There is fresh paint in the hallway. This is not good enough for you." He marched over to the front desk and said, "This is not good enough for my musicians. I don't want them to be inhaling paint fumes." His demand for room changes was actually a thoughtful act.

This was a tour of British cities and the next day a luxurious brand new coach came for us. The bottom of it was designed to store scenery and stage equipment. Inside there were three TV sets, two bedrooms, and a kitchenette. They brought a chef along who cooked on the bus for us each evening. We placed a request for what we wanted and dinner would be served between the sound check and our performance, which was a nice way to travel.

The coach picked us up at the hotel and we went over to pick up Jack at his flat. It was a beautiful day and he came walking up to the bus. Not really knowing why, I used to call him Chief. "Hey Chief, how are you? What a great day."

And he replied, "Fucking birds."

Puzzled, I said, "What?"

He said, "Those fucking birds."

I didn't know what he was talking about.

He said, "At four o'clock this morning, those fucking birds were chirping outside my window. I couldn't get any sleep, those fucking birds." He kept saying that. It still haunts me every time I hear birds singing. I could never get a normal greeting in with Jack. I couldn't say, "Hello, how are you? It's a lovely day." It didn't work. At every hotel we stayed, they had a suite for him and nothing was ever right. He hated the suites, he didn't like the bed, or he didn't like the color, or whatever. I've never seen anything like his chronic dissatisfaction.

Jack Jones' demeanor showed itself frequently. When we were in Atlantic City doing a show called *City Lights*. It was a production show and it was on ice. When we came out for our portion of the show, the trio actually had to walk on the ice and get up onto our little platform. The orchestra for that show was directed by my dear friend and Ed McMahon's former pilot, George Hernandez, who I had worked with many times. He watched me when I had to conduct our group, and duplicated what I was doing with his orchestra to pull both factions together. While we were here in Atlantic City, George and I went out to a local airport where he also conducted my biennial flight review.

We opened the first night and Jack was a smashing success, they just loved him. I went back to his dressing room afterwards and said, "Wow, Chief you really killed them."

He said "Yeah, yeah."

I said, "Don't yeah me. I'm telling you they loved you out there. It was a great show."

He said, "Yeah, I guess it was okay."

I said, "Incidentally, I walked around and went out to the front where everybody comes in and there is a wonderful placard of you. It's like six feet tall and you have a great smile."

He didn't react at all to that, but the next night he came into my dressing room before the show and stuck his finger in my face and said, "Do me a favor. Don't make a project out of trying to make me smile."

I said, "Don't worry, I won't, I've given up." I walked out of the dressing room.

In the bus, Jack had a computer, and every night he would print out the show that he was going to do. His vision was not that good and he couldn't remember lyrics every once in a while. I figured it out that if we did four songs, and he didn't forget the lyrics on one of those four songs, we would probably be okay. Sometimes he would forget, so he had cue cards stashed on the monitor cubes in front of him with the words written out in extra-large type for him to read.

I have to say again, he is immensely talented. Jack Jones is a great singer, a real musician singer, but he did some quirky things. On most nights he ended his songs on a high note, and then ascended another fifth because he had a strong high range. For the finale, he would hold that last note like it was a challenge to beat last night's record. It was fascinating that he played those kinds of games with himself. I don't think he ever realized it or analyzed it as such, but I couldn't help it.

Jack seemed like one of the unhappiest men I have ever known. He was, by most measures, an accomplished singer, but he defied all of the formulas that would have worked for him to have become a giant success. I think Jack felt like he was living in the shadow of his father, Allan Jones, who was a famous Broadway singer, and never succeeded in pleasing him.

I received a call one day from Danny Bennett, Tony Bennett's son and manager, asking if I was available to do a tour with Tony. We had worked together on several television shows, and our paths had crossed many times over the years. I asked Danny what the dates were, figuring that it would be international, and that my passport had expired. He was calling me on a Tuesday and they were set to leave for Spain on Friday.

Tony is a tremendously talented musician and an exceptionally charismatic performer. I loved working with him and was not going to pass up the chance to do this. I got an emergency passport and got booked on a flight to Madrid with no idea what Tony's music was going to be. He was enjoying a long streak of successes and, as one reviewer put it, "Tony didn't bridge the generation gap, he smashed it." Whatever the music was, I knew it would be good. As it turned out, we performed songs from his album that had just come out. The music was arranged for strings and woodwinds with his rhythm section, no brass. I was able to get a tape of the recording and listened to it on the airplane. It was simply beautiful.

When I arrived in Madrid, we went directly into rehearsal at a television studio. I was still going into this cold, but Joe LaBarbara on drums, and Paul Langosch on bass, were very supportive. The orchestra was fine, with good strings, and all worked well. We had enough time to go over everything thoroughly and the filming went smoothly, with a small audience present in the studio. Compared to the way we did things in the US, this was a less regulated approach to TV production. All the numbers were pre-selected, each one was blocked out separately, getting all the camera shots together, and then filmed individually. It took a long time to get ready for each segment.

In between tapings, Tony came over to the piano and I would say, "Do you remember this tune?" I played a few bars and he recalled it exactly. Then he said to me, "Do you remember this?" I'd recognize what he was singing and accompanied him. Between takes for the show, we must have done a dozen songs this way for the audience.

Also between tunes, while talking with Tony, he said, "Hey man, you know there's one thing I can't stand, man, and that's change in the pocket."

Confused, I said, "What?"

He said, "Change in the pocket."

I didn't know what he meant and I said, "Don't worry about me, when I get into my tuxedo I don't have anything in my pockets."

He said, "No, no, it's okay man. I just can't stand change in the pockets."

A little while later, he put his hand on my shoulder and said, "You know; I've got to paint. I've got to paint every day. Painting is my life." He continued, "I went to the del Prado today."

I said, "That's great, Tony."

He continued, "Yeah, that's the epp-ě-tōm of museums."

Taken aback, I replied, "Okay?"

He was mispronouncing epitome and I wasn't sure if he was putting me on.

After filming the show, Tony took us out to dinner and we had a wonderful meal. Before going out, some funny things happened to come up while talking with the guys in the dressing room. I was relating some stories about the people I had worked with, particularly Jack Jones. While I was relating the Jack Jones stories, they started referring to "singer's disease." I started to laugh, "Oh, what do you mean, singer's disease?"

BONADETTO

A PLEASURE TO SAY HI TO A
GREAT FRIEND —

Tony Bennett

Tony's portrait

They said, "Singers, you know, they're all alike, they all have singer's disease."

I guess they were referring to personal eccentricities. Comparatively, Tony seems to have a natural immunity. A couple days later, I was home again. It was another wonderful experience. Sometime later, I ran across a violinist who had worked with me in the studios in Los Angeles. Apparently, he was the culprit. He told me that one time, while talking with Tony Bennett, he was jangling the change in his pocket, and Tony appeared to become quite annoyed by it.

I worked with Vikki Carr intermittently over a period of a year and a half. I met her long before she was ever known for her solo effort. Trumpeter, Ray Anthony, as part of his act, had two girls stand on each side of him. Vikki had been one of The Bookends. We played engagements in Washington DC, New Orleans, Chicago, and in California with the Fresno Philharmonic. She had loyal fans who truly appreciated her shows.

They were pleasant gigs and the quality of her music was quite good. Some of it had been written by Bob Florence who had been one of her musical directors. She is not necessarily my favorite type of singer because, instead of standards, she does a lot of light Pop tunes. Vikki also sings many Latin songs, which were fun because she sang them so well. She was a fine singer with a great voice, truly a fine instrument. Vikki was attractive and I nicknamed her, "Chops," because she had a fetching embouchure. "You've got some chops, baby."

Through no fault of her own, her show didn't have the dramatic peaks and valleys that are needed to make a performance really engaging. The actual presentation stayed at one level. The irony is, she usually cried two or three times at each show. Through her ability for theatrical drama, she could bring herself to that point, usually in reference to a particular lyric. Vikki talked about herself a great deal on stage and during the show she referred to herself in the third person. I used to signal to my drummer, Tommy Duckworth, keeping score of how many times she mentioned her own name during a show. One night she mentioned her own name seven times. However, her audience seemed to love it, but when you're sitting on stage with her every night it gets a little bizarre.

Around this same time I worked for Charo. She was married to a Swedish television director, Kjell Rasten. They came out to the studio at the house when I was writing for her. Charo's style was to talk a mile a minute with her Spanish accent. She'd say silly things like "Missippippi," which were funny, but her energy was maniacal. Her husband would say, "Charo, Charo slow down nobody can understand you." She called me the computer "yeenius" because I created a pre-record that she could use on stage with the use of click-tracks. She thought the whole process was amazing. She signed a promotional picture of herself that read, "To the computer yeenius."

22

The Ground Moveth

CARMEN JONES WORKED AT CAESAR'S PALACE for many years in the wardrobe department. She was assigned to whatever artists were appearing in Circus Maximus, one of the larger and better venues in Las Vegas. Carmen helped Ann-Margret with quick changes, handled last-second repairs, and ensured that Ann-Margret and the rest of the cast did not have any "wardrobe malfunctions." She was responsible for the care and maintenance of every piece of costuming, including shoes and accessories. Carmen was one of those people you wanted to have on a show like Ann-Margret's. Someone who can create and maintain organization backstage, pay attention to detail, stay calm if something goes wrong, and knows how to prioritize when a lot is happening simultaneously. During the performance, it becomes a high-pressure job that requires a cool head, and there is no down time.

Whenever I was at Caesar's with Ann-Margret, Shirley, or Raquel, I usually ran into Carmen, and we developed a friendship. She had a deep appreciation for music and worked on many shows over the years. From the time I first met her, she struck me as a warm, loving person with a strong work ethic and a great sense of humor. As she spent long hours backstage while we were in rehearsals, we got to know each other a little better. Sometimes, when I was working with the orchestra, she watched from the wings. When she had a break, she came over to the piano and we talked. Sometimes I would play something for her or we just laughed. We discovered that we both longed to be parents, and were each coming to terms with the likelihood that would not happen. We also both knew how wonderful and how painful relationships could be.

Eventually, Roger hired Carmen to go on the road with us as Ann-Margret's wardrobe mistress and personal assistant. Some of us would sleep while we traveled, but Carmen was usually awake, repairing costumes, or tending to things that needed to get done before the next show. While we were in rehearsal, she would find the local shoe repair store, get supplies, organize the dressing rooms, and lay out everything for each cast member. When we were on the road, she did all that herself, without an assistant.

Most of Ann-Margret's team lived in either Los Angeles or Las Vegas. When we flew out for performances, we'd often depart in two separate groups and convene at the destination airport. Carmen flew from Vegas, and I came in from Los Angeles. Ann-Margret had an engagement in Atlantic City, so both groups flew into Philadelphia. The shuttle van was there at the airport to pick us up, and someone said there was an extra seat in the van with Carmen, so I ran for it. I was going to ask her on a date, but she fell asleep before the driver pulled into traffic. Still, I was glad to be there with her. After a show one night in Atlantic City, we had our first date at the hotel coffee shop.

I knew Carmen for thirteen years before I ever suggested having a drink together. I was sixty-two and she was thirty-six, so I guess it began as a May-September romance. I've never felt any particular age at any point in my life, so it wasn't an issue for me, and Carmen didn't seem fazed by the difference.

The next engagement was Lake Tahoe. I think of those few days up there as the beginning of our romance. I felt that the possibility of becoming a husband again and parenthood might still work out. At the end of the Tahoe engagement, the paramedics showed up because Carmen had taken ill with severe altitude sickness. Instead of flying back with the rest of the cast and crew, I drove her back to Las Vegas.

I've been married most of my life, it's just the cast that has changed. I first got married when I was twenty years old, and there were periods of a couple of years in between relationships. Frankly, I'm embarrassed by how many marriages and divorces there have been in my life, but if I hadn't gone through those experiences, I wouldn't have the life I have now.

Carmen and I came to care a lot for each other, but she made it clear that she was not interested in living together, so we made plans to get married. The entertainment industry adds a whole other level of pressure to relationships. BJ knew how much I wanted this marriage to succeed and suggested I get some pre-marital counseling. She knew a psychologist named, Mary Rocamora, who had a particular expertise working with people in show business. I went to see her, and when Carmen came to town, I suggested that we both go. Mary confirmed that we were well-suited for one another, and from her perspective we were ready to get married. BJ, who knew me well, also approved of the match. Carmen was understanding of my past relationship with BJ and accepted our friendship.

One day I got a call from a distant cousin in New Haven saying he was on the Hillhouse High School Reunion Committee and they were making plans. He inquired, "Do you want me to let them know where you live?"

I had an unlisted number because when I was on the air, I would get inundated with calls from people who wanted to sell songs, get tickets, or get on the show. I had never been invited to my high school reunion so I said, "Sure, have them send me the information."

That evening, I asked Carmen, "How would you like to go to a dead people's convention?"

She said, "What are you talking about?"

"Well a lot of people aren't going to be there, they're probably dead, and a lot of people that will be there are probably in the same condition."

We went to the dead people's convention and it was kind of fun. I showed her the houses I lived in as a child and we spent some time in and around New Haven.

I really wanted to show her Guilford, a little shoreline town about twenty minutes up the coast from New Haven. When I was growing up, there was a restaurant in Guilford called the Old Stone House, where my parents and I went on special occasions. I had the engagement ring, and thought I would take Carmen there for dinner. The waitresses knew what was going on and they were all giggling. I got down on my knees and proposed. Carmen tells people to this day that she couldn't eat because I proposed before dinner.

A few months later in January, we were married in Woodland Hills out on the deck by the pool. We found a minister, and had about fifty people to the house who knew us as a couple, including Ann-Margret and Roger. BJ was my Best Man. That always gets a raised eyebrow. Even BJ's parents flew all the way out from Florida. As I was walking down the aisle, which was the pathway by the swimming pool, BJ told me, "This better be the last time."

During the reception BJ's dad reminded us, "Don't you think it's about time to toast the bride and groom?" He honored us with the toast.

We had the entire event taped and a videographer walked around interviewing our guests. He went up to BJ for her thoughts, "How do you feel about this?"

She replied, "Well, I know Donn very well, he's been like a husband to me."

Before marrying Carmen, I had become resigned to the fact that everything I wanted in a marriage would never happen. I've always felt it was mostly my fault and was not going to marry again and never become a father. From early on, I saw the raising of a child as a privilege and a great opportunity to create a happy, loving environment. In my own childhood, the love was there, but it was not a happy household. I knew it could be different. One of the things that brought Carmen and I together was our interest in having a child. I resumed my dream of having a family.

A physical pregnancy was not possible, and we became totally committed to adopting. Realizing an agency would probably not look favorably on our twenty-five-year age difference and my marriage history, we decided to seek an adoption attorney, one who came to us highly recommended. Through her we learned how private adoption takes place. You develop a concise résumé describing who you are, how you live, where you live, what you do, what you like and dislike, and why you want to have a child. Then you run ads in certain newspapers letting people know that you are a couple interested in adoption. The ads are usually answered through the attorney. The attorney screens the ads and informs you of someone that's interested. That is the circumstance that took place with this attorney.

We were put in touch with a couple in Fort Collins, Colorado. They were a young pregnant woman named Rhonda and her husband, who were giving up their infant. This couple, on welfare with two children, one with a disability, was overwhelmed by the prospects of caring for another baby. We did all of the preliminary work and contacted them. They decided they wanted us to be the parents.

Calling them regularly during the pregnancy, we all became close. The time of the expected birth came and we were ready. We drove from home to Boulder to visit my flight instructor, Gary, whom I was best man for, and his wife. We let the birth mother know exactly where we were because it was getting close. The call came and, as we left Boulder for Fort Collins, we got a flat tire. I called Gary, and it started snowing. He came as quickly as he could, gave us his car, and took care of getting the flat fixed. We ended up driving through a serious snow storm all the way to Fort Collins. We arrived at the hospital fifteen minutes after the baby girl had been born.

Carmen went into the bonding room, where she got into a gown and the baby was put in her arms. We met the mother and father. The father seemed like a good person. However, there were some strange elements at play. It seemed Rhonda's family tried to arrange for adoption within the family, and they were quite distressed that she had gone with us. We felt some friction over this, but we didn't think it would turn into anything serious. A day went by, and it was time for us to leave with the baby. We started the drive home to California from Fort Collins.

As we were instructed, I called the attorney to let her know that we were on our way back and that everything had gone relatively smoothly, but we couldn't reach her. I called my answering machine from the car and found there was a message from her telling us to contact her immediately. I couldn't reach her. She was famous for not returning phone calls, which was a real irritant in our relationship with her. This kind of a situation should be a real hand-holding commitment. It should be sensitive and supportive for everyone involved. In hindsight, we didn't get that feeling from her at all.

We got back home, contacted her office, and found out that she was skiing in Colorado. When we finally made contact she said, "We're having a little bit of trouble. It looks like the birth parents now are reneging on the adoption and they want the baby back." This was within the first week. We were crushed. The attorney said we better get some other legal help with this matter. We wound up with five attorneys and over $65,000 in legal expenses.

There was no standardization for adoption in this country. The rules of adoption in Colorado were different than California, and this wasn't a California adoption. In California, unlike Colorado, the birth parents had a period of six months to change their minds. If they do, then an arbitrator was retained and a court decided what was best for the child.

The circumstances for the child within that family were terrible. Being on welfare doesn't make for an unloving household, but it went deeper than that. A nurse from the hospital called us and said, "I don't know if this will help you or not, but they did a sting operation here, and the father of that baby has been arrested on a drug charge." It became evident that this was an extortion attempt.

We did everything we legally could to keep the child. We had two attorneys in California, two in Colorado, and an arbitrator that represented the baby, not the family, the baby. We had to give Kirsten back after four and a half months. We didn't want the parents to come to our house. BJ offered her house and that's where it took place. They came to her house; we handed over the baby, and watched them drive away with her. Carmen and I were shattered. We got into our van and just drove, not knowing where we were going. We ended up in the Pacific Northwest, on Orcus Island.

Over the period that we had the baby, we were unable to get our story out to anybody. I knew Regis Philbin and thought he could be one to get in touch with *60 Minutes* or a talk show that would expose this whole mess. We lacked any real care from our initial attorney and became vulnerable to the archaic laws of Colorado. The laws are such that if the birth parents, or parent, want the baby back, in almost all cases, they will return the child. They could be murderers; it doesn't matter. Our case was never heard before a judge. We never had an opportunity to prove to anybody that ours was a far better situation for rearing that child.

Sometime later, we found out that the child was handed over to somebody in that family for dollars exchanged. The emotional devastation of our first experience lingered, but did not change our resolve to have a family. It continued to be a high priority for both of us and hoped that we could do better.

Mary Rocamora heard about our terrible difficulty with the adoption loss and called one day to express her concern for us, and how badly she felt. Later she called again, "Donn, I don't know quite how to handle this, I've never done anything like this before, but I have a client, a man who has worked in the film studios for years. He is divorced from his wife and has been living with a lady for several years. He has a daughter, who went to Europe this year, fell in love with a gentleman, and came back home pregnant. She absolutely does not want to terminate the pregnancy, even though her father wants her to. I don't know how to go about this. You'll have to walk me through it."

I said, "I can tell you what was asked of us. I can tell you about the letter that we wrote describing who we are and how we prepared ads to put in papers. I can send you that or whatever you want."

She said, "I think it might be a good idea if I send her a copy of your letter."

Mary presented the letter to this twenty-one year old girl. Soon, we heard, "She wants to meet you. She loves the letter and who you are."

I suggested we get together for dinner.

Alx was in her second month of pregnancy. There were coincidences that we learned in our first meeting. She came from a Jewish family and the biological father was from Donegal Ireland, where Carmen's family came from. She made it clear to us that she could not possibly handle the baby. She wanted to go to school, she had definite aspirations, and it was not the right time for her to raise a child. She knew beyond any doubt that she wanted to let the baby be adopted. We impressed upon her that evening at dinner that this was the beginning of her search for parents. We said, "This is a very important decision and we think you should look around. You should entertain some other couples."

She said "No, I don't want to. I've made up my mind."

We wanted her to sleep on it a while. She had made up her mind and we came to an agreement.

We went through the entire pregnancy with Alx. Carmen attended most all of her prenatal visits to the doctors. Of course, when you do this, you assume all financial responsibilities. That's what we had done with the first child. Carmen went to the meetings to learn how the birthing process would take place and what her role would be. She became referred to as "the coach."

It came time for the birth, and we drove to Long Beach Hospital. Carmen went to the delivery room with Alx. Alx's father, who had not been supportive, softened a bit and actually attended the birth with her mother. The father paid for Mary Rocamora to be there through the whole birthing process. Alx had said she also wanted me to be in the room when the baby was born, but changed her mind. I waited downstairs in the coffee shop. Mary came down about five minutes after the birth and said, "You're a daddy." The agreement was that the baby would stay with the mother for one day. Twenty-six hours later, we were home with Sara.

Alx asked us to give her monthly pictures of the child, and we did. As advised, in the beginning we never let her know where we lived. She did have our phone number, which she could have easily traced, but she never abused that privilege. She called twice in the first two weeks to find out how the baby was doing. She called maybe two more times in the first year. In the beginning, Alx would not acknowledge the name of the baby because, when born, the baby is given the birth mother's choice of names until the adoption becomes final. The adoption would become final in six months as long as there is no contesting voice. If something had come up, in California there would have been a trial where you present your case and the court would then decide which home would be best for the child. When the adoption was finalized, previous records were removed and a new birth certificate was drawn up with our choice of name. We asked BJ to be Sara's godmother and she gladly accepted.

In the beginning, Alx would occasionally write or send a little gift referring only to Sara as "the baby." The second year she presented us with a little four-legged stool with a big "S" painted on the seat. We continued to stay in touch with Alx and it has been a good relationship. Sara has known from an early age that she was adopted and knew what "birth mom" means. I know people who have tried to keep it a secret. It can be difficult for a child who may find out in their teens or in their young adult life. It can feel like abandonment and Sara was never abandoned. She has had many giving people in her life. We mailed Alx pictures once a year. We recognized Alx's birthday and sent her a gift, and she received our Holiday letters. She has written a few times with expressions of deep gratitude that she chose us.

Sara, Carmen, and I had settled into a wonderful routine in Woodland Hills, but life had other plans for us. On January 17, 1994, at 4:30 a.m., "the ground moveth." The Northridge earthquake struck. The official reports said it was 6.7 on the Richter scale, but other seismological studies from University of California suggest it was closer to 8.0. This felt like a disaster of Biblical proportions for everyone in the region. Our house and property sustained quite a bit of damage. Fortunately for us, it was mostly cosmetic. Even so, it amounted to several tens of thousands of dollars.

The Federal Emergency Management Agency provided meaningful assistance, but in the final analysis, the real estate lost hundreds of thousands in evaluation. For many reasons, it was time for us to make a change. Leaving California would be lengthy processes. Timing is everything, and I managed to time our move to coincide perfectly with a momentous occasion in the entertainment industry. I found myself scheduled to be in two places at the same time.

23

Mr. Burns

ANN-MARGRET COULD NEVER CALL him George. It was always, "Mr. Burns," not only on stage, but at home, as well. She had enormous respect for him and never passed up an opportunity to work with him. He was still performing from time to time, but in 1994, just two years shy of his 100th birthday, George had a bad fall in the shower. He was unable to perform after that, but in 1996 we wanted to put together a live show for him in Beverly Hills to celebrate his 100th birthday, and of course Ann-Margret was willing to do whatever was needed to help make it happen. Before we even started working on the production, I felt it was going to be one of those truly memorable experiences.

By the time we started planning this show, I had already come to the conclusion that it was time to make some personal changes. Carmen, Sara, and I were living in the house I had built with Mary Ann and had shared with BJ and Susan, and it was time to move on. The Northridge quake was just the catalyst for finally making a decision. Carmen and I decided that if we were going to move, we would go back East. Whenever I had a gig in New York or Boston that allowed some free time, I would rent a car and drive to the Connecticut shoreline. I always loved the area. Carmen and I now preferred a slower lifestyle than that of the Los Angeles suburbs, especially for us as a family. We were attracted to the idea of raising Sara in a smaller town with a good educational system.

This change in our lives was much more than just a move. My professional life was going to have to evolve into a different routine. I had no idea what I was going to do, or how it would work out with touring and gigs, but I knew we needed to be back in Connecticut. I knew I wanted to travel less and be home more. Life on the road was strenuous and not conducive to family life. It was time for me to prioritize, and now the most important thing in my life was my family. I waited all my life to have a child and wanted the simple joy of seeing her get on the school bus, and being there when she came home. I was ready to start making the shift, but it wasn't going to change overnight. I had commitments and wasn't ready to drop everything at once. I really enjoyed the performers I was working with.

We had not yet sold the Woodland Hills house, when we made final preparations, confirming flights and moving trucks. Then I discovered the George Burns celebration had been scheduled to coincide perfectly with the dates we planned to move.

My friend, Felicitas, came all the way from Munich to help Carmen pack up the house. She drove with me across the country, which took us just four days.

Twelve hours later I was on a flight from Hartford back to Los Angeles for the George Burns birthday party. I didn't want Carmen and Sara to have to deal with the logistics of multiple flights, especially with our family pets, so Carmen, Sara, Hershey, the dog, and Abba, the cat, flew from Los Angeles to Boston on a nonstop flight. My friend and fellow musician, Paul Broadnax, met them at the airport and drove them to our new house. On the flight, I was looking forward to the show, but feeling guilty for leaving my family and friends with the work of settling us into our new home. Our new family-oriented life was going to take some time to coordinate.

We spent a lot of time choosing the music for the show. There was a special lyric written by Sammy Kahn some years ago and Roger Smith got hold of it for Ann-Margret. We adapted it so she could sing it to George Burns. It was necessary for her to say his first name in part of the lyric. I remember rehearsing this with her in her living room. I was sitting at the piano working with her and she said, "Roger, I can't sing this lyric. I can't sing 'George.'" I adjusted the music to allow room for her to say 'Mr. Burns,' because she just couldn't do it otherwise, not even in the privacy of her own living room. She felt so respectful of "Mr. Burns" because he had discovered her. Unfortunately, he wasn't able to be at the show because he wasn't feeling well. So they videotaped the whole performance and then took it over to his house.

24 Get Off My Rug

TOM AND DICK SMOTHERS are wonderful friends. Tom used to come over to my Woodland Hills home quite frequently. I remember riding on an airplane with him just before I got married to Carmen. Tommy asked about my wife to be, "How old is she?"

I said, "She's a lot younger that I am."

He said, "Tell me about that. I'm about ready to marry a girl that's about twenty-five years younger than I am."

I said, "That's the case with me."

Maybe we both needed some self-assurance.

I think Dick was a real daredevil. He was involved in some risky ventures, such as scuba diving and acrobatic flying. I had been continuing my flying lessons, and I was looking to get a little time in an aerobatic plane. I wanted to learn something about spins and inversion that aren't necessarily required. I went to a field outside of Reno, where they had the air races every year. At the time, I was converting from a low wing airplane, which was a Piper Warrior, to a high wing Cessna 172, and that's where I transitioned. There was a Citabria parked inside the hangar. That was an aerobatic airplane designed for inverted flight that could be flown upside down and the carburetors won't malfunction.

I asked my instructor about it and he said, "Oh yeah, that's Dick Smothers' plane. Would you like to do a little training?"

I said, "Absolutely."

211

So, we used his plane because they had a lease-back arrangement. Any time that was charged for use of that airplane went back to Dick. I did two twenty-minute periods of aerobatics, executing loops and rolls.

Years earlier, as with everyone, I was thrilled by the moon landing. Astronauts had become American heroes, and I found the technological developments very exciting. All of this took on a little different significance, when I did some recording with a comedic character that appeared regularly on *The Steve Allen Show*. Bill Dana's real name was William Szathmary, and he wrote comedy for the show. His brother, Irving, was a film score composer, who wrote for the *Get Smart* series starring Don Adams. Bill Dana was known by, "Hello, my name is José Jiménez." He would speak with a broken Spanish accent. It was funny because his delivery was dramatically straight, but filled with gags. I did a couple of albums with him where we supplied a quartet. One was called, *José Jimenez the Astronaut*, where he did a routine about being an astronaut. Through this character he created, Bill became friends with a few famous astronauts, like Buzz Aldrin, who came in to do the live album with him.

For a short while, we had a director with *The Steve Allen Show*, who was a wonderful gentleman and comic, but not such a great director. Allan Sherman became quite well-known for his song parodies, such as "Hello Muddah, Hello Faddah (A Letter from Camp)."

Allan was a jolly gentleman, who was always fun to be around. He was well-off financially from devising and maintaining some kind of contractual arrangement with a TV game show that he produced called, *I've Got a Secret*. He died early from chronic conditions related to obesity and over indulgences.

Allan called and asked me if I would do a show with him at the Hotel del Coronado. It's a famous old hotel, old for California, on a small island across the bay from San Diego. Marilyn Monroe and Jack Lemmon shot *Some Like it Hot* there. Many classic movies were filmed at the Coronado. I knew that Allan did a couple of his parodies, and that was fine, but I didn't know what else. We rode down to San Diego on an airplane, which is about a twenty-minute trip from Los Angeles.

I kept asking, "Don't you want to talk about your show a little bit?"

He just replied, "No, we'll get to it later."

We got down there and it came time to rehearse. They had sent a small band of elderly musicians. I saw some instruments I'd never seen before. The bass drum, instead of it being normally on its side, was set up like a floor tom with the foot pedal hitting the bottom head of the drum.

The hi-hat was almost down on the floor. I thought, How can he play a normal hi-hat ride? I was set up as usual, on the left-hand side if you're looking at the stage, which is actually stage-right. As always, I sat facing the orchestra, profiling the audience, so that I could see the musicians. For a reading light at the piano, they had and old gooseneck desk lamp. The base of it was on the piano next to the music holder. There were three trumpets and four saxophones.

We started rehearsing, and when I looked over to the band, I saw one of the trumpet players playing a relatively high note with such incredible force that his face was changing into a red tomato. This person looked like he was going to need an ambulance call any minute. I stopped the band and said, "There's no need for that. We're not out front. This is a comedy show we're accompanying so just lay back. If you want, play it an octave lower. It doesn't even matter. Just don't play so loudly."

We got through the rehearsal okay, and Allan and I went out for something to eat. I said, "Let's discuss how you are going to do this. How much and how quickly do you want me to segue from one number to another? I'm good at analyzing audience applause. When I hear the applause reaching its peak and starting to decline, I'll begin the next number. Unless you tell me that you're going to speak at that point. I don't let any stage delay happen. I can't stand that. It feels wrong and it's unprofessional."

He said, "Great, that's fine. I'll talk after the second or third number."

Well, we started the show that night, and Allan did what he felt he needed to do with regard to speaking to the audience. I glanced over at the end of the second number to see if he wanted to talk. I didn't read it that way, so I started the band. As soon as I did, I realized I had made a mistake and tried to stop the music. This was a task that I thought would be easy enough, but became totally impossible. I conducted a cut off. I waved at them. Then I whistled like I was hailing a taxi. Nothing worked. They were into that music, playing as loudly as they could. I finally picked up that gooseneck lamp and I waved my arms like an old train conductor. Allan saw this and started laughing so hard he couldn't stop.

Most comics don't have much music in their shows, unless they are comics that sing. I've worked with professional impressionists, who are also comics. A great impressionist has a unique parallel to a musician with exceptionally good ears because they duplicate the sound of the people they are imitating. It is their phenomenal aural proficiency that gives them that ability. They also practice expressions a lot in front of a mirror. Some impressionists, because the aural definition of their impression is so accurate, can do something subtle with their face and take on the whole persona of the person they're impersonating. When accompanying them, we play cues, but they may also sing a part of a song and this requires them to have good musical accompaniment.

A couple of them that I worked with are Bob Anderson, Scott Record, and Fred Travalena. Bob does a great Tony Bennett. He talks and sings like Tony and he does Tony's twirl.

Bob really gets into the character. When he does Sammy Davis Jr., he gets one of his eyes crossed and his jaw stuck out to one side and looks just like Sammy.

Scott does one of the cleverest pieces I've ever heard. He talks about earlier days when juke boxes were important. He'd say to his audience, "I don't know if you know this but, in the last ten years the most often played piece of music ever on a juke box is "New York, New York," sung by Frank Sinatra.

Very often, when you go into a place, the juke box will be in terrible shape and the records are completely worn out. I would like to do an imitation of Frank Sinatra singing "New York, New York" as heard on a juke box." To represent the skips in the record, the arrangement is written metrically incorrect. It has a bar of three, a bar of two, a bar of five followed by a stop and so on. It is just a masterful piece and really funny. It's hard to play because your natural metric sense tells you that there's got to be another beat in that bar, but there isn't. Scott had a lot of fun music to play, as did Bob. They worked a great deal in Las Vegas. Fred Travalena was our opening act with the Shirley MacLaine show.

For the past few years, I've been playing with a comedy ensemble called Yarmy's Army. The group is named in tribute to Dick Yarmy, a talented actor and director, who was the brother of Don Adams. Among others, its membership includes Shelly Berman, Jack Riley, Ronnie Schell, and Peter Marshall.

Shelly Berman is a legendary improvisational comic. Jack Riley, known to many as Mr. Carlin on The *Bob Newhart Show*, is a dear friend and graciously puts me up whenever I am in California. He's a shy, humble, giving and thoughtful man, who is very retiring, much like the character he plays. Jack is un-showbiz that way. Ronnie Schell, starred in *Gomer Pyle, U.S.M.C.* and served as Honorary Mayor of Encino California. The five of us did a show for the Iowa Special Olympics called *Comedy Iowa*. Ronnie had done a lot of work with the Special Olympics and he put the whole thing together.

Peter Marshall is a dear friend, whom I have worked with many times over the years. Most people know Peter as the host of the television game show, *The Hollywood Squares*, and don't realize that he is a wonderful singer and knows hundreds of tunes. He has many television and movie credits and starred in such musicals as *La Cage Aux Folles*. I first became associated with him through Alan Copeland, who wrote the material for Dick Haymes. Peter Marshall's older sister was Joanne Dru, a well-known movie actress, and one of Dick Haymes' wives.

Peter was close to the Haymes family so he also knew Dick's bother, Bob Haymes. Bob was a wonderful singer and pianist, and an important song writer. He wrote "That's All" and many other great tunes. Bob stayed at my house in California for a couple of weeks, while we spent several hours recording his songs in my studio. Peter Marshall had an association with all of these people because it was part of his extended family.

Peter is one of the most confident men you could ever be around. He speaks with great gusto and there's no pause in his conversation. He is straight ahead and has hundreds of stories and everybody likes to hear them. He makes me look like a junior member of the experience society. He might start telling a story about years ago where Sammy Davis Jr. opened for him in Las Vegas, when he was part of a comedy singing act called Noonan and Marshall, and just keep going. It's not as egocentric as it might sound, it's just that one thing relates to another when he starts to tell these stories. He might mention somebody's name and we would tease him by saying, "Yeah, didn't they open for you somewhere?"

To begin the *Comedy Iowa* tour, I flew to Los Angeles and stayed overnight with Jack Riley. The next day, we went out to Van Nuys airport, which is a big general aviation field. It used to be the busiest airfield in the world with the number of take-offs and landings per hour, per every day, per every week. I used to fly out of there all the time when I parked my airplane there. The Pioneer Hi-Bred International seed company, from Iowa, sent their corporate jet to pick us up. My heart just went nuts when I walked into this airplane. I got to sit up front right behind the co-pilot in the jump seat. It was fascinating for me to realize how far the electronics and avionics had come. The airplane is configured to seat ten people comfortably, so with five people it was not loaded. We took off with great gusto and a steep angle of ascent.

We opened in Des Moines. To start the show, they had me go out and play a number, which I felt uncomfortable about because Jack Riley loves to play piano and is my only piano student. Jack plays a solo piano number when he begins his act, then he accompanies himself on some of these funny little comedic songs that he sings. When he finishes he says, "See what $12,000 can do? Donn Trenner is my teacher. We work together in California and recently Donn told me that if I keep practicing diligently for another four or five years, I will probably be able to get a gig playing at Wal-Mart."

I played each of the acts on and off. I accompanied Peter on the tunes that he sang. Also, I would play a lot of little comedy punctuations, as I had done with Steve Allen, with whatever comes out of my brain at the moment. I have no fixed piece of music and I have no idea what the show is going to bring, because comics can opportunistically turn left or right reacting to something that happens. That's what a good comic will do. They can respond to a fixture falling out of the ceiling or some woman getting up to go to the bathroom. They might make a spectacle of her, which isn't always nice, but that's what can happen.

Shelly Berman closed the first half of the show doing several of his comedic bits that he became so famous for. I didn't accompany Shelly. I played him on and got off the stage. When he is getting to the end of his segment, I would come back on stage to play him off and close that portion of the performance.

After the intermission, we come back on, and there are director's chairs set up with each comic's name on them, and they sit in a semi-circle. Then, they start egging each other on to tell different jokes: A woman goes to the dentist and asks, "Doctor how much is a root canal." The doctor says, "Well, we have two methods. One is a brand new procedure that we do with lasers. You're in the chair for about two hours and there is no pain, there's no blood and there's no discomfort." She's says, "Good, how much is that?" "That's $1,800." She says, "$1,800? Forget it!" He says, "Well, we have the normal way, where you're in the chair for about four hours. We drill the tooth out. It's a little bit messy and you're not very comfortable." "How much is that?" "That's $1,200." She says, "Forget it!" He says, "Wait! I've got an older gentleman that works for me now. He's from Cuba and he's got his own drill. You're in the chair about twelve hours and it's quite messy with a lot of pain and discomfort. The cost is about a $147." She says, "Very good, book my husband for next Wednesday." It becomes sort of like a comedic jam session and the jokes that come out are just incredible.

One night, we got into Henny Youngman jokes: This guy goes to the doctor and says. "Doctor, doctor I'm peeing constantly what should I do?" The doctor says, "First of all, get off of my rug." Another guy goes to the doctor and says, "Doctor, I just can't urinate, I don't know what to do." The doctor asks, "So, how old are you?" "I'm 92." The doctor says, "You've peed enough." They just go on, one after another, with all these old one-liners. It was so funny to see all of these people in the audience borrowing each other's handkerchiefs because they were laughing hard.

It is a great joy to be on stage with a great comic or a spectacular show and feel the value of the entertainment that is emanating from the stage. It reaches the people and brings them to a place where there are not any problems in their life. It provides a moment of joy. I used to go through that with Bob Hope. I used to think what an awesome thing this man is able to do with forty-thousand GI's sitting in the snow in Korea. He is making them laugh constantly, just one joke or one kinetic after another. There's a great value in entertaining

We did five shows in five consecutive days. Each day we did a sound check at 5:00 and the show would start at 7:30. I was involved in the sound check because I had some knowledge in that area. A couple of the places were inadequately supplied. I mean, they just didn't have what was necessary. They didn't know what stage monitors even meant. These performers need to have monitors because they have to be able to feel the presence of what they are saying. If you work a big auditorium, and the sound is only out in the house, with no immediate sound on stage, everything sounds like an undecipherable echo. So, we had to rectify some of those situations.

Ten o'clock at night is not my favorite time to eat, but the guys didn't want to eat before the show, so they would take us out to dinner afterward. They wanted to treat us really well, so they'd go to the best restaurant they could find that was open at that hour, and often a restaurant stayed open for us because they knew there would be some celebrities there. With the five of us, plus several people accompanying us from the Special Olympics, there were a dozen or so seated at one table. We were served many hors d'oeuvres followed by our dinners. They treated us well, but it's difficult for me to eat at that hour, especially having to get up the next morning to drive three or four hours to the next city, with a stop for lunch.

These comics are pretty much always on, so lunch and dinner provides them with another opportunity, some more than others. Jack Riley tends to be the quieter member of the group, yet when approached he can do some dynamic things. Peter Marshall, with his deep confident voice, is always out there with a story that everybody loves. Shelly Berman, of course, can go into a ten minute bit about the food that he is getting.

Comics are continually set up to perform. For lack of a better term, the opportunistic ones can take any moment and make it work for them by coloring it, usually negatively. They will take some wonderful experience, and make it look like a terrible happening, like talking about airline food, which so many comics do. I'm a little over the top about flying, but I still marvel that you can sit in this machine and go from one side of the country to the other in five hours, and have food and drink. So what are you complaining about?

We came to the end of our tour and, on that fifth night, the Pioneer Hi-Bred International held a little reception for us before the show. Now, all of us were kind of displeased because it appeared we were going home commercially. The last date was in Davenport and we would have to drive to Des Moines to catch a flight. We'd be going from there to Denver, and from Denver to Los Angeles. Everybody was throwing punches trying to get the corporate jet. I met the head of the company at the reception and said, "We really love that airplane and we really feel badly that it's not taking us back home, but we certainly understand."

Ronnie Schell got on the show that night and said, "We just want to take this moment to thank the Pioneer Hi-Bred International for how wonderfully they have taken care of us and for that wonderful airplane that they sent. We just loved it so much. We'll be talking about it all the way home, on the Greyhound bus."

Well, we didn't have to drive back to Des Moines, because their jet came to Davenport to pick us up. We rapidly flew back to Van Nuys.

After landing back in Los Angeles, I extended my trip a little bit. I spent Sunday and Monday writing music with Gordon Hunt, who I had started a project with, and visited with BJ. Then, I went to Bob Cox for my haircut and continued down to San Diego to see my friend from the service, Leo Adelman.

25

Life Is Beautiful

I FIRST MET CHIC CICCHETTI when I was working on an album for Paul Broadnax. A friend, who had been in my band during high school, was playing in Chic's orchestra, so I went to the 880 Club in Hartford to hear them. I knew how talented my friend was, but I frankly I didn't go that night with high expectations. However, I was blown away. There are many "rehearsal bands" that exist in major cities, but this one is different because of the value and expertise in Chic's writing, the cohesive attitude of the players, and the deep commitment to playing well. The Hartford Jazz Orchestra has been in existence for more than fifty years now.

Chic was an extraordinary arranger. He knew what a jazz orchestra should sound like. The standard contemporary big band instrumentation consisted of eight brass players, with four trumpets doubling on flugelhorn, and four trombones. There were five saxophones, with two altos, two tenors, and baritone, all doubling on soprano sax, clarinet, flute, piccolo, and bass clarinet. The use of lighter woodwinds offers a much more delicate and significantly warmer sound than if they were just playing saxophones all the time. Add to that, a three-piece rhythm section with piano, bass, and drums. Chic's band was designed to produce the broad spectrum of colors and textures that he created in his orchestrations.

For years the band featured a wonderful singer named Bobbi Rogers, and much of Chic's finest writing is found in his vocal arrangements for her. Many skilled big band arrangers don't write well for singers. The backgrounds are often too busy, along with too much full ensemble writing that can be a deterrent to the vocal interpretation of the singer. Chic understood the nuances in the balance between voice and instruments.

An experienced arranger includes detailed dynamic and articulation notation in their arrangements. Dynamic markings indicate to play with force or without force and to expand or decrease over the length of a particular phrase. Articulation markings indicate how a particular note or phrase is to be punctuated. Chic took great care to incorporate both elements in his notation.

Playing Chic's arrangements requires exceptional musicianship. It's not enough to be a good technician. It's the difference between just playing the notes and really playing the music. First-rate musicians make notation sound musical. One might think that all of this information, if performed as written, leaves less room for input from the player, but that's not the case. There's plenty of room for interpreting the music. Also, detailed arrangements don't preclude improvisation. There are always choruses written in for a specific player to improvise.

A soli is a passage written to feature a section generally of the same instruments within the ensemble. The lead player is influenced by the dynamics and articulations found in the music and the section players need to blend in and honor that interpretation. In full ensemble passages, the interpretation comes mainly from the lead trumpet player. That's a critical chair in the orchestra. Of all the instruments, it's absolutely necessary for the lead trumpet player to play every day because of the physical musculature required. Daily exercise of the embouchure is essential for staying in shape. It is a workhorse position and requires stamina. I've had the privilege of playing with brilliant trumpet players over the years, but the collective reputation of the "lead trumpet" player is, shall we say, deserved. Generally it's an attitude issue, but that can be exactly what is needed to get the job done. Before I get myself in any further trouble, we'll leave it at that.

When Chic Cicchetti called me, he wanted to make a change in the piano position, but he was morally obligated to a gentleman of failing health. Later on, Chic called me again and said, "Now's the time." I joined the band in 2000. With every Monday night engagement, I became increasingly aware of the depth of Chic's writing. Chic spoke with some of his band members a couple of days before he passed away and asked that I take over as musical director. A few short months after I started, I was playing piano and conducting. Some would say it's not like playing in Las Vegas. My response is, "Thank goodness for that."

I used to fly my airplane over Las Vegas, and over the years you could see the breadth of the expansion stretching in every direction. They brought so much water into Las Vegas, to create enormous waterfalls and care for landscaping and golf courses, that it has affected the weather conditions. Although I had some great performing experiences there, I never liked the place and wouldn't trade my current circumstances for anything.

Business in Las Vegas has changed dramatically. The enormity of some of the establishments is hard to believe. Entertainment has changed dramatically, as well. The difference, from then and now, is there are hardly any hotels doing shows with live orchestras. Occasionally, an artist like Tony Bennett may require an orchestra, but they also book many people like Willie Nelson, who come in self-contained. Hotels like Caesar's Palace no longer run weekly shows because they don't want to deal with an artist who comes in needing ten hotel rooms for their band. It's not so much the expense, as much as they don't want to give up rooms that gamblers would take. The scene is now made up mostly of a few lounges that book small groups or acts for a weekend. There are numerous small acts, that in order to maintain their star-power, come into these places because it is important to say they played Las Vegas. The representative agency, or agent of a particular artist, pitch to the entertainment departments. The entertainment directors look at the package to determine how much it would cost, how much money can be made considering what will be brought to the hotel, and what the hotel has to provide for how long.

It is tragic to see what has happened to music in general. The so-called economic advantage of synthesizers has had a frightening impact on the industry. Orchestras do not exist anymore because of pre-recorded shows and the synthesizing of whole productions. Some may think my critique ironic, but the pre-records I engineered never replaced the employment of musicians. With the possible exception of the theaters in large cities, especially New York, there is no longer any place for a working musician to go and expect to make a weekly wage, that's good enough for a lifestyle that hopes to support a family. Innumerable accomplished musicians have been put out of work. One laptop is used to replace an entire orchestra. Where is the human expressiveness?

A couple of years ago, I was asked if I would be interested in doing a theater piece in Chicago. It was staged in the Athenaeum Theater. The play was called *Lady Day at Emerson's Bar and Grill*. The show called for only two people to be seen on stage. I would be playing for Ertha Kitt and have a few acting lines. I took my family to Chicago. Carmen did wardrobe and we had a baby-sitter, who began teaching Sara Ebonics.

We did talk about doing the show to include bass and drums. I started rehearsing with a trio until realizing it would absolutely not work. Ertha did not have a metric problem really, but her mind changed so rapidly that she jumped around a lot. Without the visible ability to cue the musicians, it would be impossible for me with a trio. I could handle it better by myself.

The show was a musical drama that ran about an hour and twenty minutes with no intermission. All the songs were Billie Holiday tunes. Ertha Kitt was certainly not the best person to imitate Billie Holiday's sound, but it was kind of ethereal. She was not supposed to actually play Billie Holiday. It was a reflection on the life of the legendary singer and required Ertha to physically decline over the course of time we were on stage. I actually had to help her off stage sometimes. There is one number she sang with a little dog, which was part of Billie Holiday's life. At that point in the show, she was to be totally deteriorated. She got to the end of the song, and the little dog was up on her knee howling with its head pulled back and pointing upward. Well, that was an audience catcher and the dog never failed, every show, a howl right on cue. The show made me reflect back to the time I saw Billie Holiday in New York. We were picked up for two additional weeks and were there for seven altogether.

For several years, The Donn Trenner Orchestra did the music for the Directors Guild of America annual awards dinner. The gala event is done at one of the major hotels, like the Beverly Hilton. It usually takes place about two weeks before the Academy Awards, and is a telltale. Director Howard Storm was involved in this event every year and is the one that originally sold them on the idea of using me with an orchestra. They started talking about not using the live orchestra because they were thinking about going to some kind of digital performance, using a couple of synthesizers, which really upset me. Howard, who was on the entertainment committee, was strongly opposed. He said, "We are not supposed to represent the elimination of talent by substituting electronics."

The Director's Guild chooses performances from the previous year's television shows and motion pictures that represent outstanding achievement. The nominees are voted on by the Director's Guild members and final winners are elected. It is not the best actor or actress, it always pertains to best director or producer and others involved with production. Of course, there is a celebrity Master of Ceremonies and celebrity presenters, such as actor Helen Hunt, Gordon Hunt's daughter, who was also a recipient.

My contractor was John Setar, who had been with me for all these years. While we stayed in constant communication, he did most of the

With Ertha Kitt in Chicago 1996.

preparatory work, researching and accessing the music needed and communicating with the various committees. I would go out to Los Angeles a week in advance and spend a lot of time with John at his house. When the cues were done we got somebody to copy the parts, or sometimes we had to do the copying ourselves because of the budget. We had a full brass section, reeds with woodwind doubles, piano, bass and drums. The budget did not provide for a string section or percussionist. The musicians were paid a good studio rate, but the powers that be, were always looking for ways to save money and threatened for years to eliminate the orchestra by using some kind of digital performance.

The preliminary work is difficult for awards shows because we're given the five or six contenders for each category, and we have to dig up their music, if possible, from each of these properties and get it written so that it can be played by the orchestra. I write maybe an eight measure cue that can be repeated with some kind of a tag or button on the end, so that whomever you play on, you can play off and button it up for a clean ending, which is the way I prefer to do it. I don't like a staggering trail off. I want it to be buttoned up properly. A good orchestra always sounds great when it's clean and glistening.

For productions like this, there may be sixty cues that we have to write and we end up playing a fraction of them. The cues are numbered and, at the last possible second, we have to get our fingers together to signal the orchestra. A couple of times, I've said number three and stuck up two fingers. Then I've got to get my hands up and give a downbeat, and all of a sudden re-associate myself with the music I have in front of me. Every awards show is like that, live, with five times the music as you'll ever need to play.

I don't think a lot of people realize how secretive the awards process is. It would be much easier on the musical director to have any kind of clue as to who the winner will be. It would make it smoother, and remove the hysteria that exists at the moment of the announcement, but there is no other way to do it. The names of the award recipients are contained in sealed envelopes.

It is always tricky when you're doing the show because they don't necessarily mention the name of the film or the television show, but usually a specific episode. For example, *Mad About You* was a weekly sitcom starring Helen Hunt and Paul Reiser, who also did some writing and directing. Each week, the show had a specific title that depicts the theme of that show. So there are several nominees representing particular episodes in several categories, Best Comedy Show, Best Dramatic Show, Best Musical, Best whatever. The winner is announced by name and episode title, often without the name of the show right away, making it very difficult to immediately cue up the appropriate theme music. A timpani roll takes care of it for me. It gives me a moment to determine the correct cue for the orchestra. I'm always glancing over to my drummer to be ready. We did not have percussionist so we had to use a fast mallet roll on the floor tom for my timpani until I get my brain in gear.

Roberto Begnini was nominated for the film, *Life Is Beautiful.* He is such a clown that he is five degrees away from being obnoxious. He's got blazing energy and his wonderful accent takes him through everything. He wants to be funny, but sometimes he's funny not even meaning to be. It's not an abusive use of the language, but it's kind of like Norm Crosby's malapropisms. He just confuses words choices once in a while.

Begnini that night was something. When he was announced for winning an award for Outstanding Directorial Achievement, we played the music from *Life is Beautiful* to bring him up. It was a fairly lively theme, the way we reproduced it, and he came dancing onto the stage. He passed by me smiling and was all arms and legs. His body language reminded me of Pee Wee Herman, he was so loose, like he had a rubber body. After the presentation, we played the music again to take him off stage. As he passed by the orchestra, he caught my eye, grabbed me, and we danced circles as he exited the stage.

Postlude

CARMEN AND I DIDN'T LAST as a married couple. We did manage to stay close friends and raise Sara together. Sara lived with me throughout her childhood, but her mom was nearby and we saw each other regularly. For a while, I took a job at a local school as an accompanist so I could work close to home and my schedule fit Sara's. Carmen's job, at the nearby casino, also accommodated Sara's life. I took tour engagements that fit into school vacation times so we could travel together.

Sara came home from school one day proclaiming she wanted to play in the school band. As much as Carmen and I both love music, we didn't have any specific expectations for Sara as a performer or musician. If so, I wanted her to learn to play a non-transposing, concert-pitch instrument, and she chose the trombone. (When you see an A-flat, you play an A-flat; unlike a trumpet or clarinet, when a notated B-flat really sounds an A-flat in concert pitch.) Also, with no valves or manual keys, the slide trombone can quickly develop the ear for note accuracy. As it turns out, Sara made a great choice and became a contributing member to her high school ensembles. Much to my delight, Sara also developed and interest in singing and became a music major while attending college. Now nearing graduation, she has become a fine vocalist and instrumentalist. It has been more than ten years since she started pursuing music, and time has flown by.

I'm still busy performing, recording, and traveling. The opportunity to play in a variety of settings is a great joy. In addition, I have been a music contractor for the Mohegan Sun, one of the larger entertainment venues for high profile artists in the Northeast. It's become a family business in a way; I supply the orchestra for the headliners, Carmen does the wardrobe, and now Sara has joined us as an audio intern during the summer and college breaks.

Working with touring artists has been a perfect fit for me. From time to time, I've conducted orchestras, played piano, or coordinated undertakings as needed. There's a terrific collection of musicians in Connecticut and I've been fortunate to connect with them. Working with Mohegan Sun allows me to bring them together and offer more opportunities to perform professionally.

I play with the Hartford Jazz Orchestra most Monday nights, and have regular local gigs at a wonderful restaurant in my adopted hometown of Guilford. Interestingly for me, I'm now receiving calls for interviews and speaking engagements. I am humbled by the attention and support of so many who have become dear acquaintances. I still frequently fly to California to make music and socialize with friends, and, as always, to get my haircut.

A Postlude may provide music for bows at the end of a show, but I prefer to think of it as a bridge in a 32-measure AABA song form. The band plays on.

At the Guilford Library in 2014.

Acknowledgements

THIS BOOK WOULDN'T HAVE HAPPENED if it were not for the extraordinary amount of time, patience, encouragement, and sheer determination of Tim Atherton. Tim teaches at Dartmouth College and Westfield State University and is an outstanding trombonist I first met nearly twenty years ago while contracting orchestras for large productions at Mohegan Sun Casino. During suppers between rehearsal and performance, I learned he was also a jazz ensemble director and lectured in the history of jazz. Soon, Tim sent me a letter proposing what would be my autobiography. I'm glad I took him up on it! From that point, Tim spent countless hours interviewing me and surveying my archives. Through continued research, he cohesively organized the events of my life and my thoughts and wrote my story.

I'm also eternally grateful to his wife, Karen, who lent me Tim for all those hours and then transcribed the tape recorded interviews. An active musician, Karen is busy as an educator and trumpet player, and has been remarkably supportive and patient.

Endless thanks to Marian Breeze who, with the support of Tim, guided me through an editorial pass of an early draft. This was a critical point for me.

Elizabeth Coburn has compiled and contributed perhaps the most substantiating document of my musical existence—a discography. To the founder of my fan club, Liz, thank you for your continuing support and generosity.

Dr. Joseph Cardinale has been an extraordinary friend, neighbor, and quite literally a life-saver. Words can't express my and my family's gratitude for Joe's support, caring, and kindness.

I'm blessed to still be working, and to enjoy the company of so many talented and wonderful people. For these past years, I've been a member of the Hartford Jazz Orchestra. They inspire me (and they've been after me to finish this book) so I'd like to acknowledge my fellow musicians: Dick Prestage, Jack Nedorostek , David Stangerone, Patrick Lennon and Donald West on trumpets, Ben Griffin, Dan Hendrix, Fred Bagnall, and Dan Innaimo on trombones, Sebastian Giacco, Bob DePalma, James Antonucci, Erik Elligers, Lisa LaDone and Zeke Vasquez on saxophones and woodwinds, Jeff Thompson on drums, and Lou Bocciarelli and Michael Asetta on bass.

Here's to the other two-thirds of my faithful trio: David Daddario on bass and Tom Devino on drums.

Recently, I've been accompanying and recording with some fabulous singers, including Nicole Pasternak, Shaynee Rainbolt, Sylvia Mims and my dearest friend, B. J. Ward. It's been a privilege to share the stage with each of these talented performers, and I look forward to continued collaborations.

I'm grateful to the many other groups I've been working with, as well, including Dr. Joe and Friends: Joe Cardinale, Dave Daddario, Kenny Palmieri, and the other musicians who join us from time to time.

To Corky Hale, a longtime friend and talented vocalist, musician and producer I was lucky enough to perform with. We have joked for years that I would include her in my memoir. Well, here she is!

To all the others who I failed to mention in this book or in these acknowledgements, please know that it's my failing alone, and that your presence in my life is no less meaningful.

A List of Recordings

1952	*On the Coast.* Charlie Parker, Chet Baker, Sonny Criss; Jazz Showcase
1953	*L.A. Get Together.* Stan Getz, Chet Baker; Fresh Sound
1954	*Rodgers and Hart.* Dave Pell; Fresh Sound
1955	*Jazz and Romantic Places.* Dave Pell; Atlantic
1955	*Les Brown All-Stars.* Les Brown; Capitol
1955	*Down In the Depths On the 90th Floor.* Helen Carr; Bethlehem
1956	*Take the "A" Train/ September in the Rain.* Bette Roché; Bethlehem
1956	*In a Mellow Tone/ Time After Time.* Bette Roché; Bethlehem
1956	*Summertime/I Just Got the Message, Baby.* Bette Roché; Bethlehem
1956	*Life is Just a Bowl of Cherries.* Howard McGhee; Bethlehem
1956	*Relaxin' With Frances Faye.* Frances Faye; Bethlehem

1956	*The Sound.* (box set) Stan Getz; Royal Boost
1956	*Take the "A" Train.* Betty Roché; Bethlehem
1957	*I Had the Craziest Dream.* Dave Pell; Capitol
1957	*Swing Song Book.* Les Brown; Coral
1958	*Concert Modern.* Les Brown; Capitol
1958	*Plays Hi-Fi Music for Influentials.* Steve Allen; Coral
1959	*Voodoo!* Robert Drasnin; Tops
1959	*Live at Ellitch Gardens.* Les Brown; Status
1959	*The Les Brown Story.* Les Brown; Capitol
1959	*Jazz Song Book.* Les Brown; Coral
1959	*Dave Pell Plays Harry James.* Dave Pell; P.R.I
1960	*Impact! Band Meets Band.* Les Brown, Vic Schoen; Kapp (reissue of *Stereophonic Suites for Two Bands* 1957)
1960	*Swingin' On the Moon.* Mel Torme; Verve
1960	*Steve Allen Presents Terry Gibbs.* Terry Gibbs; Signature
1960	*The Swingin' Sound.* (Songs by Steve Allen) Les Brown; Signature
1960	*My Name...José Jiménez.* Bill Dana; Signature
1960	*José Jiménez; The Astronaut.* Bill Dana; Kapp
1960	*A Tribute to Harry James.* Big Band All- Stars; Radio Recorders
1961	*The Warm Moods.* Ben Webster; Reprise
1961	*I Had the Craziest Dream.* Manny Albam; RCA Victor
1961	*Double Exposure.* Les Brown, Vic Schoen; Kapp
1962	*Comin' Home Baby.* Mel Torme; Atlantic
1963	*Gravy Waltz/Preacherman.* Steve Allen with Donn Trenner and His Orchestra; Dot

1963	*Three Guitars in Bossa Nova Time.* Herb Ellis; Wounded Bird
1963	*Love.* Rosemary Clooney; Reprise
1963	*The Andrew Sisters Presents.* Donn Trenner and His Orchestra; Dot
1963	*Hollywood: My Way.* Nancy Wilson; Capitol
1963	*Jose Jiménez Jollywood.* Jose Jiménez; Kapp
1964	*Songs from the Steve Allen Show.* Steve Allen; Dot
1964	*Jennie.* Jennie Smith; LP Time
1965	*A Swingin' Touch.* Frankie Randall; RCA
1966	*I Remember You.* Frankie Randal; RCA
1967	*Lush Life.* Nancy Wilson; Capitol
1968	*Welcome to My Love.* Nancy Wilson; Capitol
1968	*Sound of Nancy Wilson.* Nancy Wilson; Capitol
1972	*Live! at the Cocoanut Grove.* Dick Haymes; Daybreak
1972	*Texas Waltz/Leave It to Me.* Herb Ellis and Donn Trenner; Epic
1973	*Live at Ellitch Gardens.* (Denver, 1959 –Part Two) Maynard Ferguson; Status
1973	*Anita O'Day Sings Bob Friedman.* Anita O'Day; Private/Unissued
1974	*Vocal Ease.* B. J. Ward; Catfish
1976	*Shirley MacLaine Live at the Palace.* Original cast; Columbia
1992	*Inglewood Jam: Live at the Tradewinds.* (Reissue 1952 recording) Charlie Parker; Fresh Sound
1993	*Luck Be a Lady.* Mel Torme; Delta
1993	*'Round Midnight.* Mel Torme; Verve
1994	*It's About Time.* Paul Broadnax; Brownstone

1995	*The Complete Bethlehem Collection.* Helen Carr; Bethlehem
1995	*Lullaby In Rhythm.* Les Brown and his Band of Renown (1954-1955); Drive Archives
1996	*Shaken Not Stirred.* Various Artists; Rykodisc
1996	*Plays Hi-Fi Music for Influentials.* (reissue of 1958 recording) Steve Allen; Varese Vintage
1996	*Here's to Joe.* Paul Broadnax; Brownstone
1996	*Greatest Hits.* Rod McKuen; Delta
1996	*Exotic Excursions: Original Exotica for a Bachelor's Den.* Robert Drasnin; Pickwick
1997	*Great Jazz Artists Sing Strayhorn and Ellington.* Various Artists; Blue Note
1998	*The Capitol Big Band.* Charlie Barnett; Capitol
1998	*Return to Me.* Dean Martin; Bear Family
1998	*Music of Bob Friedman.* (13 CD Set, rereleases of 1970's recordings) Various Artists; Private/Unissued
1999	*Swingin' at Capitol.* Various Artists; Capitol
1999	*Discoveries, Instrumental Stereo Oldies.* Various Artists; Varese Sarabande
1999	*Great Swing Classics In Hi-Fi.* Various Artists; Capitol
1999	*Gravy Waltz: Best of Herb Ellis.* (Epic and Columbia recordings 1962-1964) Herb Ellis; Euphoria Jazz
1999	*Basie Street.* (Capitol and Tops recordings1955-57) Ronnie Lang; Fresh Sounds
1999	*After Dark: Jazz Ballads.* Various Artists; Charly
1999	*A Work of Heart.* Harry Skoler; Brownstone
2000	*Many a Wonderful Moment.* Rosemary Clooney; Bear Family. (8 CD set of recordings starting in 1958: Columbia, MGM, Coral, RCA, Reprise, Capitol)

2001	*West Coast: 1945-49.* Charles Mingus; Uptown Jazz
2001	*Bandland/Revolution In Sound.* (reissue of early 1960's recordings) Les Brown; Collectables
2002	*The Lerner and Loewe Bandbook/Richard Rodgers Bandbook.* Les Brown; Collectables. (Reissue early 1960's Capitol recordings)
2002	*Shirley MacLaine Live at the Palace.* (Reissue of 1976 recording) Shirley MacLaine; DRG
2002	*Rawhide.* Frankie Laine; Bear Family
2002	*Complete West Coast Recordings1945-1949.* Charles Mingus; The Jazz Factory
2002	*Best of the Capitol.* (1955-1958) Les Brown; Capitol
2002	*Now, with Tommy Mara.* (live in Manhattan, April 1999 at Danny's Hideaway); Lost Crooner Music
2003	*It's a Wonderful World.* (early 1960's) Les Brown; Collectables
2003	*Greatest Hits.* Rod McKuen; BR Music
2003	*Double Image.* (recordings for Discovery Records in 1949 and Coral in 1952 Georgie Auld); Ocium
2004	*Say It With Music.* (reissue of 1950's and1960's recordings) Dave Pell; Group 7
2004	*Modern Jazz Archive.* (compilation of 1946-1954 recordings) Charles Mingus; Harmonic
2004	*Big Band Buddy: Studio and Live1945-57.* Buddy Morrow; Jasmine
2004	*A Proper Introduction to Sonny Criss: Young Sonny.* Sonny Criss; Proper
2005	*The Great American Songbook.* Nancy Wilson; Blue Note. (2-disc compilation of late 1950s and early 1960s Capitol recordings)

2005	*The Early Years.* Chet Baker; Proper
2005	Save Your Love for Me: Nancy Wilson Sings the Great Blues Ballads. Nancy Wilson; Blue Note (compilation of recordings from 1959-1968)
2005	*Portrait of a Great Jazz Artist.* Don Fagerquist; Fresh Sounds (compilation of a series of recordings from 1955-59)
2005	*Guess Who I Saw Today: Nancy Wilson Sings Songs of Lost Love.* Nancy Wilson; Blue Note (compilation of recordings from 1961-1968)
2006	*Rod Mckuen, the Amsterdam Concert.* (The Concertgebouw, October 1971); Stanyan House
2007	*Les Brown's In Town.* (recordings (from 1956 and 1964) Les Brown; Jazz Beat
2013	*Nancy Wilson.* Nancy Wilson; Soul Music (reissue of Capitol recordings The Sound of Nancy Wilson1968 and Nancy in 1969)
2013	*Four Classic Albums: The Dave Pell Octet Plays Rodgers and Hart (1954)/The Dave Pell Octet Play. Irving Berlin (1953)/The Old South Wails (1961)/ I Remember John Kirby (1961)* Dave Pell; Avid Records
2013	*Comin' Home Baby.* (reissue of 1962 Atlantic recording) Mel Torme; Midnight Club
2013	*Two For the Road.* Shaynee Rainbolt
2014	*Where Lovers Live.* Sylvia Mims
2014	*Double Feature.* B. J. Ward

Index

45356270R00141

Made in the USA
Middletown, DE
01 July 2017